G000124109

Happy Hour

Patrice Chaplin is a novelist who lives in London and south-west France. Her fifteen books include *Albany Park*, *Siesta* and *Into the Darkness Laughing*, a biography of Modigliani's mistress.

Patrice Chaplin

Happy Hour

PAN BOOKS

To Gerona

First published 1998 by Macmillan

This edition published 1999 by Pan Books
an imprint of Macmillan Publishers Ltd
25 Eccleston Place, London SW1W 9NF
Basingstoke and Oxford

Associated companies throughout the world

ISBN 0330367463

Copyright © Patrice Chaplin 1998

The right of Patrice Chaplin to be identified as the
author of this work has been asserted by her in accordance
with the Copyright, Designs and Patents Act 1988.

All rights reserved. No part of this publication may be
reproduced, stored in or introduced into a retrieval system, or
transmitted, in any form, or by any means (electronic, mechanical,
photocopying, recording or otherwise) without the prior written
permission of the publisher. Any person who does any unauthorised
act in relation to this publication may be liable to criminal
prosecution and civil claims for damages.

3 5 7 9 8 6 4 2

A CIP catalogue record for this book is available from
the British Library.

Typeset by SX Composing DTP, Rayleigh, Essex
Printed and bound in Great Britain by
Mackays of Chatham PLC, Chatham, Kent

This book is sold subject to the condition that it shall not,
by way of trade or otherwise, be lent, re-sold, hired out,
or otherwise circulated without the publisher's prior consent
in any form of binding or cover other than that in which
it is published and without a similar condition including this
condition being imposed on the subsequent purchaser.

Chapter One

Beyond the cherry red roofs with their friendly old-world charm, Mount Canigou spread across the sky magnificent. Canigou, the sacred mountain, sacred to the Catalans for centuries. Before that, before the Catalans, when north-east Spain was called Iberia, the Phoenicians came in boats to take from this mountain a vital mineral substance, which Madame Beaumarchais said was radium. But her grasp of history was worse than mine and could not be relied upon even for essential matters concerning her own house. When I asked how old it was she said promptly, 'A hundred and fifty years'. But in my bathroom the local architect had uncovered stone flooring at least two hundred and fifty years old.

'Well, then, two hundred and fifty if that makes you happy. What's a hundred here or there?'

She'd said a later date because she felt that would make me secure. That the house was really old might displease me, make me reconsider investing further on the second floor. Madame Beaumarchais knew plenty who disliked the 'very old'. They were busy buying villas in modern materials just outside the village, villas with pink walls; when the sun shone they looked false, the pink like candy-floss.

Of course, I found out later to my cost, these modern dwellings had a point. The old houses had charm, character, soul. They also had neglected roofs, destructive pests called 'termites', mould, weakened beams. They needed constant love and attention that cost money.

Mount Canigou was gay today, its snow-covered summit sharply etched against blue, sun-bright sky. A good sign. Sometimes you couldn't see the mountain, the cloud around it was so thick. The worst clouds were black and morbid, and if the sun shone they turned a sinister green. On these days, sinister things happened. The Catalans sang songs to Canigou praising it, asking for its blessing. They made pilgrimages to its lower slopes and told it their secrets. I made sure it was the first thing I looked at in the morning. You could get used to almost anything, as well I knew. Even beautiful things. So I made a ritual of looking, really looking, at the mountain. After all, that's why I was here, near the border between France and Spain, to really look at and absorb beauty, to do my soul good.

I had come from London, and during the last months there I hadn't looked at anything. In fact, I had made a point of not looking. When I was lying ill in the rented room full of petrol fumes and acrid pollution, I was suddenly frightened. I didn't want to die. Not in that horrible room. And then I thought, Not die in it? What was I doing living in a room I wouldn't die in? And I made a vow to move to a place where I could open my eyes and look out every day and say, 'God, life is beautiful.' So I moved to Castel in the Pyrénées and said, 'God, life is beautiful'.

Madame Beaumarchais held her glass in that meaningful way that showed she wouldn't say no to a refill.

'I've only got red left.'

She waved her glass impatiently. I opened the fridge
and got out a bottle of dry fruity Roussillon, which I
didn't open because I knew she had a preference for
white. I'd taken to liking red wine chilled. In the
popular roadside restaurants, packed with every kind of
client, they offered red wine *naturel* or *frais*, from the
refrigerator. It was a custom Madame Beaumarchais
deplored. She insisted it stay at room temperature and
be allowed to breathe.

'But you don't like red,' I reminded her.

She blew out her lips childishly. 'I prefer white but
this won't kill me.'

The chemist had told her that alcohol did not mix
with her medicines so she'd given up the medicine.

'Neither of us can drink it if you don't open it,' she
said, sensibly.

The shutter banged in a sudden wind. 'It's the
mountains,' she said. 'The weather here changes from
one minute to the next.'

She was probably in her early seventies, with a
disquieting childishness that mocked the bourgeois and
teased the angry. She took risks. She had a way of
drawing very close. What saved her? Her intelligence.
She had all the intelligence she needed and could make
unbeatable remarks to deflate any adversary. She didn't
get to the point. She was at the point. Today she was
dressed in a dark green silk blouse, like a bad cloud, and
a conservative skirt. Her hair was dyed the same
midnight black as other elderly villagers', only well

styled. She wore meaningful jewellery and expensive shoes. However much she drank, her appearance didn't suffer.

The light changed around Canigou. All in a minute white clouds had fluffed up yellow in the sun, like a soufflé mixture. Overheated, they disintegrated and drifted off, mere foam, leaving the vast, scarred body of the mountain exposed.

'The air will make you well,' said Madame Beaumarchais, coughing. 'After all, they come here for the cure.' She took a generous drink, and looked at me through her good eye. 'Always wear makeup. You never know who will come to the door.'

She'd bought the apartment downstairs twelve years ago. It had splendid rooms filled with paintings. The antique furniture fitted her life. No discordant note of excess was allowed. Born in Toulouse, she'd married twice and talked about a daughter with a good job. At some time she'd owned a bar on the coast just above Spain. Many of the artists whose work appeared on her walls had personally appeared in her bedroom. She had a certain style. She was educated in the real sense. She was also a drunk. She'd mentioned serious illnesses and hospitalization. Then she'd moved to Castel, and its clear air had given her years more of life. She talked about it as a gift. Castel, famous for its cherries, its beauty, its painters. They'd all lived here: Picasso, Braque, Soutine, Juan Gris, Chagall. Castel was also known for its art museum and one-star *Guide Michelin* restaurant.

My apartment curved from the front door to the final wall in the kitchen and seemed to flow, an oval, harmonious sanctuary and off the oval were the bedroom, the bathroom, the terrace. The rooms were empty and newly painted, white walls, the original stone floor uncovered from beneath the grisly red flooring that the postman – the previous owner – had stuck on with pride. I'd also scraped off his snow-white pebbled wall effect, which horrified his wife. It was newly done, she said. Not cheap.

I'd so wanted these empty rooms with their longed-for space and indisputable simplicity. The building had been designed when they knew how to build houses. The staircase had a grandeur and it gave me real pleasure to walk on those stairs.

The apartment divided simply into the side facing Spain, the social side with a door leading on to the terrace above the main street, and from there out on to the plane trees, the church, the fountain with nine jets. Here was noise, people, company. The other side of the apartment faced unspoiled countryside, the shrine of the local patron saint of wine, St Ferréol, and the mountains. This gave peace.

The studio next to my bedroom was empty and Madame Beaumarchais encouraged me to buy it. 'It will give your apartment more value and you can have your guests in there.'

And *she* wouldn't have to have unknown lodgers in there.

The first stars were out in the now turquoise sky. The sunset still flamed over Canigou. I watched stars come on like lights, hundreds of them. A clear, pitted sky. No fog of pollution. Madame Beaumarchais pointed to a light that moved visibly around the mountain's girth.

'A comet?' I watched it speed off towards Spain, then disappear.

'They say many strange lights are seen around Canigou. They appear and suddenly flash off. They say they're spirits and the mountain attracts them. That's what they say.'

'Why did you come here?' I asked.

'I like the light and the nature.'

'The people?'

She indicated 'some'. 'Why are you here?'

'To breathe air and see stars.' Neither of us, I realized, gave much away.

I walked with her to the door and put on the hallway light. Nimble as a mountain goat, she flicked down the stairs for her simple evening meal of broth and salad. 'Don't forget to have the terrace retiled. When it rains it comes into my bedroom.'

Every source of water in my apartment always seemed to land, she said, in her bedroom. I explained, as usual, that it was scientifically impossible. 'But it's the pipes. Don't you see?' She was fed up with geography. So what if my bidet was yards away from her bedroom? It still had pipes.

How had the postman dealt with the water problems? I wasn't going to find out. He'd fled with my money, the romantic English woman's money, to the new estate with the pink villas. He'd bought one of these prefab horrors. Why, after living in an apartment that had such spirit? It puzzled me. I found out later. I found out a lot of things later.

Madame Beaumarchais smiled up at me, generous with her big teeth. She had great confidence in her smile. 'And buy the studio.' She could see that I still hesitated. It meant a big investment in this still untried house.

What a mixture she was. Sophisticated in the old manner, tricky, childish, astute. Certainly she was someone to reckon with. She liked the Bohemians, the artists, the outsiders. But she could drink elegantly with the wealthy and powerful men from the south. She'd met a lot of well-known people in her time and it hadn't been in her bar across the border.

I thought she told half of her story and that that was all anyone was going to get.

The sound of the river lulled me, healed the memories, took away anxiety, even time. The river never let me down. It lapped along beside me as far as the first hill into Spain. Then it spilled down the rocks and disappeared behind some allotments. I loved the sound. I'd longed for it all my life. Inside, I was thirsting for this river and all I had to do was leave the apartment, run down the wide, curving staircase, across the spacious hallway belonging to an atmospherically richer time and out into the modern world. The bustling Castel evening where, like the Spanish, the locals walked in the twilight and sat at outdoor cafés.

At one point the river became a stream between the gardens, speeding and hissing until it got back to its naturally fuller shape further along. I walked along the edge, balancing on narrow stones, and like a child jumped to and fro across the fast-flowing water and the locals cried, 'Doesn't it make you feel dizzy walking so close to it?'

No, it never did. It made me feel joyous.

The sky was light blue and absolutely clear up to the heavens tonight, and suddenly a wisp of wayward moon came into view around the side of the mountain, a bit late, as though drunk. The plane trees were rustling in the scented draughts. Oh, yes, it was lovely beyond thought. And I knew I'd see him tomorrow because a night so resplendent promised only good. He would show up and the love I had and had always had for him matched the evening. So I didn't feel cut off, not able to be part of it.

Madame Beaumarchais knew I'd come from London and wanted to realize my love of tango, and that I'd spent a lot of my past over the hills in Spain.

But she only knew half of my story as I only knew half of hers.

Chapter Two

I'd never meant to find Castel. A mistake took us off the coast road above Collioure and we went round the same roundabout again and I said, to stop this craziness, 'Go inland.' Marie was fine at the wheel as long as she knew where she was going and where the road was going. Crossroads were her *bête noire*. Ever since she had started studying psychotherapy, she'd had a funny attitude to a crossroads.

I'd been told that what I was looking for could be found in Collioure. Everyone I met said, 'Collioure is the place.' I meant to go there and I did, in spite of Marie's ambivalence at the wheel. We'd stayed two days and I'd tried to like it. But all the virtues I sought, the light, the atmosphere, the beauty, were to be found in a place I'd never heard of – Castel – and a mistake took me there.

Years ago, around my sixteenth birthday, I'd gone to Collioure with the Spaniard. We'd come up from northeast Spain, a short distance but a long journey because in those days trains were very slow. Then we had trouble with the frontier police because Franco didn't like his countrymen moving around too much. I remembered the soft crystalline atmosphere of Collioure, the extraordinary light, the fishing nets spread between the boats, the artists painting around the harbour, the friendliness. We sat with them on the beach and ate bread smeared with oil and tomato. Everything was perhaps heightened because I was already in love with the Spaniard, had been from the first moment. I didn't realize it would be a lifetime's business. It was no surprise that Collioure had attracted Picasso, Matisse and many great artists from earlier this century. I'd always wanted to go back.

But thirty-five years later Collioure was a disappointment. Too many tourists, too much trading on a time that was gone. Everyone was looking for the same thing, the thing that had inspired the artists. All they got was the effort of getting through the crowd, overdone painters in Montmartre costumes. No more bread with tomato — everywhere huge complicated ice-creams adorned with strawberries, chocolate confetti, tiny tinsel windmills. Yet the light was unchanged.

Before Perpignan another mistake took us off towards the mountains. 'Go to Le Boulou,' I said, trying to sound as though I had some part in what was happening. Road signs indicated it was a spa town. I felt intrigued and half expected to see couples walking too and fro under sunshades carrying glasses of sulphur water, a band playing waltzes, a genteel style that worked, had always worked. Why change it?

Le Boulou was a small town like many others. No bands, no strolling couples. The water source and baths were tucked away just outside the town next to a modern casino. People from all over France had come to take the waters, the mineral makeup of which suited their aching joints, done-in livers. The social security provided this yearly cure, which included a three-week medically supervised spa treatment, hotel accommodation, meals. It was no longer glamorous. *Thé dansant* in the afternoon took care of the entertainment.

Marie stopped for petrol and asked the attendant about a place for lunch. He suggested restaurants frequented by curists. Marie did not want a medical atmosphere. It was a beautiful day, the sky patterned with pure white clouds like fleecy Bo-Peep sheep rolling in from the sea. Marie wanted to eat out of doors.

'Then go to the Résidence du Soleil. Go to Castel,' said the attendant.

The way he said it – I could tell it was something special. I was so hungry I wanted to eat then and there, but Marie wanted to go to the place with the evocative name and she was right. We didn't find the restaurant but we found Castel: The original fortress village, high on a hill, and around it the new town with its smart villas spreading down to the river Tech. There was a dramatic medieval bridge, the Bridge of the Devil, and signs everywhere stating, 'Castel the Creative'. Overhanging everything, the magnificent mountain range dominated by Canigou.

Plane trees lined the streets, mountain water rushed down the gutters. The Saturday market filled the old quarter. Whichever way you looked, the hills and countryside started literally at the end of the buildings. There was no ugliness. Everything was clean and bright. Church bells chimed the hour and the sound, unobstructed, lingered in the pure air. I'd never seen anywhere like it. The place had body, quality, and couldn't have been more different from the highly recommended Collioure. Any tourists were absorbed into the daily-life atmosphere, dwarfed by the drama of the architecture. Standing in the middle of the short main street, I could see an art museum, two art galleries, medieval arches, fortress walls, fountains, pleasing cafés, prosperous shops, the church. A pack of ownerless dogs ran in circles. Tall plane trees swept together in gusts of jasmine-scented wind. It wasn't a poor place. It wasn't bourgeois. What was it? Beautiful.

Marie asked in the newsagents for a traditional-style restaurant. The proprietor came out and stood in the street to do justice to what he was about to say. He pointed with respect at an old square building surrounded by trees. L'Hostellerie. One star *Guide Michelin*. Seventeen *toques Gault Millault*. He couldn't say enough about the food. He spoke as only a Frenchman could. 'People think nothing of driving for hours to eat there.'

L'Hostellerie was a haven. That was the first thing. Nothing ostentatious or socially challenging here. The dining-room was simple and stylish with two huge prize-winning paintings, wall-sized, dramatic and ritualistic; one presented a bullfighter preparing himself for the ring, the other a woman carrying a lantern about to enter a passage into the unknown. You could sit and eat safely at the edge of these dramas. They provided the necessary diverting ingredient, the dash of Tabasco in the sweetness. The table linen, cutlery and glasses were so clean they demanded comment. Waiters moved in unison, trained and subtle. That the restaurant had *Guide*

Michelin rating and that the *sommelier* had recently been awarded a national prize wasn't referred to in action or attitude. They were glad you were there, the staff, and they were going to give their best.

Francine, friendly and receptive, managed the dining-room. Slim to the bone, she wore French designer clothes effortlessly. Her hair, fashioned in the latest Parisian style, suited her thinness. It became obvious Francine did not buy her clothes in the village or visit the local hairdresser. Later she admitted, 'I don't know Castel at all. I do all my shopping in Perpignan or Paris.'

Marie believed Frenchwomen were thin without struggle because their nervous systems were totally different. They were hyperactive from birth. Marie liked Francine's style and said so. We got an extra delicacy for that. Francine commented on Marie's impeccable command of French, how sick she was of all the foreign approximations – she'd forgotten I was at the table. And how they liked it, the French, if you could change the workings of your mouth and placing of your tongue to produce these sounds that did not occur in any other language, as far as I knew, except on the Viking coast of Norway. Marie, from Bergen, had only to glide along the grammar and tenses. The rest had been there from childhood.

Outside, the branches clashed in the wind and white blossom fell. An elderly glamorous woman stood stark among it. She stood as though she was at her wedding.

'That's Madame Beaumarchais,' said Francine. And then, realizing that possibly we may not know the person, added, 'She comes from Toulouse. She's had an amazing life. What shall I say? She's a —'

'Courtesan?' said Marie hopefully.

'Grand hostess.'

Madame Beaumarchais entered the dining-room surrounded by men. I thought, This woman knows how to handle herself. She was no different, I suspected, when she was on her own. In spite of her age and weight, she was graceful and distinctively made up. Her damaged eye was just part of her face, accepted immediately. I liked her laughter.

Other lunch guests arrived and as they sat down they too became soothed. There was a generous, calm space between tables.

Francine suggested ravioli in daube sauce, pigeon quenelles in a chestnut sauce, an orange and red-pepper dish with fresh anchovies from Banyuls, and the speciality of the region, duck with cherries. She explained that Castel was famous for its cherries and its painters. As each dish arrived, she came to the table and introduced it as if it was a person she wanted us to like.

'Roasted lobster in its own juice with a ginger cake and fresh berries from the region and a *compôte* of local vegetables, and rice flavoured with freshly picked jasmine. *Voilà. Bon appétit.*'

There were two chefs. Francine's brother Vincent cooked the fish and her husband Guy the meat. Vincent was married to the celebrated *sommelier* Marie Belle, which made her Francine's sister-in-law. Two couples together non-stop six days a week. Yet they looked relaxed enough.

Marie Belle, sturdy, pulsing with ox-like energy,

poured the wines, her boyish hair sleek, gleaming, clothes chosen to accentuate power. She was invincible. She was used to being on show, being tested. She liked to win. She looked as though she ate the meat and Francine the fish.

We were given a delicate white sparkling *brut* wine from south of Carcassonne, Crémant de Limoux, better than many champagnes. Then followed the regional wines by the glass, the Banyuls, the Côtes du Roussillon, the Rivesaltes, the Muscat *sec*. Before the dessert, a thick creamy white cheese on slices of dark bread that neither of us had tasted before. It was an experience not to be forgotten, and when they dropped this delicious dish from the menu there was no equal. The dessert was everything it should be. But there was one surprise, simple unbeatable. *Mel y mato*, a Catalan soft cheese with honey but frozen like ice-cream.

After the first course I wanted to stay for the weekend. After the meal, for life. I asked if Francine could recommend a hotel.

'But you stay with us. We have a suite which we rent out upstairs.'

I had found Paradise.

While I was having one of the best meals of my life the postman from Marseille went to Marcel, the local estate agent, and put his Castel flat up for sale. He wanted thirty thousand francs, which he would use as a deposit for one of the detestable pink villas. What the villas had, but I didn't realize it at the time, was no immediate neighbours. But Paradise has a price.

Marcel considered the deal reasonable because the apartment was '*plein centre ville*' – right in the middle of

Castel. It had wonderful views, which was rare, and spaciousness, also rare. Marcel, thin, intelligent, looked like a humorous monk. He liked small sharp jokes and inserted them into any conversation. They had nothing to do with humour. He'd come from Paris nineteen years before, and had made Castel, and its abundance of architecture, his life.

He noticed Marie first. Most people did. It made being her friend difficult. Running with Viking blood, she was forthright and got into trouble. Her beauty got her out of it. She knew how to project her smile, gave it everything. Simple Vaseline took care of the laughter lines. Psychotherapy had been her life-long ambition but she'd had to wait until her children had grown up, her marriage dissolved and her mind settled before she was free to study. She'd chosen London because it had more to offer.

Marie loved old buildings and beautiful surroundings and tried whenever possible to live accordingly. She flicked through Marcel's available properties, sniffed out the real buys from the rubbish and asked how long they'd been on the market. Marcel's downfall was his refusal to be dishonest, a terrible failing in an estate agent. But the postman's flat was so new it hadn't even appeared in his window. Was it only impulse that took me to see it?

The flat was full to bursting with the postman's family eating Sunday lunch. Two tables at right angles covered with paper cloth. The postman carved a huge joint of lamb. His wife served cooked fresh cherries and rice. Her sister dressed a salad. They offered us Muscat from Rivesaltes. We met Grandma, two grandpas, an aunt, another sister, her children and the postman's children. I tried not to react to the postman. He was gorgeous. Everybody knew it, including him. The children left the table and ran on to the terrace. Church bells were ringing. One grandpa sang a Georges Brassens song. They were a happy bunch.

I saw many flats in the next few days, but that one was happy.

Sardanas were danced outside the Pablo Café. All in a moment dozens of people wearing canvas and rope *sardana* shoes gathered and the woodwind band played lively Catalan music, with a hint of melancholy. The dancers formed circles, and, holding hands, produced complicated rhythms, the long, the short, on delicate feet, confidently. I decided I would learn the *sardana* again and the tango and the card game *belotte*. And the French language and Catalan. But I lived in London.

There was a light-hearted feeling in the postman's flat that I couldn't forget. Marie was worried. Was I foolish enough to consider buying it? I liked the gaslight on the stairway and the stone floors. Marie loved stones but distrusted them. They were unhealthy, held in the cold. Stones could literally kill you. I said I liked the view from the windows.

'You can't live on a view.'

I could. I could certainly live on a view, I discovered. The views from all sides in the postman's flat gave me an urgency to live, to explore. A rebirth, if anything. Why live anywhere else? I asked to see the flat again. As I was going up the stairs Madame Beaumarchais was coming down.

'This house suits you,' she said.

'Why?'

'I've no idea. But you look as though you belong here. Better than Collioure. That is so ordinary, these days.' She was wearing a hat swathed in veils. She was perhaps the one person it suited. I asked how she knew I'd been there. 'You were seen eating in Les Templiers. But you ate better here in Castel.' She continued down to the front door, trailing a subtle perfume and a definite mystery. She lived, I found out, below the postman in a large, grand apartment.

Should I? Shouldn't I? Buying it, I was like an uncertain bride. The commitment terrified me, but the place was so persuasive. It was full of new sensations, colours, smells, sights, dramas, so different from anything I was used to. I looked at Mount Canigou and thought, I could get myself well here. And the apartment – it had *âme*, soul. Shall I sign the purchase agreements? As if in answer, the church bells rang jubilantly. It was, as the French say, *un coup de foudre*.

Chapter Three

From the apartment above the restaurant I could see across to the hills north of Castel. In certain lights they seemed to undulate, these low sharp-backed hills, like a juvenile snake, and make their way further east towards the coast. And north would seem east, and west, south, and I'd be like a compass gone mad. But the light could change anything. It provided all sorts of entertainment.

Below my window, waiters from the Pablo scraped chairs across the pavement and shook them into place around the zinc-topped tables. The proprietor, Monsieur Nadal, a kind man with a sensitive face and substantial moustache, greeted the mayor as he walked a tiny dog towards the town hall. The animal obviously embarrassed the mayor. It was a woman's dog, spoilt and whining. Probably his wife's. To be in the company of that dog did him more harm than any mistress: it showed whose thumb he was under and that it was she who insisted on these terrible excursions. The pack of ownerless dogs stopped fighting over something dead and unspeakable, and turned to sniff out this little yapping brat. Should they eat it or mount it? It was beneath contempt. You could almost feel their sneers as they turned away to real adventures.

Before the mayor got to the corner, an expensively dressed woman with over-dyed hair accosted him. Shouting, she picked up the minuscule dog. Shame-faced, the mayor felt in his pocket and found the courtier-designed dog-coat with bells. Still abusing him, the woman fitted the coat around the dog and called him Baby – the dog, that is. She replaced the animal on the pavement. 'Now go walkies with Papa.' She didn't keep her voice down. The poor mayor, more humiliated than if he'd lost an election, stumbled on towards the town hall.

'She's fed up with small-town politics,' said Marie. 'She wants him to lose the next election.'

I had to agree that you didn't need much else to do that. The dog was enough.

The window was a good vantage point because from behind the sweeping branches of the plane trees I could see the comings and goings of the village. There was a great deal of activity until one minute to noon and by one minute past the place was deserted. The Frenchman's lunch cleared the streets throughout France. Spain and its languid habits, a mere eight kilometres away, was not allowed to influence this ritual, which was punitive, nationalist, even sacred.

Castel had always been Catalan, but these days there were more French. It seemed at first sight that they mingled together effortlessly, the only distinction the luxuriant moustaches, old men wearing black berets and sudden bursts of Catalan like gunfire in the shops and back-streets. The Catalan stronghold was the Pablo Café, and Monsieur Nadal ran the cultural activities, concerts, plays, recitals, *sardanas*. He fervently wanted the Catalan traditions to continue, and they seemed to be more in evidence here than in Catalunia itself, just over the Spanish border.

Francine's husband Guy brought in a silver tray so loaded he could hardly carry it. He placed it bumpily on the low table.

The breakfast was superbly laid out and irresistible. The black coffee had a creamy smooth taste, the croissants were small and newly baked, the butter unsalted, pale, from Normandy, the jams home-made, the bread compact and moist. He'd added slices of mountain cheese and local grapes. The *tour de force* was the spiced cake. It was rich yet not sweet, and could accompany everything, but there were only two slices. I told Marie to order a couple more in her pleasing French. The only thing Guy's skills couldn't improve was the fresh orange juice. Marie forgot all about her dietary plans of the night before and ate as one would expect.

'Why don't you just live in here?' she said, reaching without hesitation for the last piece of cake. 'You won't have all the responsibility of buying a place. Here you can come and go, or go for good. You can visit other places. Once you've bought a second home you have to spend all your free time there.'

I wasn't so sure about the 'second'.

The apartment above the restaurant was decorated in an art-deco style with an easy luxury, two bedrooms, a sitting room, a large-screen television, a modern bathroom with a pressure massage bath. It had a light, off-key atmosphere. To me it was a kind of home. Francine said the prize-winning foreign painters from the worldwide annual art competition stayed in the apartment.

Well-known French actresses passed a night or two. A famous writer, a concert conductor. She didn't mention the businessmen, the bourgeois couples. She knew how to build atmosphere.

'I mean it,' said Marie. 'All that work you'll have to do in that old apartment. It's always more than you think. And buying a place – you're not made for it.' She stopped. 'You're not really going to live here, are you?' I didn't answer. 'It's just a rush of blood to the head. London's your place. You can't live here.'

Suddenly I could. For all the colours, evocations, joyousness, purity, I could pay the price, whatever it was.

She already knew it, the price. 'You can't live with these people. The Catalans are totally ingoing and are even proud of it. They don't like outsiders.'

'That's not right.' I thought of all the ones I'd known when I was with the Spaniard.

'No,' she agreed. 'It's not that they don't like outsiders. They hate them.'

I reminded her I'd put down the holding deposit of ten per cent of the price and signed the agreement.

'Lose it. That money is nothing compared with what you will lose. It was just a grasp at – Paradise.'

I knew it wasn't.

'Then give that up and live here and have all that marvellous food.'

For a moment I almost went for it. Then I did the awful counting. A year in here could almost buy my flat. A night in here equalled a week in the attractively run-down hotel across the road. Marie wasn't having it. Compromise wasn't what it was about. She was willing to pay for quality of life. That's what it was about. I agreed she had a point.

Mid-morning crowd at the Pablo tables, coffee replaced by wine, the voices louder, laughter gayer and among the sounds I heard the Spaniard's voice. 'Wait for me at the train station. Twelve o'clock.' I rushed to the window and looked down. The Pablo crowd moved tables as the sun moved. They looked a well-heeled lot. As Marcel had said, Castel was a money town. The Spaniard wasn't there. I thought I'd heard him because I wanted to hear him. Along the town-hall wall the old Catalan men gathered, wearing black berets. They were there every day, one tooth between the lot, talking about the way it used to be. They'd certainly know of the Spaniard.

The fountain opposite splashed upon layered stones. The sound was pleasing. The fountain was old and had enough of a past to be celebrated. Its date and name were printed first in French, then Catalan on an imposing plaque. Castel had always been Catalan since records were kept but France had taken it over, then Spain, then France. This disputed place, no stranger to war and adversity, had finally found its role in the seventeenth century. Negotiator and keeper of the peace between the two countries. Two huge defences, reminders of the constant wars, stood at either end of the village: the Porte d'Espagne and the Porte de France, each with a massive stone archway through which narrow streets twisted, sharp as hairpins, and unexpected hollows in the walls filled with mountain people playing violins or flutes for money or the love of it. Castel was essentially a light-hearted place.

Through a shaded arch opposite I could see part of

the back-street, roughly cobbled and intimate with its secretive doorways. Madame Beaumarchais came out of the wine shop, her bag full of bottles of white. I could see from that distance that she liked an established wine and would pay for quality. As always she was conservative in her dress. Nobody would get anything on her. An artistically turned out willowy girl with long black ringlets, smoking a cigarette, suddenly joined her and they had some kind of altercation. The blinding sun reached even that alleyway and cast their shadows forwards into the square for all to see. Beaumarchais and the girl stood innocently apart but the shadows told a different story. The woman pressed a rectangular object into the girl's hand, her movements furtive and brusque. Then the shadow hands slid apart.

'Money,' said Marie.

I thought it might be a letter. The shadow had enlarged the operation, given it drama. Drugs?

The girl hadn't finished arguing. Madame Beaumarchais gestured, 'Enough.' The girl looked smoked out, exhausted. It didn't mean she couldn't argue. Finally, Madame Beaumarchais charged at her like a wild boar, all teeth and bulk. Was this some local custom? The girl stood her ground. I could see she had had plenty of practice. Being in the wrong place at the wrong time? Everyday for her.

'It's about money,' said Marie.

I thought it was much deeper than that. In fact, it was about the house, and how could Madame Beaumarchais allow a stranger to buy the postman's flat, a foreign woman who had nothing to do with their lives? Had Madame Beaumarchais lost her cunning? Was she ready for the retirement home? The girl's face, pale, oval, was beautiful and ravaged.

Then they moved from the archway into the square, into the public gaze, and the treacherous shadows moved forward to the safety of the gutter.

I could hear the girl's voice clearly. It was surprisingly pleasant – young girl well brought up. It was also full of slang. They both looked across the square, their eyes level with the upper windows of the restaurant. For some reason I bent down, not wanting to be seen.

A child danced around the two of them, taunting. The girl tried to restrain her and lost the initiative. Madame Beaumarchais flung a few hard facts at the pair of them and that was that. She had won. She kissed the air insultingly around the girl's face, French fashion, and crossed to the hairdresser's.

'That will do you a lot of good, going in there, I don't think,' said the girl. 'With what you've got left, spend the money on a wig. Or why not chuck it at the first beggar?'

'Haven't I already?' said Madame Beaumarchais, pointedly. So the rectangular shape had probably been money.

The child skipped up to the fountain, arms outstretched, and touched the water through which the sun shone, making rainbows. Then she jumped into the fountain and splashed about with the pure joy of it. People gathered but the girl, ringlets flying, turned away. Another cigarette lit from the first kept the life chain going. The two women. What was it? There was something seductive between them.

There were as many hairdresser's shops as bars in

Castel. Francine said it was because you couldn't get a good cut however hard you tried. There was one each side of the front door of the house where I planned to live, another, more sophisticated, further along and beyond that, opposite the town-hall, another about to open. And in the old quarter and the new smart stretch towards the river Tech, hair salons of every category. Yet everyone I met seemed to go to Perpignan for a haircut.

Opposite the Pablo was the pharmacy, owned by a Spanish doctor, Carlos, and next to that a food shop specializing in Catalan products, and then the haberdashery, which had been in the Bonnay family since the last century. The jeweller's beside that was always full. Carlos – they said he was a millionaire – came out of his pharmacy and stood in the sun. He lifted up his face, took the golden heat fully and every part of his being was infused with happiness. Like the sun reflected on a coin, which in turn reflects upwards on to a mirror, so his happiness shot up to me and from me to Marie.

'It's going to be all right,' I thought she said.

I knew what she was talking about and it couldn't be all right and never would. Unless God chose otherwise.

I didn't want to move or speak or let go of this moment. I wanted to grasp this happiness so rare. No, I did not want to go on to the next moment or the next, I'd rather die now, said my practical mind.

'I'm dying to go out,' said Marie.

Castel had begun as a border village in the tenth century and probably before. Marcel said the original village was still intact although naturally rebuilt during the centuries that followed. You could trace it, he said, from the church up to the square with the fountain of nine jets and across to the clumps of fortress wall and as far as the agricultural sector. The streets, too narrow for cars, thankfully, swung sharply, curving, clamorous and echoing. The houses leaned across towards each other as though for comfort and solidarity. Centuries back, they'd certainly needed it. Marcel said a single building would consist of different parts spanning nine hundred years. Among the old, touches of the very old. He strode ahead, his thin body looking enormous in the tiny impasse. He stroked a broken wall with pleasure.

Walking through the village with Marcel was a pleasing experience. He loved architecture and history and wanted to share it. Surprisingly, the main street where I planned to buy the apartment wasn't nearly as old as the rest. Marcel believed the buildings dated from the eighteenth century. Further down towards the river was another very old sector, stairs with a fountain, just off the commercial shopping street – the Fontaine d'Amour, a splash of the old, full of legends, and around it on the stone seats, people gossiping, fanning their faces or washing clothes at the public sinks. Marcel believed this was as old as the original village higher up. The tenth-century inhabitants were prepared to live here outside the protection of the village walls because of the water source, which enabled them to farm their land. I happened to be looking at the recently opened branch of the super-modern chain store Yves Rocher as he spoke. He laughed. 'They're glad of the fountain too. In the summer. In the drought.'

Marcel hoped I was an artist. I wasn't. But his speech pleased me anyway. He described Picasso's love of the village, how it was for him the most beautiful village, how he had brought many of his group to live and paint here. Much of their work now hung in the well-established art museum in the main street. Marcel knew where they'd all stayed: Chagall by the river, Soutine by the bread shop in the old quarter, Krémagne and Picasso near the agricultural area. Braque had been to Castel, Juan Gris, Miró, Dufy, Matisse.

Then he described the local festivals, concerts, parades, fiestas, exhibitions, the bullfights. He said the *sardana* contest was one of the most important in Catalunia. They even sent their best dancers from Barcelona. There was always something going on. 'You can't be lonely here,' he assured me.

Yes, I could see Castel was considered rich financially and in its spirit.

He was doing very well, he said. More French from the north coming to live here, and foreigners were buying in the small hamlets around or in the new *lotisse-ments* outside the city wall.

'What kind of foreigners?' asked Marie.

He said, 'Scandinavian.' In fact, they were Dutch, German and Swedish.

He said over two hundred artists were living there. Some of them had come for the annual art competition and had fallen in love with the place, but also creativeness was here, endorsed by nature. To the west of Castel, Amélie-les-Bains, an historically established spa town, light-hearted, gay, full of *thé-dansant* and *bal musette* for the locals and thousands of curists. The brochures stated that Amélie enjoyed a micro-climate with three hundred and sixty days of sun a year. But since that had been written global changes had turned it into a microwave climate. These days they had savage storms. Beyond Amélie lay the mountain spa, La Preste, then the ski resorts and Andorra. To the north-east, the Mediterranean town Perpignan which, during the years of Franco's regime, gave the Spanish forbidden cultural experiences, theatre, film, newspapers. In those days, as I understood it, the Spanish, especially the Catalans, could not get news, only the doctored variety from Madrid. In the fifties I used to go to the frontier town Port Bou with the Spaniard and his friends. For a Spaniard, getting into France – even on a day visit – was a dicey business: if the Spanish frontier police didn't like your papers or, worse, your face, you could end up in jail or just end up. Perpignan was the Mecca for the intellectuals. Politically sympathetic French, including Jean-Paul Sartre, printed a newspaper for the Catalan nationalists trapped in Spain; it was distributed in Perpignan. I knew of this struggle because I'd lived through part of it with a man who'd fought through all of it. So 'Catalan' had a significance for me whereas Marie, seeing them as they'd become since independence from Madrid, had a slighter view altogether.

We chose the Café de France because of the shade instead of the Grand Café opposite. There was a luxury in just choosing. Marcel suggested a pre-lunch drink. Marie decidedly wasn't having lunch but I knew L'Hostellerie's menu would soon change that. Marcel bought a bottle of local rosé, a delicate pale pink, which went down effortlessly and copiously. 'It's refreshing in the heat.' He ordered three small tins of Spanish olives stuffed with anchovies and slices of local sausage. He would talk about Castel for the rest of the day, the rest of his life – not because he was selling it but because he valued it.

'The Harrods of Castel is the old quarter by the church.' Marie looked across at my house. 'You've got Woolworth's.'

The sea was to the east, a mere twenty-five minutes away, and the mountains to the west, Spain to the south, ten minutes by car, and the Cathar country to the north. I felt I was in the centre of the universe.

'I know all that,' said Marie. 'But you won't leave London. In the end it comes down to people.'

But I could. I looked at the café tables, full of new people, the luminous light that enriched the most habitual sight. And the air, pristine, that you could breathe with pleasure. Yes, I could leave anywhere for this. The artists had.

'Wait till it rains,' she said.

Chapter Four

I had to pass that door again because I couldn't believe what I'd seen. Amélie-les-Bains, the most southerly spa town in France, full of well-being and those searching for it. These people were conventional, mostly middle-aged, with Charles Trenet on their turntables and ordinary ailments. Everyone was ordinary. That was the thing. Nobody was ever on show. Nothing confronted you in this place. You didn't even see a beggar. Yet in that doorway another world altogether – a slice of 1950s Pigalle.

Today there was a real holiday mood on the streets, a live band playing outside the cafés, a jostling for places at the pavement tables, waiters – virtually under the eyes of the police – carrying out extra illegal chairs and tables, until the customers spilled to the street's edge. And the police looked the other way and accepted a glass on the house. Everyone was out enjoying the sun, drinking, laughing, strolling, playing *belotte*, looking for a companion, romance, excitement. And there, inside the largest and most prominent café, was another reality altogether, a scene from a fifties French movie, Jean Gabin and his co-star, in this case a mixture of five French film actresses from the fifties with a touch of

Lana Turner. She stood there behind the bar aloof and so beautiful. Dyed ash-blonde hair piled up in a Gibson Girl hairstyle catching the light, and a stunning theatrical makeup. Her neck was long and shapely, her body curved and toned and long in all the right places. She looked as though she'd been poured into the sky-blue suit. Yet for all that she belonged to another time. Her air of nostalgia seemed to endow all this glamour with respect. It gave distance. And the barman beside her, Jean Gabin's double, lifting a crate of beer. And all around them ordinary people, the ones you would never notice, leave alone look at. And she in the middle. Why? Was she a ghost? Had she come here in the fifties, a showgirl from Pigalle, and the mineral-water treatment hadn't worked and she'd died of TB?

Marie whizzed down past the casino towards the road for the mountains.

'Wait a minute. I did see her,' I insisted.

For once she didn't disagree. There had been something unexpected in that café and she turned back along the one-way system.

Only a few kilometres from Castel, this place had a completely different atmosphere, lay-out, purpose. A narrow town lying in the river basin with green sheer slopes rising up like walls all around and mountain peaks above. It made me feel as though I was in a pot and it would not have suited the claustrophobic. The noise of a gorge thundered like a factory machine, a racing, never-ceasing pulse, day, night, giving an edge to this tranquil place. The river Tech flowed through the centre of everything; important, crossed by many bridges over which after a very good lunch the old and infirm staggered towards the bowls game. There was no obvious history except that most of the shops were forties' style. The buildings were nineteenth and early-twentieth century. There were no artists. The microclimate pleased the French, especially those from the industrial north, and they poured into Amélie-les-Bains, thousands of them all year round. The water treated most things, and what it didn't, Valium and its Diazepam brothers did. The doctor to see was Seurat and he wasn't prescription-shy.

In spite of the medical overtones, there was a gaiety here and the holiday mood was permanent. Marie agreed it was a good spot in which to grow old. The most famous hotel, the Reine d'Amélie had housed curists for decades. It still retained something of the grandeur. There was plenty of competition, these days, from other hotels, well-run, friendly, offering good food, daily entertainments, excursions. People were looked after.

We stopped the car in front of a shop, its window full, not with Scholl foot-correction sandals, but with glamour shoes, gold-rimmed, transparent creations like narrow boats with skyscraper heels. Black velvet pumps sprinkled with diamanté, gold and silver ankle boots soft as gloves that rang bells as you walked. Shoes to give dreams. In those, like Cinderella, you stepped out and got your man.

The Café des Arcades, romantic and thrilling like a Paris brasserie from the forties and earlier. Mirrored walls, advertisements for Byrrh and Suze, globe light zinc tables, sawdust on the floors, plump banquettes, everything scrupulously clean and filled to the brim with curists, locals and people from the region who liked to dance. At the back a raised dance floor, and upstairs, a hotel. The front windows were folded back to let in the gentle spring air, the pavement tables already filling with people in their pleasure clothes wanting a good time to start early.

Above the dance floor a spinning ball threw flecks of coloured light, like confetti, on to the dancers. The *bal musette* music was live, accordion and drum. And behind the bar there was her, the phenomenon reflected over and over in different mirrors. What *was* she doing in Amélie-les-Bains? Simenon would have written about her in the Maigret books. She'd have been in the well-known Parisian gangster film *Le Rififi*. She'd have filled the *femme fatale* parts in a dozen French low-life movies. She celebrated the artificial, which so often hid plain looks. Her face was, and would always be, beautiful, courtesy of its perfectly set features and an enviable bone structure. The makeup gave the sense of unreality, yet was faultless in its application. She was made up for a performance. She had enviable poise and a dancer's body, her extremely high-heeled shoes obedient to every body twist and turn. No slouching into a bad posture because she was tired, or suffering on those demanding heels. She was disciplined to the last polished fingernail. She was a performer – more, a performance – and had the stamina to go with it.

'How often do you notice a neck?' Marie was staring as uncontrollably as everyone else.

Marie tried to guess her age and decided she must be older than she looked. Plastic surgery? It had to be. We moved closer, trying to decide where artifice ended and nature began. Yet the nearer we got the more perfect she became. A waiter didn't like too much staring for free and asked what we wanted. Quite a lot, actually. Who the woman was, where from and why. We said, Iced tea.

The eyebrows, yes, they were gone and replaced with a delicate grey arch. Her mouth was unspoiled. A full-lipped sensual mouth, exquisitely shaped, with its sudden smile. Life, and she'd obviously seen plenty, had not diminished it. It was probably no different from how it had been when she was seventeen. The lips were painted a bright glossy red and outlined with a darker colour. The teeth were large, even, very white and looked like a dentist's creation. Her eyes, blue-grey behind long curly lashes, were large and slightly slanting. They were expressive eyes, lingering, dreamy, not at all hard. The powder brushes had been out, highlighting this, hollowing that. She was there behind the counter, not a hair out of place, to be stared at – and the clients were staring. She moved. Their eyes followed. She was the entertainment, their fix. She stroked a glass with a tea-towel. It had all the importance of a conjuring trick. In comparison with her, even Marie lost out. She looked human whereas this person was a fantasy.

She was new to Amélie. She and Jean Gabin had arrived at near enough the same time as I'd discovered Castel. The locals, who sat separate from the curists, told Marie that the couple had come from Paris and that she was a hairdresser. Marie had trouble with that one.

'I heard she owns a clothes shop,' said a woman.

'No, she's a dancer at the Lido. That's what I heard,' said a man.

'She's a –' An old man waved his hand. 'A *poule*. That's what I heard.'

'More a madam,' corrected the first man, and winked.

She could be a dancer, a showgirl, a whore, a madam. The locals suggested one after the other. But she was all of them. A sex purveyor from Pigalle, hard, professional, yet there was something sad about her, tragic almost, and that gave her dignity.

Marie decided Jean Gabin was her *mec* – pimp.

'Oh, no. They're married,' said a local woman. 'A waiter told us.'

Some weeks later, the customers started to copy her style. She wore different and immensely viewable outfits every day with jewellery and shoes to match. Everything was clean and absolutely fresh. The fabrics were more than new. They looked alive. Since she'd moved in, shoe sales next door had gone up. Had the owner anticipated her arrival and ordered such robust stock? Or had she some percentage? The curists crippled themselves in the gold skyscraper glamour shoes. She was their dream. In fact, you either wanted her or wanted to look like her.

'Why is she here?' Marie asked, on this first day.

'To make money like everybody else,' said JoJo, a handyman from Castel.

'Do barmaids make that much?' Marie was amazed.

So was the handyman. 'She's not a barmaid. Oh, heavens, no. She's the proprietor. She owns the establishment. She and her husband.'

The woman still stood, not doing much, but that didn't matter. Her eyes didn't avoid the stares of the curious. They just didn't connect. Jean Gabin was pugilistic in build – and probably temperament too, if he had to be. You didn't notice him, not when she was around. But he had hair and a face and, yes, strong blue eyes. She turned and talked to him and laughed. I wanted to hear her voice and moved nearer. She stopped talking and completely ignored me. I thought she might be an impostor. Her and him. They were in there pretending to run the bar – and the real people? Anyone's guess.

The locals reckoned she'd never survive in Amélie-les-Bains. On the face of it it was too straight and the areas that weren't were well hidden. No one had ever seen anything like her. The police chief, the mayor, the tradespeople, the women and the church, in that order, would see her off. So they thought.

I looked out at the people passing. No one looked like her. No one even in Paris would look like her. How could she get away with it, in this town?

Her health – was that why she was here? She needed to breathe, for heaven's sake.

Didn't I? She needed fresh air, sun, even a water cure. Or was she running away from Pigalle trouble. Police? The mob? Or her life's dream had been to own a *thé-dansant* establishment in the south. Or she was an impostor.

Young men, waiters from hotels and restaurants, came in to see for themselves if what they'd been told was true. They, too, stared and went on staring. Jean Gabin was always around to move in, if necessary. She never served or seemed to work. The waiters did all that.

At seven in the evening the dance music stopped and that session was over. Waiters laid the tables with white paper cloths and red napkins. The curists staying in the hotel took their places for dinner. Then she came from around the bar and, wiping her hands down her skirt, said hello to her clients. She went from table to table, shaking hands, smiling. She had a lovely smile.

'*Bon appétit*, Monsieur, Madame. Have you had a good day?'

And her voice wasn't anything like I'd imagined. It was a pleasant, well-modulated voice. Marie, the expert on French, said she was obviously well brought-up. It wasn't the voice of a street girl. It went with the warm smile.

The shoe heels were so lofty and tapering they could have thrown her weight forward. She was one of the few women I'd seen who could be perfectly balanced and at ease in such elevated shoes. Then she was gone.

The food looked good. Grilled fresh sardines then puréed potato, mashed with milk and butter and sprinkled with pepper, and a large spiced sausage with sharp yellow mustard, all steaming hot and delicious. I had such a yearning for that potato, sausage and mustard, and the fresh green salad dressed with oil and garlic, and the Camembert that came with it. And the strawberry tart made that afternoon. Even the coffee.

'Are you hungry?' said Marie. 'You can't be.'

'Aren't you?'

She said she wasn't but she'd stared too long at that mashed potato. We sat beside the curists and the waiter poured red wine into a jug to let it breathe. It was cool, light and tasted of fruit. It could be drunk bottle after bottle eternally. It was the nectar poets wrote about.

'It's like drinking gold,' said Marie. She asked the waiter its name. He thought she meant his name and was pleased. JoJo the handyman lowered his voice and told us, 'He's the best lay in town. He's supposed to be incredible. All the women go with him.'

Was he joking? The waiter was thin with a slightly hunched back, sad brown eyes – no, they weren't sad when he looked at a woman. His hair was long and straight to his chin. He was good at his job, concentrated and efficient.

'Are you sure?'

'Of course,' said JoJo. 'Why d'you think he works here?' He eyed the female curists.

'He came with the others from Paris?'

'No, no. But the *patron* heard about him and coaxed him out of the casino grill.' He indicated money. 'Livens the place up.'

Before the night was over I could see that the Café des Arcades was a very sexual place: men looking for action, a few professional street girls wandering in, the waiter always available and a sex-hungry under-age girl from the next town. This was the place where you could let your hair down. Madame didn't. She remained as cool and unavailable as she'd been at four in the afternoon. Clients didn't go home disappointed. The *patron* made sure of that.

I wrote down the name of the wine and the year.

'Don't even bother,' said Marie. 'The next bottle will be quite different. I'm so used to that in France. These local wines. So unstable.'

Around dinner-time, Pigalle types started to gather. They kept to themselves at a table near the dance floor. Jean Gabin left the bar and came across to shake hands. Their table was laid and they ate the same as everyone else. Marie tried to ask the waiter the name of the *patron*'s wife. Questions were discouraged.

The *bal musette* started up again and we went into the dark, secret room and danced with the curists. We found that our disco style, of which we were confident, was not enough. How well they danced – as though they did it every day of their lives. Tango, paso doble, foxtrot, quickstep, mambo, waltz, Madisón, rock and roll, cha-cha-cha. Was there nothing they couldn't do? Something in that small hot dance room gave it allure. It was sin. Just the right amount.

I'd forgotten how heady and free it was to dance. I hadn't, I realized, danced these dances for years. And, gradually, all preoccupation and strain dissolved, then memory, and I felt lifted up, part of these people's enjoyment and, like them, I danced all out, rhythmic, free, until I became simply a spinning energy, part of the music, joyful. For a short while I experienced freedom.

We danced with JoJo, his brother, his friends, then a Corsican curist, a teacher from Alsace who suffered from gout, taxi-drivers, croupiers. No shortage of partners. Everyone was sharing and friendly. No exclusion here. Through the crowd I glimpsed the girl who had argued with Madame Beaumarchais. In the near dark her face was pale and calm, like a half moon.

We went to the bar to cool down. The local wines were so good there was little point in drinking anything else. Madame sat at one of the café tables behind us with

Jean Gabin and an old man, wearing a beret, with his poodle. The old man's eyes were mournful, mouth grim. Madame smiled at him, but nothing doing. He looked like hard work. She got going on the small dog, also gloomy, and that was easier. Another man finished his dinner. He had the bright wise eyes of a bird and they'd seen enough. A mat of hair sat oddly: if it was a wig it was the worst wig ever made. He looked interesting, a man of substance. He was possibly an entertainer from Pigalle, from one of the older clubs, past his best. These four people became part of my inner world long after that outer one was no more.

Close to, the ash-blonde Gibson-Girl hair was bright and generous in shape, like a gleaming fruit bowl. It absorbed the light, then gave it out. It was the brightest thing in the room.

She was aware of us but not giving anything away. Marie, after all her dancing, looked dishevelled and glowing like a schoolgirl. Gone was the Monaco smart life-style. She hadn't danced in a place like this since — perhaps never. She indicated the woman's near-full wine glass. 'She doesn't drink.'

'Talk to her,' I said.

'And say what?'

'Tell her you like it here.'

'She couldn't care less,' concluded Marie.

It was hard to catch the woman's attention. She had a good avoiding technique. She might be concealing something. I thought it might be age. Age lurked behind all that painted artistry.

'I think she's shy,' said Marie.

I asked the Corsican if he knew her. He looked at

her directly. He at least could do that. I asked him why she was here. I hadn't been so interested in anyone for years.

The four at the table spoke but not for the gallery. Their mouths moved, but not for lip-readers. How different they looked from the rest of the café. They'd look different anywhere. I supposed they'd come from Paris together. After patting the dog, Madame walked – it was more than a walk, it was a lifetime of practice – back behind the bar. She smiled at the waiters and gave an order or two. She definitely knew how to do that: they worked fast, faster, professional, disciplined. The Corsican went to the bar and asked her a question. She turned to him and her eyes widened, accepting him. The man with the sad face and the even sadder dog left. Jean Gabin lit a cigar and turned his eyes on the television. A waiter gave the woman a freshly squeezed orange juice with ice-cubes, which she drank delicately, with pleasure.

'I think she's given up the sauce for one reason or another,' said Marie. 'It's inconceivable she doesn't drink.'

The Corsican got talking to her with noticeable ease.

'She likes men,' said Marie. 'She's a man's woman. Doesn't trust anything else.' JoJo asked us back to the dance floor. The place was filling up, atmosphere hotting up, the music louder, beat stronger. The discussion even here was about 'La Parisienne'.

After a fast waltz with JoJo I lost him in the crowd and seemed to be dancing with a much cooler man.

'I'm Herbert,' he said. 'From –'

The Corsican came back and swung me towards the musicians. He wanted to sing. I wanted to hear about his conversation.

'We talked about hair,' he said.

'Hair.'

'How long it takes to put her hair up like that.'

'And?'

'Ten minutes.'

'And?'

'No and,' he said.

She – her name was Colette – had a natural discipline that would never allow her to slip into excess or parody or disappointing intimacy. She was simply a refugee from Pigalle, thirty years ago.

Just as I'd signed for the flat so she'd signed for the café. Everything seemed to happen around April. Herbert, the English solicitor from Lancashire, had reason to remember that date. By chance he'd met Madame Beaumarchais in the Toulouse area and given her a lift back to Castel.

Three in the morning. No dent in Colette's impeccable style. She was still very hard to get, out of reach. Just because she was Pigalle did not mean you could have her – her attention or literally.

The Corsican asked what I did. I told him I was a singer. He was thrilled.

'Sing here.'

'I couldn't for a million.'

'A million what?' He rattled in his pocket.

It all seemed out of my range emotionally, stylistically.

We danced the tango, the conga, and now it was all

effortless. Bodies belonging to the music, all thought of tomorrow gone. Yesterday – that had never been. I felt a wince of excitement. Like the old days when I was first in Spain. On the drive back to Castel in the sunrise I felt high, higher.

'Ssh. Don't flaunt your luck,' said Marie.

Chapter Five

No one had told me who lived above my apartment. In fact, people were reticent about my neighbours. Marcel's partner, Juan Pamello, who used to be chief of the railway station when trains still ran through Castel, had an absolute knack of shifting the issue. He'd counter a hard question with another hard question. Only the Spaniard was as good at that as him. Juan Pamello was Spanish. He'd left Valencia for France after his obligatory military service and he'd worked for French rail for twenty-five years. When the exquisite nineteenth-century station had closed in Castel, twelve years before, he had joined Marcel as an estate agent. He was married to a French midwife who worked in the main Perpignan hospital and had two sons at university. He was fiercely proud of them, undeniably ambitious for them, and couldn't help showing it, although he played a close hand about everything else. For himself he wanted to live his dream and go round the world by rail.

'So who's above my apartment?'

'God.'

'Neighbours are a deal-breaker.'

'But you English love bad neighbours.'

'Never.'

'I read it in one of your more reliable newspapers. Most English hate their neighbours.' He puffed on a pipe, which stained his teeth and displeased his wife.

'So what's up there?'

'I'm not selling up there so how do I know? Why? D'you want someone up there?'

'I probably don't.'

'Think yourself lucky. No one's up there. It's a granary up there.' He had a lovely laugh, dry and full of amusement.

Then he said that if I had doubts about the apartment I shouldn't buy it. Doubts would turn into unhappy certainties later on.

Juan Pamello had fine, frizzy, greying hair, a cloud around his head, and a sensitive intelligent face. He had a sensual understanding of things and probably understood women, which gave him an advantage over the majority who did not. His wife knew all that and kept an eye on him, the one she didn't keep on his pocket. She ran a tight show and wanted a civilized retirement. Getting old was bad enough, but getting broke? She was lemon-blonde and should have been pretty, but her mouth was hard. She didn't exactly make friends with Marie. When she saw her, she said sharply, 'Oh, you're the woman my husband runs around with at all hours. I didn't realize you were middle-aged. I wouldn't have worried.' Then she laughed, turning it into a joke. She thought.

Because of the expensive lengthy legal rigmarole, the final purchasing signature was delayed. I still stayed in the apartment above L'Hostellerie and every day turned into a holiday, an adventure. Marie hired a car and we went, often with Juan Pamello, into Spain, or across the Pyrénées to St Jean de Luz on the Atlantic coast, or down to the French coast below Perpignan, or up to the Cathar country. Sometimes we just drove ten minutes to the frontier, with its main street filled with duty-free shops, flamenco dolls in every window, hotels, restaurants. We ate in a Spanish tapas bar and in the afternoon danced tango. Filled with men, it had an extremely lively atmosphere. It took us a visit or two to realize it was a brothel. Then one day Juan Pamello came round, all excited with a proposition. 'There's a house just coming on the market and I'm telling you first. You must see it.'

It was a proper house, lived in by proper people, a nuclear family, professional, part of the intelligentsia of the Castel community. It was all the things Juan Pamello was excited about. In excellent condition, superbly restored, but it was on the edge of the village towards the agricultural area. Also, it was expensive. Not by English standards but seventy thousand francs was a real investment. But the windows were too small and there were no views. Juan Pamello said windows were meant to be small to keep out the terrible summer heat. I thought of the views from the postman's flat – not thought, could not forget.

'That apartment is not usual,' said Juan Pamello. 'This house is a very good buy and I know I'll sell it quickly. You could offer fifty-five and they'd settle for sixty-one. I could get you a mortgage.'

Parts of the house were over four hundred years old, other parts much older. Some of the stonework and the arches dated from the tenth century. Well, who was to say that they didn't? It had been restored with respect, modernized with taste. The walls were painted lemon and tangerine and sharp green, all citrus colours, and then a patch of deep blue. The blue tiles around the tangerine walls of the bathroom thrilled Marie.

'They went to Spain to get those. For ceramics you have to go to La Bisbal.'

It was a good house. It was at the top end of a narrow, sloping, uneven street, with the clear mountain water coursing down its sides, named after Pierre Brune, who had built the Picasso art museum.

Showing me the house was the worst thing Juan Pamello could have done. I was now confused – worse, ambivalent. So to break all that up he showed me a third property above the main grocery shop, Casino. It was decorated in the Spanish style and easy to come into and leave.

Juan Pamello believed he knew me. 'You don't want to settle down. You want to keep going, travel. With this you just pack a bag and lock the door. Go where you want. There are no overheads and it doesn't need anything doing to it either.'

Did the postman's flat?

'Let's say this is a *pied-à-terre*, which is really what you want. And when you're away I'll look in and check it's all right. And it's easy to let if you ever need to.'

As I couldn't make up my mind I decided to buy all of them. I ended up driving myself and everyone mad. I'd live in one and let the others for income. I'd organize art and adventure tours to Castel. Greed would change my life. It took two days to shake my head clear and I decided to forgo my deposit and live in the L'Hostellerie apartment.

'She'll get over that in forty-eight hours too,' Marie told Juan Pamello. 'And she'll be back in the first flat. But then she'll back out altogether and leave for London.'

For the first time he remembered his commission, all the running around he was doing for something he might not get. He decided to laugh. 'Madame Jane, you're like a woman before her wedding day.'

'But I think she's right,' said Marie. 'It's ambivalence, but a wise ambivalence.'

How I disliked being spoken about in the third person. She did that a lot, I noticed. Juan Pamello treated us equally. Which one he preferred, if either, was a secret among the hundred others he protected.

Marie still saw every available property because she loved old buildings and longed to restore them. She'd spent two years restoring a medieval village property in a fortress village in the Côte d'Azur. It belonged to her previous married life and she wanted to sell it and do something fruitful with the proceeds. With Marie, Juan Pamello developed another dream, of opening a cultural new-age centre where people could live in peace hopefully. It had spiritual overtones. The clients could have companionship or not, create, meditate, discover, be fulfilled. Juan Pamello thought it was realistic. 'It's what people want, these days. There's too much isolation.'

I thought it was just another way of describing an old people's solution.

'Well, yes. And I'll be the first in there. I'm sixty.

And I know three widows who'd sell up their houses and buy immediately. Why should we get old and have to be lonely too? It's a good thing. We can do all the things we've never had time for and promised one day that we would.'

Marie would buy the property and he would run it.

'Better sell your house first,' I said.

'There's no harm in looking and I enjoy it.'

She took Juan Pamello speeding around the countryside. His wife was furious, but he liked it. The three of us got on well together. Perhaps we all shared a sense of impermanence, a hankering after adventure and replenishment. Juan Pamello didn't drink any more because he believed he had the beginning of an ulcer. He took us to a hidden-away health store off the main street, surprisingly well stocked. They baked him a special bread.

'That won't help as long as you suck on that pipe.' Marie loathed smoke. He said he'd chuck it in and get really fit before he did the long rail adventure. He just had to wait for his younger boy to settle at university. Although Castel was a paradise for me, for him it was a compromise. He'd obviously forgone many dreams and wishes for the wife and kids, the job and the retirement fund. If he didn't get on that long-distance train soon, he'd be too old. Marie said he'd never make it, but the thought of it kept him going. He was moody, ungossiping, almost mathematically discreet, especially when it came to my neighbours. He admitted he may have seen Madame Beaumarchais.

Francine at L'Hostellerie said she owned a villa up in the nearest hills. On hearing I was about to buy the postman's flat with actual cash, she suddenly had a lot of neighbours who were happy to up and go at a moment's notice if I offered the right price. These villa neighbours were all well-to-do, their houses were their castles. They invested and improved and upkept and outdid each other. The villa neighbours all had magnificent lawn mowers. I saw just one villa. 'It's an investment, a real investment in every way.' I found myself almost apologizing to Francine.

'But you don't want to live in hotels.' She was horrified. 'That's dead money.'

Then she remembered that she ran one.

Marie was fascinated by the L'Hostellerie family. How did a brother, sister, sister-in-law and brother-in-law manage to run a business, spending six full days a week close together? How could they stay professional, friendly, and keep it good behind the scenes? 'It takes discipline,' said Francine.

Marie thought there was more to it than that. It didn't interest me particularly. They got on with each other to survive. But I did notice that the billboards advertising this exclusive place mentioned only two names yet there were four people. Sacrifices were, perhaps, part of the discipline.

While Marie and Juan Pamello looked at deserted estates and hotels for sale – they were on to the big stuff now – I went back to the apartment. The postman and his family had gone back to Marseille, but had given me the keys and said visit whenever I wanted. They'd come back for the final signing.

The atmosphere, the structure were harmonious and life-affirming. It was a sanctuary. But could I really live here? Had I enough inside me to keep it going and be on my own? Like the two couples in L'Hostellerie I'd need discipline. Perhaps I should get to know the area and rent for a while. But already I loved the area. 'Loved' rather than 'knew'. Perhaps that was more important. I could see that the house was a better investment and the Spanish flat an easier deal, but this place – it made my day. If I was going to take the jump I had to do it now. It wasn't something you thought over. It would only confuse the issue.

Shall I take it? I seemed to ask not myself but the stone walls, yellow with sunlight. At that moment the church bells rang for a wedding, and I had no problem in taking that as a sign. And I'd be near him. He, who was a mere hour away across the border. After all, I couldn't live in his city or even, perhaps, in his country. I felt like a bird perched high above him in the distance, unseen, with the freedom to go to him and leave him when I chose. And nobody would know where I came from or went to.

Although I had now made up my mind, I still asked Juan Pamello what he thought. He was surprised. Who would ask an estate agent a question like that? Perhaps because I trusted him he told me the truth.

'The house in the Pierre Brune is a very good buy. That's first choice. Second, the Spanish flat. It's easy to manage or resell. This is third. But it's what you want to live in that counts.'

The house was too far out and I didn't fancy walking back there at night. The Spanish flat didn't have views or charm. So I took the estate agent's third choice and would make the best of it. Like marrying the guy they warned you was no good but you knew you could turn him around because love was there. The postman's flat was right in the centre of everything. Sometimes, it seemed, it was at the centre of the world.

Chapter Six

Juan Pamello stopped me in the street. 'Ah, I was looking for you. I want you to meet Monsieur Garcia. He lives on the same floor as you.' He was so proud to produce a neighbour, a good one. 'He's just having a shower and change of clothes. He likes to look his best.'

We sat at a pavement table outside the Grand Café, and Juan Pamello bought the drinks and an assortment of hors d'oeuvres. The café was known for the freshness of its snacks. Today they had small pieces of duck, little dishes of perfumed rice, roasted peppers, salt anchovies. I asked for olives. Out of olives. Although the area was packed with yards of olive trees, vast plantations of olive trees, I could never find one to eat. There were none in the bars and the Casino grocery only sold tins or packets from Morocco or Greece. What happened to the local ones?

Juan Pamello asked the waiter, who said his father, the chef, was a specialist on olives.

'So where are they?'

'He only serves olives when he cooks rabbit.'

Even Juan Pamello thought that was strange. 'So where can we get some?'

'They have very good olives in Spain. Filled with anchovies or peppers. In small tins.'

'What about French olives?'

A generous shrug took care of that.

'Maybe they destroy the local ones,' said Juan Pamello. 'To give priority to another country. A lot of corrupt and stupid things happen in the EEC.'

I never did find out where the local olives ended up. Perhaps in Spain, in those much-admired little tins.

Monsieur Garcia was a taxi-driver in Paris, had been for forty years. He was wiry, thin, fiery and loved life. He certainly gave it his best shot. He was full of energy, laughter, and lived it all to the last piece. He didn't keep himself in the bank. No rainy-day philosophy there. He had a colourful voice, and used all the range he had, accompanying it with skilful gestures. He was watchable. Yes, he was an actor, an entertainer. That's what he really was. He made his living driving a cab and that didn't stay in the bank either. He said immediately that life was for the living and he didn't bother with savings. He simply bought what he liked. He had a boat moored in Toulouse, a house on the Catalan coast in Spain and, of course, his apartment in Castel.

'I fell in love with the place so that was that. Nineteen years ago.' He caressed the words, closed his eyes with pleasure. 'Here were all these marvellous trees in the breeze. It was so hot I forgot a breeze could even exist. I just arrived under them. My wife saw this house, looked up at my very flat. She loved its style, the windows. And at that moment a woman came out and said it was for sale.'

He also had an essential base in Paris, which his wife

also liked. It appeared that she was a sophisticated woman and liked town life. She'd been to Castel twice and found it parochial.

Juan Pamello cut in swiftly, 'You mean something else. She wouldn't know what parochial means. She's used to the big city. That's what you mean.'

Garcia opened his mouth to speak, then changed his mind. Instead he opened his arms wide, embracing the whole street. 'Dear lady,' he said to me, 'what I love about the place – there are no shops. Where can you buy Armani here?'

'Buy Armani?' said Juan Pamello, amused.

'She likes to *look* at Armani then buys something similar. She said to me the other day, "I think I should become a Catholic." So I said, "you already have a religion. The avenue Montaigne is your church and Armani your god."'

'The avenue Montaigne is the *haute couture* area in Paris,' Juan Pamello explained softly. 'I didn't realize taxi-drivers made so much money. I'm in the wrong business.'

'I work the hours,' said Garcia, with a gentle shrug. 'I have the property. She has the lifestyle.'

Garcia spent time on his appearance and was always strikingly clean, his clothes fresh, vibrant colour, never faded, immaculate. The only odd note – he looked like a fox but it said something for his charm that you didn't notice it. He was somewhere near seventy and no stranger to the tint bottle. The sharply trimmed moustache and well-cut hair saw some dye. He spent part of the year working in Paris, the rest travelling between his boat, his apartment and his house by the sea. He agreed that he had a lovely life. He liked to eat well and drink and play cards. Many of his Parisian taxi-driver friends had moved to the Roussillon area.

He pointed to the mountain, the abundance of white blossom, the sky. He breathed the scented air deeply. 'You'll love it here.'

I believe that everyone has a unique voice, more a sound. Most people live without really uncovering it except during intense occasions – joy, sorrow, making love. He'd found his. It was a sound in the upper register that almost sang out of him from the heart. 'I love.' That's what the sound carried.

He was eager to show us his apartment which, after a modest beginning, swept into gracious interlocking rooms, and finally a salon with large mirrors, generous plants in tubs, delicate sofas on spindly legs, a piano, framed French posters from the turn of the century. The place had a *belle-époque* style, easily attained. He called it the Music Room. Everything was scrupulously clean, personally scrubbed and polished by him. He told Marie that he'd had the beams restored and the fireplace uncovered. But the paper was coming off the ceiling in the corner of the kitchen. A flood? From upstairs?

Somehow the house was more vast than I'd imagined, with unending doorways leading to grand apartments. Garcia's doorway was nothing much, although when I came to think about it later, it looked over-sturdy and too tough, as though it was the last door possible that could keep whatever it was out.

I didn't think any more about the ceiling stain because Garcia sat at the piano and gave a marvellous recital of the old French songs sung by his celebrated passengers. He had a vibrant voice, strong on the high notes. He'd known all the singers – Jacques Briel, Piaf, Freya, Mouloudji, Ferré.

After 'Un Jour Tu Verras', he sang the one Charles Trenet made famous, 'La Mer'.

'Charles Trenet lives just up the road. He owns the Résidence du Soleil.'

I went back into my flat via the terrace we shared.

'Anything you want, ask me. Day or night. I know you'll be happy here, dear Madame. I'll take you to Vidal's for supper. And even to the Relais Chartreuse, a Moroccan restaurant near Le Boulou.' He lifted his fingers to his mouth. 'Exquisite.' His hands swung out of the life-affirming gestures and he held them together, clasped in a gesture I hadn't seen him make before. He looked uneasy. 'Of course, you've seen Mademoiselle van Zoelen?'

I gestured that I hadn't. His gesturing was catching.

'Oh, well. There's so much to see.'

I did not pick up the note of warning.

Because the postman, Monsieur Augustin, had allowed me free access to the apartment before the final signing, I made a list of the things I'd have to do. I definitely wanted a new kitchen.

Marie was curious about Garcia. 'He must make a helluva lot driving a cab in Paris to let that wife strut around in Armani.'

'Yet he's a simple guy.'

'Oh, no, he isn't. He just seems a simple guy.'

I supposed Garcia had not declared every *sou* of profit to the French tax inspector.

He obviously had a certain kind of marriage, in

which he and his wife could live apart amicably. It would be amicable: he was described as a man with a warm heart, big as a house. He was obviously self-sufficient, did his cooking, looked after his clothes, dealt with any loneliness he might have, while she enjoyed all the complexities of the big city.

But when I mentioned it to Madame Beaumarchais, she said, 'Oh, no, it's not the city or the shops. That's not why she doesn't come. She has to stay behind to look after his dog.'

I replied, 'Everyone here seems to have a different answer.'

She laughed drily. 'Don't be fooled. Wolves never eat each other.'

Chapter Seven

The house had been built after the French Revolution in the late eighteenth century and was supposed to be a listed building. It was right in the centre of the village on the main boulevard. Monsieur Rey, aged ninety-three, worked in his travel agency opposite. He advertised trips to Lourdes and owned most of the buses in the area. He was a millionaire but I saw him go through the public rubbish bin attached to his outer wall. At his age, perhaps he'd mistakenly thrown something away. At my age, at any age. I felt that living opposite him, some of his money luck might rub off on me.

On either side of the magnificent hallway was a hairdressing salon, Sophie and Elle, and squeezed beside the front door a bookshop with stands on the pavement. A respected French-Moroccan author with an intriguing dark face and green eyes often worked in this shop. He also arranged readings for local authors, of which there were very few. It was painters in Castel.

Madame Beaumarchais owned the first-floor flat. On the second floor there were several doors. Next to me was a small empty studio owned by a Monsieur Gato and his wife, who had left Castel and made an upmarket move to a villa with a pool. And opposite, the life-loving Monsieur Garcia.

The third floor, the granary, was unused. Around the back, on the ground floor, was a courtyard with hanging trees and bits of statue. It was a stately house, with a solid, cool atmosphere. The stairs were generous with lovely old maroon tiles bordered in wood. They were at least a hundred years old. They were washed and polished by Madame Beaumarchais's cleaner.

Marie understood houses and how they should be – she had an instinct for that. She decided to stay and get my apartment into the right condition before she went back to London. I'd said what I wanted: all the postman's decoration scraped off, white walls, and the red, juicy, plastic floor-covering lifted. She included that the shutters should be painted, the walls made flat, the floor-covering lifted, yes – but take it further: uncover the original stones and polish them up. Yes, I agreed, that was what I wanted. She called in Marcel and, in French faster and more acute than even his, got an estimate. Then she got it down.

She was very excited. Old houses, apartments – her love. She was far more excited than me. The place offered me a new way to be alive. It offered her a chance to turn the acceptable into the superb. Lights, furnishings, a new doorway to the lavatory, all in old original materials. Not modern approximations. She measured doors and windows for net curtains or blinds. At Colette's she'd found a handyman, JoJo, who was not only a splendid dancer but had a complete understanding of her renovating ideals. He loved the old stuff, could handle it, could find it. She grabbed him immediately and showed him my apartment. They planned to turn it into a work of art. I was not consulted. Perhaps she believed I had no understanding of this sort of thing. However, I presumed I was going to pay for it. They stood, the two of them, beside the slim brown tree trunk that rose from the floor and into the ceiling in the middle of the main room, and made a list of prices. I hoped the tree trunk actually supported the ceiling because it looked decorative and unreliable. JoJo, a thin little fast guy, like a jockey, with a constant hand-rolled cigarette in the corner of his mouth, knew the house very well because he'd worked on it and had often had to protect it. The stairs. How often over the years someone had wanted to tear up those tiles. He slapped a hand on the tree trunk.

'Is that holding the ceiling up?' I asked.

'No, no. I put that there twenty years ago.'

In came old stones, old tiles, old lamps. What he couldn't find he could construct from the bits he did find. Marie was pleased. 'He's an artist. Someone like him is so rare.'

I explained I was happy about JoJo working but I wanted more involvement in the planning.

She couldn't waste time on all that. 'Go out and walk and have a coffee. You can have this place done adequately or it can be done really well. I know how to do it. So does he.'

She, of course, also spoke excellent French.

JoJo bent over an old door, sawing and banging, little dark eyes like currants, lips whistling around the gone-out cigarette.

'He's got five brothers. They all work with him. They'll come here and have this done in a week.

I couldn't object. There was nothing to object to. She did know what she was doing and would do it infinitely better than me. I shrugged Garcia-style and went out for a walk. Marie had a good heart. She was absolutely straight. She was, in essence, a good friend. She was so good-looking and yet that wasn't enough. She had to control everything as well. I found it sad.

Then I saw the beautiful girl with the moon face, Madame Beaumarchais's antagonist, running down the stairs from the granary above. She introduced herself as Eliane van Zoelen. She said she hoped I'd be happy in the flat – if I took it. I wondered why there was any doubt. She went on down the stairs on high-heeled speckled noisy shoes into Madame Beaumarchais's apartment and called out to her with a certain rough familiarity.

I told Marie about the meeting.

'Eliane Van Zoelen? Who is she?' asked Marie.

'She is –' For the first time JoJo was caught off guard. 'She owns the house.' He went on whistling and sawing.

'I do want a new kitchen,' I reminded them. 'And this floor-covering off and the walls. That's all.'

So Marie told me why 'all' was never a term used when refurbishing a place. JoJo agreed immediately. In speedy French he listed the absolute changes, the improving ones and, finally, the adornments. I couldn't understand any of them.

'He'll do it for a fabulous price.' Then Marie said softly, 'Who is Eliane van Zoelen?'

One thing about Juan Pamello: he made his confusion genuine.

'Van Zoelen? Do you mean the young woman?'

'Who owns the house,' I said.

Juan Pamello looked puzzled at first. He was good at that, too.

'She's in the house,' said JoJo, matter-of-fact, and surprised us all.

'Is she?' said Marie.

JoJo liked understatement. 'Up above you. She's doing up the granary. I'm doing it up for her, actually.' He added casually, 'I'm laying the floors.'

Juan Pamello gave him a look — one I'd seen only on the faces of attacking animals in children's books. Then he remembered he was civilized and lived by certain values and the look was gone.

'I don't like the sound of that,' said Marie.

So Juan Pamello decided he knew more about it. 'I didn't know she was back.'

JoJo didn't have time for diffidence with the truth. 'She walks up and down past your office enough.' He didn't care if he blew away Juan Pamello's commission. He didn't like too much fiddling around the actualities. He liked Marie, respected her, and I, her friend, was spending hard-earned money.

'I'm working, not looking out of the window,' said Juan Pamello. 'As far as I knew the girl lived in St Jean-de-Corts.'

'With a croupier,' said JoJo. 'They've split up.'

'And now she lives in the granary,' I said. And then I thought, What are we getting so wound up about? What's wrong with Eliane van Zoelen?

'Van Zoelen? Isn't that Dutch?' said Marie. 'Is she from here?'

'Yes,' sighed Juan Pamello. 'She's French by her mother and Dutch by her father.'

'Has she got a small child?' I remembered seeing her with Madame Beaumarchais.

'She must be three or four.' Juan Pamello looked at JoJo. 'By the croupier?'

'Not necessarily,' said JoJo.

'But how can she own the house?' I asked.

'Let's go to the lawyer,' said Marie.

Maître Aznar was busy. She was always busy. It seemed she was the only lawyer in Castel. The waiting room was full.

'There is another,' said Juan Pamello.

'But no one likes him,' said Marie.

'Exactly.' He put some change into the drinks machine and got us a Coke. 'You don't want to listen to every rumour you hear,' he said.

'No,' said Marie. 'That's why I'm here. I want to hear some truth.'

Finally we sat in Maître Aznar's room in an oval, Marie, Juan Pamello and me. She opened the file and flicked through the notes, then looked at me. 'We've got to get your marriage certificate.'

'I had it faxed.'

'I need the original.' She closed the file. Her face

was pale and drawn with exhaustion. She had remarkable eyes: they lit up and dimmed down depending on who she was talking to. She liked a laugh. On this occasion she wasn't getting one.

Marie put the case in her perfect French but Maître Aznar turned to me with her answer. 'Van Zoelen doesn't own the house. She owns the façade for some peculiar reason. She did own the house but circumstances have changed that. She does, however, retain the top floor.'

'She's in the process of doing it up,' said Marie.

'Well, that can happen,' said Maître Aznar. 'It's not against the law.'

'It could be very noisy. Laying floors.' Marie knew all about that.

Then I had a good idea. 'Why don't we go up there and ask her?' I said. 'She seems nice enough.'

'You can try,' said Maître Aznar drily. She rustled some extra papers. 'You should be able to sign in another week.'

'What's taken so long?' asked Marie.

'By French law we have to check that there's no outstanding loan or mortgage on that apartment. That protects Madame Jane.' She looked at me straight. 'And I advise you to have the property checked over before you sign. In this country we do not have surveyors but Marcel, I'm sure, will be able to advise you on your prospective purchase.'

She got up. We stood up too and shook hands. She was conservatively pretty, spoiled, the daughter of a famous Catalan judge. Her hand was dry as a twig. She was married to a man from Spain who was less powerful than her. She had two children. And she was a very good lawyer.

From the Second World War on, the house had been owned by Eliane van Zoelen's family. Her grandparents, wealthy and bourgeois, had left it to her mother, who was courted by the eligible men of the province. But in the late fifties a German painter crossed the mountains from Spain on foot and arrived in Castel broke, exhausted, his espadrilles glued by sweat, blood and wear to his swollen feet. Nobody ever forgot the sight of those exhausted espadrilles. Eliane's mother fell for him, took him in, supported his painting career. In 1959 she gave birth to their daughter, Eliane. For a time they lived well and apparently happily in the house. Van Zoelen was considered an excellent painter but the marriage became unhappy and, when Eliane was eleven, he committed suicide. His widow took to drink, drugs and men. Eliane was propelled into adult life. Money dwindled; the house had to be divided, bit by bit, into apartments and sold off. JoJo had done the dividing and tried not to damage the essential character of the house. Madame Beaumarchais had bought the first apartment, seventeen years ago, in 1968. She came for the air and the nature. Eliane, her mother and their two lovers moved up to the second floor. That in turn was sold off, and they moved up to the granary. A falling-out occurred: the mother and her new lover moved to Amélie-les-Bains and Eliane moved with the croupier to St Jean-de-Corts, while he worked in the casino at Le Boulou.

That was the story I got in part from Madam

Beaumarchais and Marcel. It had a lot in it. I thought a lot was left out. Some tricky lawyer tactics had allowed Eliane to keep at least part of the house she loved by owning the façade. But she was broke.

I saw Eliane again on the stairs and was taken aback by just how beautiful she was. She had a pale perfect face, voluptuous mouth, black hair, glossy and thick, hanging in ringlets in a fringe over her forehead and down the side of her face, and pulled back at the nape of her neck. Her eyes were startling in their power, clear green, slightly slanted, imperious, elusive. Sometimes they seemed to swim away into her inner world of private dreams. She'd look at you from two worlds at once and it was disconcerting. Her nose was slightly hooked, skin creamy, flesh taut. She looked like a Picasso model. More, she looked like the result of Picasso's having dreamed and painted there. Somehow she'd escaped in the flesh from one of his pictures. She had had a horrible life. She came to symbolize what I experienced there. Undeniable beauty and the bitter side of things.

She told me openly that she was in the process of doing up the 'attic' and invited me up to see the work. The higher we got, the dirtier the stairs. Madame Beaumarchais's cleaner wasn't evident here. Eliane swept a giant spider to one side and pushed open a door which had seen some abuse: it had been hacked at, chopped around the lock. It gaped where a foot had kicked it in. I didn't give much time to its injuries because what was on the other side took all my attention: it was a bomb site, a devastation.

The floor had been lifted and we were standing on wooden beams. There was a lot of mud and dirt and rubbish. The windows were mere holes and the stonework of the wall was uncovered. Dotted here and there, like objects left stranded by a raging sea, were what had once been kitchen furnishings, a stove, a fridge, a washing-machine. In one corner isolated, as though on a jetty, were four chairs on which people sat, around their feet newly cemented floor tiles, and beside them a new table. Deep in the dust and mud, JoJo bent, his shoulders shuddering as he shovelled and scraped. He'd abandoned Marie and her ideals for the old true employers upstairs. He'd forgotten his loyalty and they remembered it for him. He scarcely knew me. Like a duo in a circus act, Eliane and I walked along a pipe and joined the group on the perfectly laid jetty of new floor. She waved at her empire of the dirty, lost and broken, and said, 'I'm having it all done in these tiles.'

I agreed they were tasteful.

She showed me the room around the corner, where a new kitchen range, dazzlingly clean, was waiting to be plugged in. On the floor, old rescued tiles from the house's former glory. The walls were painted pale lilac. An expensive cloth was spread across the table. New plates, glasses, goblets were still stacked in boxes.

'I'm having an open-plan kitchen.'

Further along was a half-finished bedroom, with brass and copper adornments and a new luxury bed with drapes.

Then she took me back and introduced me to the people. They were drinking wine, Pernod and whisky, and the new table was strewn with glasses and full ashtrays. Around this devastated room lay mountains of rubbish. This squalor must have come from generations back: no one lifetime could have produced all that. From a black sack a long tail moved and a dusty rodent came into view. I gave the appropriate cry. Eliane laughed. 'It's nothing. It's my daughter's pet mouse.' The quartet at the table got a good laugh out of that. I looked from the broken areas of clean, new, bridal-suite-pure renovation to this excavation site. It reminded me of some of my nightmares. I felt so over-come my legs shook.

'This is my mother.' She pointed to a sullen, blowsy woman in her late fifties, who was lapping up the Pernod. Her extraordinary beauty was still in her face, but in clumps. A patchwork of good and bad, like the apartment. On the next chair her most recent lover, a drug-dealer from a *marginaux* community in Arles-sur-Tech, the next village on from Amélie-les-Bains. He was so stoned he rarely got a word out. The mother, on another sort of substance, couldn't stop talking. Eliane's croupier sat on the third chair: he was tall, thin and bitter, with hot eyes and magician's hands, always moving. On the fourth chair sat a flabby red-faced man, who was Eliane's latest admirer but, in fact, had to make do with her mother. He had a good car and paid for the drinks. The little girl ran around the territory, treading mud into the main kitchen.

Eliane did not, it seemed, get on with her mother. Or the croupier or the new fat friend. The little girl was wildly hyperactive. The two thin men were entirely at odds with each other. The croupier spat words of French obscenity.

Eliane waved a hand around, and said proudly, 'I'll just have this repaired and I'll live here with my daughter.'

It sounded all right. Then I saw JoJo cross his eyes.

The mother said something unintelligible and gruesome. Eliane retaliated. Her anger was superb and her eyes flared with points of fire.

I thanked them for their hospitality and balanced my way along the pipe to the outer door. I turned to wave goodbye. What did this scene remind me of? What did it sum up? I couldn't think of it. I should have. It summed up a brothel.

Chapter Eight

Colette stood behind her bar in the Café des Arcades, perfect as always, a star in a real-life show, and in just entering the place you became part of the performance. Her pale gold hair was as usual in the Gibson-Girl style, every strand up and in order, not one lost or forgotten, not a molecule out of place. She was dressed in a lilac silk suit, which reminded me of the walls in Eliane van Zoelen's new pastel kitchen.

I wondered why she made such an effort for this out-of-the-way café.

'But that's how she stays alive,' said Marie. 'Attention. She feeds off it.'

Colette smiled at me, surprisingly shy, and at that very moment a French song played, a song that you'd want to hear again and again. The singer's voice – I'd know it anywhere, yet I'd never heard it.

'What a marvellous song. Who is he?' I asked.

Colette answered, 'Mouloudji. He's been around since the fifties.'

I thought again how clear and well-rounded her voice was. There were no traces of night-club life in it. No Pigalle. Then she turned to look at Jean Gabin. She was never, I saw, engaged in conversation with anyone for long, especially not a woman.

Curists from all over France and Corsica swept in from the street and jostled on to the dance floor, the live music began and they danced waltzes, the paso doble, the mambo, old couples with beautiful posture – and one or two very old – others middle-aged, as Juan Pamello's wife would describe them, and some young. If there weren't enough men the women danced together. It was apparently not certain that they'd arrived in Amélie as couples or that they'd ever seen each other, but their relaxing treatment and Colette's place put them together anyway into 'curist couples' and Colette referred to them as Monsieur and Madame. The place certainly had something.

JoJo sat in the café playing *belotte*, his eyes long and cunning. When he saw Marie he threw in his cards, joined us and bought a round. The white wine was rough. 'You need *blanc sup*,' he said. The waiter, with the hunched back and long straight hair, who supposedly slept with all the women in Amélie, changed my wine. JoJo, looking at him, gestured, 'very hot'. 'They say he can do it around the clock but would these women even know? That's what I say.'

The waiter certainly hid his talents under a bushel. He couldn't have looked less like a seducer. He was like an illustration from a child's fairy-tale. Not sexual, not avaricious, just innocently there. He stood patiently and smiled almost sweetly as I approved the new wine. It was definitely *supérieur*.

'What about her?' Marie indicated Colette.

'She's a mystery, that one. The woman who cleans for her is my fiancée. Sort of.'

'Does she live here?'

'D'you mean upstairs in the hotel? Too rough for her. She lives in one of those palatial villas opposite.' He pointed it out across the road, with trees in front, late nineteenth century, next to a very proper curist's hotel where they played bingo, all correct, then crept out for a dance and a drink at Colette's.

'She's got an apartment on two floors. Rented.'

'How long has she been here?'

'About when you came. A month.'

Marie nodded towards Jean Gabin. 'Is he her *mec*?'

'Luc? They say he's her husband. My girlfriend says her father lives with them. He's very old, hardly goes out. They take his food over to him.'

We wanted to know everything about Colette's life: the apartment; what she was really like; her things; how did she look without makeup? We asked the questions all at once and I was aware that Luc and then Colette were suddenly watching us. We'd caught their attention. Did they sense we were talking about them?

Marie tried to change the conversation, but JoJo couldn't care less. 'From the place you couldn't tell anything about her except she doesn't need a cleaning woman. She's very clean and very tidy and keeps it that way. And empty. Just cupboards full of clothes and in the bathroom bottles of the stuff she puts on her face. Not even a photograph. It could be anyone living there.'

Suddenly Luc was beside our table. He reached out, took hold of JoJo's hand, shook it. They exchanged a greeting. JoJo's entire hand disappeared into the large clasp of the bigger man. JoJo got the message and shut up, and Luc sat seemingly relaxed on the next banquette watching football on television.

JoJo was somewhere between thirty-five and forty, and lived with his mother and five brothers. He'd done some semi-professional jobs but really worked as a handyman. He worked black, he explained. Nothing declared, no tax. He liked black. He'd never married and took care of his mother. He had a variety of tiny ailments that he spoke about with pride. He was victorious because no doctor had yet got the better of them. Medical talk? He could go on for hours, longer than the waiter could supposedly perform. The curists, both sexes, loved him. Then, he said, very quietly, 'I don't know if the old man is her father, you understand. He could be someone who stays in and doesn't go out a lot, for whatever reason. He's got a small dog.'

I remembered the gloomy man with the poodle on the first evening. He hadn't struck me as her close relation.

Marie indicated Luc. 'Tough?'

'Very.'

'A boxer?'

'A bit of everything. He can take care of himself.'

The hunchbacked waiter was at the table: did we want anything else? We got another round of *blanc sup*.

'As it's so clean why does she have a cleaner?' said JoJo.

'So the cleaner says it's so clean,' said Marie. 'So people can't speak about what she is and how she lives. The cleaner tells them. That's her real job.'

JoJo liked that idea. 'You could be right. But I don't think a place like this will allow a couple like that to stay.'

'It's a paradox,' said Marie.

When it had been explained to him what a paradox was, JoJo said, 'The whole place is. The area. It's never made sense.'

'Talking about which, how is Eliane's flat coming along?'

A cutthroat gesture took care of that.

'No good?'

'No money. She's *kaput*.'

He let his hand slip down slowly, as though he was drowning to show just how *kaput*. 'I can't go on working for her. It's a shame because it's half done.'

Colette stood behind the bar, not avoiding anyone's eye exactly, but not letting anyone catch hers. I could see she'd had practice at that. Dancing in Pigalle? Modelling? Stripping? She didn't *not* look at you, but she didn't look at you. Yet she had a certain class, a natural elegance. Just walking along the bar to the coffee machine took the attention of the entire room. Then she leaned on the counter. She looked out at the darkening street, her chin cupped in her hand. It had all the importance, that simple movement, of a drama. What happened when she actually did something?

A couple of locals came in and ordered beer. She talked to them briefly, her cherry-red lips full and smiling. The men were shy and thrilled.

Eliane hadn't paid JoJo anything for the work so far on her apartment or for the materials. He'd told her he'd have to return the paint that was left.

'She says the croupier will pay.'

'Will he?'

'They fight like hell. Her mother's got no money left.'

Then he, like everyone else, found himself staring at Colette. 'She's amazing for her age. I wonder how long it takes her to put all that on.'

And these were the two comments I mainly heard from men on the subject of Colette. A cautiousness prevailed. 'For her age.' And 'How much time?' It was a masculine consideration. Women never mentioned it.

'I wonder why she's here?' said Marie.

'I wonder how she's here,' said JoJo.

And all around the cries, '*Blanc sup.*' 'Deux Ricards. Deux blondes. Un espresso.' In the *bal musette* interval, the Mouloudji song came on again. I looked at Colette, and she smiled. I thought she gestured, 'For you.'

Marie dealt with that as though squashing an insect. 'For you? It's not in her vocabulary. It's nice. That's what she meant.'

Mouloudji's voice – there was joy in it, a rasping sweetness evoking summer, bees swarming, black-berries, richness, beneficence. It had in it a break, a catch that was thrilling. And I realized I was happy and then I thought of the past and that stopped all that. Just one forbidden thought had broken through and wouldn't leave and I hurried on to the dance floor to dance with the first person I saw, man, woman, child, and then the panic subsided and I was back in Paradise.

Mouloudji, and I heard him often after that, always reminded me of Colette. What he sang, she was.

We left JoJo to dance and went to eat at Le Pont, a small recommended restaurant on the riverbank. It was full to the last chair with curists and the owner now did two sittings. The food was cheap and wholesome, with not too many choices. He liked everything fresh – a dish of the day and then a vegetarian dish, a steak and fries or local fish. He didn't use tenderizer and picked the herbs himself. We had Galia melon, filled with local Banyuls dessert wine, fresh grilled sardines, grilled aubergine, hot garlic bread, salad, a piece of cheese and home-made crème caramel. The white wine was light and *pétillant*.

I felt a definite sense of let-down. I always did when I left the Café des Arcades. That was where life was, and it made everywhere else seem dull. All I wanted was to go back there. I felt there was some mystery, some rare excitement in that place from which I was excluded. I used to feel that around Jay. Jay – someone I didn't want to think of – that thought belonged in London.

Marie wasn't keen. 'I can only go there once a night. I'm sorry. And you should only go once. It looks –' For once she was at a loss. 'Well, she knows you're looking at her.'

'Who isn't?'

'You're different from the others. You've been around and she knows it. It's some mother thing you've got.'

When Marie got going on my family, or lack of it, I wished I'd been an orphan. I felt I had to defend my childhood and its occasional but definite happinesses.

Colette reminded me of a time I'd loved. Paris and Pigalle in the mid-fifties. In some moods I thought that that had been the best time of my life: full of hope, on the edge, glamorous ambitions. The total unconditional optimism of my sort of youth. The unknown. That's what I felt in that bar. It wasn't so much staring at the proprietress. I should have known that song. Perhaps, in those days, I did.

The restaurant owner thought Marie was a French TV celebrity, Christine Okrent, and urged us to taste his wife's lemon meringue pie. 'It's not industrial, manufactured. She makes it herself.' It was the best I'd ever tasted.

He introduced himself as Lucky. He came from the middle of France where he'd got no work; he'd come to the south and never looked back. He was equally attentive to all his clients, there among us, looking after us. With the coffee he gave a little glass of *digestif*, which he made from whisky, orange, honey, poured over ice.

'I'd like to do a more exotic menu. I love Thai food but there's no demand for it here and the curists will be put off. I make my living from them, not the locals. They're here three hundred and thirty days a year, excepting Christmas and the two weeks in January when they close the baths. Many of them are on diets and like the food simple, as they say "inoffensive". I always have a plain dish on offer, steamed fish or boiled chicken. I now let them give me their diet sheets and prepare some menus especially. A lot of them come for their liver, although the waters are mainly for arthritis, bad backs, aching joints, breathing problems, ladies' ailments. You go and take the waters at Le Boulou for your liver, and at Molitz–les–Bains for skin. They've got a white paste they put on that takes years off. And further on St Christau in the Hautes Pyrénées for mouth disease.'

He looked so young and fun-loving and fit, a million miles away from all those chronic ailments and decaying bodies.

'But I love to help people,' he said. 'Share my energy. Every year I go along to Lourdes and help out there, pushing the sick. And I've come round to thinking that perhaps it's better always to have a little something wrong to keep the immune system on its toes. You know what they say about a creaking door. Whereas the confident fit are suddenly felled with something and that's it. I am, Madame a *guérisseur*.'

I asked what that was.

'A healer. With the hands. And in this area, near Canigou, you can get a lot of power.' He showed us his hands. They were quite steady. And then they started to vibrate slightly. 'It's the mountain. A lot of people around here are healing their animals. They'd be criminals anywhere else. I tell my clients to walk half an hour every day and get the heart-beat up. Then they rest completely. A good relaxation in the fresh air. They do simple stretching exercises and make sure they laugh and eat here.'

It was a luxury to sit outside and watch the river on this humid night with the stars as big as plates. 'He's been loved by Mother,' said Marie. It was the biggest vote of confidence she could give anyone. In her view it divided society: those who had been and the others. That mother-love made life easy and flowing: the person was full of sun. And the others? They were ambivalent, damaged, and always trying to deal with it. I could guess which category that put me in. But she never mentioned a father's love. I was dubious anyway.

I didn't think love or the lack of it from wherever made any difference. We made our own destinies.

'The river's not always so well behaved,' said Lucky. He pointed inside the dining room at a tide-mark high up around the walls. 'September the twenty-sixth. I'll never forget it. Last year. Come and look.' He took us inside to do justice to his fearsome tale. 'One minute it was too hot, a burning, funny heat, and I took in the rum babas from the outside table because I feared the cream would go off. I crossed the room here, where several customers were still on their main dish. I carried the rum babas into the kitchen, put them in the fridge and turned round to come back into this room and then I heard it. A roar like a lion and the sky turned black. The storm hit. It was the worst storm I'd ever heard of. It was an inferno. And the water came piling in. I started to go into this dining room but there was no dining room.'

He had the full attention of the present clients in the now existent dining room. They stopped eating and watched him. Even the regulars looked up, quite entranced by this gruesome tale, performed each night between the second-sitting main course and the cheese and salad.

'This room was filled with five feet of water halfway up to the ceiling. Plates and bits of bread were floating on top, and it was rising. I prayed.'

His wife came out of the kitchen and stood in the doorway. 'I was terrified,' she said. The thought of her husband suddenly religious had literally done her in, upset her more than the adverse elements. 'I've never seen him believe in anything so to whom exactly was he praying? It's the last thing I'd have expected. And the customers clung to the floating furniture or stood on the steps.'

'And it rose to the top of that dresser.' Lucky pointed to a dried-out piece of old family furniture filled with china. 'I thought I'd had it. And I remember hanging on to something and two rum babas floating past in the water like breasts.'

'Lucky, be quiet,' cautioned his wife. The show was becoming too 'artistic' and belonged to the exotic menus. He was straying away nightly from the safety of the inoffensive dishes. He'd upset the curists next.

I thought Marie was going to come out with some crap about mother-love and his identifying the last desserts he might ever see with the feeding part of his mother's body. I thought she'd say, 'I told you so.' She didn't. I was quite disappointed.

'And where were your clients?' asked a client.

'They were all right. They could swim.'

And then he pointed to the high-water mark above the dresser, a mere foot from the ceiling. 'It suddenly stopped and the sun came out. So maybe a sinner's prayers have more effect than the practised ones. All this in a few minutes. Ten minutes that changed my life. I'd hung on by the last brick.'

It was a wonderful tale, which he enriched with each recounting. A few weeks later it had become a near-death experience with white light and a figure like Jesus in the kitchen. Had the experience made him a better cook? It had filled his till.

Chapter Nine

Marie understood houses, and buying and selling and bargaining. Just before I had seized the pen in the lawyer's office to make the first part of the down payment, the unreturnable ten per cent, Marie had sped in and got the price lowered to the equivalent of twenty-seven thousand pounds, which slightly embarrassed me.

'Don't be ridiculous. No one expects to get their asking price.'

Now she was moving in the other direction and risking money I wasn't sure I had. She'd also met Eliane on the stairs, a dreadful meeting, because Marie had had a rush of blood to the head and, on my behalf, asked to buy the unfinished 'attic', the half above my head. She wanted to build a terrace directly facing Canigou.

This rashness put me in immediate proximity to the croupier, the mother, the drug-dealer from Arles-sur-Tech and the fat man, a showy group I could have done without.

Eliane displayed a certain reserve, an ambivalence, in front of the others, which Marie sorted out for her. 'You've run out of money. With the money from the sale of the one half you can finish doing up the other.'

And then she corrected any ambivalence I still had left. 'Your apartment is charming enough, but with this addition it will be really something. And at the bank. You'll resell at a good price.'

I wasn't mad about the croupier's gaze or the drug-dealer's lack of contact or the fat man's hysterical sigh. I turned to the least worrying of the group. I asked the mother if she thought it was a good idea.

'You mean for my daughter or for you?'

'For your daughter, obviously. Not even I know what's good for me.'

Marie nudged me. 'Don't speak to them like that. Be businesslike.'

I saw a look of amusement pass from the mother to the lover. I thought she knew a little more English than she cared to admit. I thought 'businesslike' was a bad thing to start being with this group. I'd never been businesslike in my life.

We were invited to join them to discuss things on the jetty with the four chairs and the drinks table. The mother poured me a Pernod which all but lifted me off the chair. She didn't spare the liquor and went easy on the water. I turned my back so that I could not see the squalor mountain I was presumably buying. Marie, however, stared at it unflinching. 'With this over your head the only thing to do is own it.'

Suddenly, the mother and daughter flared up into a disagreement that shook and echoed around the stone walls like thunder. The croupier put in his share. The fat man tried to save Eliane. He landed in the muck of the unmade floor for his trouble. Hissing and spitting, they all seemed to swim across from the jetty to the safety of the stairs and descended in a pack to the calm reason of Madame Beaumarchais's grand flat to sort it out. We followed, uninvited. It seemed Eliane and her mother hated the house being no longer theirs. They still felt it was. Madame Beaumarchais listened to all the arguments and made her judgement.

Eliane should accept the offer and use the money to make a good place for her and the child. It was better for the child to go to school in Castel. What she really meant was that they would be better off away from the croupier. I should pay ten thousand francs more.

Marie called in Marcel to draw up architectural plans. A stairway would rise from within my hall cupboard and lead into the attic, from which a terrace would be built overlooking Mount Canigou. Marcel was thrilled. JoJo watched her admiringly. They weren't used to sudden grandiose flights of household fancy, not on this scale. Plans were drawn up and prices agreed, materials decided, and JoJo would start work as soon as the final signing took place. Eliane, after long hours of arguing with her mother and both lovers, agreed to sell the unfinished part of her property known as 'the granary' for sixty thousand francs. The deal was drawn up and we all trooped into Maître Aznar's office.

Marie, Juan Pamello, Marcel, Eliane were in the first row; behind her, her mother, Madame Beaumarchais, the mother's lover, Eliane's lover, the child and me. My feet were cold before I even sat in my chair. The mother started attacking Eliane and got plenty back. Then she turned on me. 'I don't want my daughter to let go of what is her house. It's where she grew up. But you've offered her this money and she wants to take it. You've come into our life like a snake in the Garden of Eden. We don't want your money, Madame.'

'I do,' said Eliane.

Maître Aznar intervened. 'I don't want to waste my time. You obviously have not decided what you want.'

'Not you, Maître Aznar,' said the mother. 'Not handling my legal affairs. Your father made "his" selling off my house when I was down on my luck. He robbed the rich and the poor.'

'Who are you talking about? Robin Hood?' said the drug-dealer. It was the first time I'd heard him say something. 'He's an English dealer and he'd not been around for a long time.'

The mother turned on him. 'Shut up. Why d'you have to keep putting yours in?'

'Maître Aznar's father was a judge,' continued the drug-dealer. 'What have they got to do with the law? They're paid to make it up.'

Maître Aznar, with considerable dignity, told him to shut up. She turned to the mother. 'If you want different legal representation, get it.' She closed the file with a snap.

'I will,' said the mother. 'I'll go to my own lawyer, the best, in Amélie. He deserves the title *Maître*. You're just a foreigners' lawyer.'

Juan Pamello and Madame Beaumarchais tried to suppress her. Eliane apologized gently to everyone and said that her mother had been ill and wasn't herself.

Maître Aznar asked firmly whose property it was. Eliane said it was hers.

'Do you wish to sell it?'

'Yes,' said Eliane.

At that point the child rushed up to Marie and said, 'You have to fuck well. Make sure of that.'

There was a dodgy silence. Eliane said innocently, 'I wonder where she –'

'You should wonder,' interrupted the mother. Then she muttered expletives and the croupier added his own.

The drug-dealer said, 'Then ask a proper price. Don't let them have it all their way.' Then he turned to me and apologized. 'It's always emotional, selling your place.' He even managed a smile.

'It can be more emotional when you can't,' said Marie sharply.

And suddenly I realized I'd be living next to this tribe of ill-assorted angry French, some down on their luck, others never had any luck. My feet now ice, I realized I'd never wanted this expensive extension. I wanted my simple, innocent apartment, empty with its miraculous views. I wanted a toehold in this village, not a commitment. Sixty thousand francs to Eliane and double for the work. I should not invest that much in a place I didn't know. I was strung out on indecision. In fact, the minute I'd paid the initial ten per cent on my apartment, ambivalence had set in like a physical condition and not gone away. I'd kept it to myself.

'Of course you want that terrace,' whispered Marie. 'It *makes* the apartment. Don't you see? And you want peace over your head.'

'But they'll be next to my head if I move up there.' I turned to the mother. 'I agree with you that Eliane should keep her inheritance. I shouldn't interfere with something like that.' I let them see I was making a sacrifice for their well-being and got out of there. Now the mother was furious with me: I'd let her daughter down.

But Eliane blamed Marie, who was now busy getting the keys to the empty studio next door. She talked about turning that into an extension of my apartment and I knew she'd overdone it. Some ghastly property-acquiring bulimia had overcome her.

Chapter Ten

The rain came, and with it reality. Scuttling across a deserted village from the Crédit Agricole cash-point to the Pablo café, sitting soaked in the endlessly empty bar, splashing up to the L'Hostellerie apartment for a change of clothes and a change of plans made me see the advantages of a big town. Where should I go? What should I do? Marie was ahead of me on that one. 'Get out.'

She felt to blame because she'd insisted on pursuing her interest in old houses in the first place, allowing me idle time to put down that ludicrous ten per cent deposit. And now the rain had come. She unfolded a huge, aggressive map and planned the route back to London. 'We'll drop the car in Perpignan and take a train to Montpellier. It's supposed to be a lively town, light atmosphere, full of doctors, so you'll like that. Start packing.' She didn't like my hesitation and flapped the map severely. She wanted to spend a day or two in civilized Montpellier because there I'd get a different perspective.

'You don't belong here. There's absolutely nothing to do. You've fallen into the same trap as everyone else who thinks they're going to be more alive in a foreign land.'

And then I fully understood what she was saying. 'After all you've done, all the people you've stirred up, the arguments, all you've promised, you're just going to leave? Like that?'

'Of course. They understand. It's the property business.'

I said I liked Castel. The noise of the rain drumming on the window was too loud. She didn't hear. More forcefully I said I loved the place.

'Of course you do. But it's a holiday romance.'

'What about JoJo? All those walls? The colours?'

'I'll send him a cheque for his time.'

I still didn't pack anything. Perhaps I might have if she'd said nothing and allowed the idea to come from me. I thought it must be my childhood lack of brothers, sisters that allowed me to be so bossed about. And by a woman. I would never take it from a man.

Always an elegant traveller, she was packed in two minutes flat and already at the door. 'What do you think you're going to lose by leaving London? Your problems? Your self?'

'Do psychotherapists know everything?' They seemed, at any rate, to have an answer for everything. And if they did get it wrong they'd say it was just to test the client's responses, resistance, sanity. So that way they were never wrong. Marie wouldn't be, anyway, because she'd learned early to fight her corner.

Rebellious, I went back to the Pablo and drank another *cortada*, coffee in a small glass with frothy hot milk and sugar. Monsieur Nadal, the owner, leaned on the counter watching the rain. His black moustache and hair gleamed in the greenish light. He said what he could to cheer me up. 'The earth needs it. It's better than the drought they've got over there.'

Almost eagerly I asked where 'over there' was.

'The other side of the Pyrénées. The mountains stop the weather fronts on this side so the rain falls here and Spain gets a drought.'

He asked when I was moving into the postman's flat. I didn't know. Suddenly, I didn't know much about anything. The weather had undermined my new life. And the realization that Marie could leave without me. London was her place. And I knew, how I did, that somewhere, some time, she'd been enchanted by a village or a person that seemed to offer a new life and been duped.

Monsieur Nadal had lovely dark glowing eyes. He was kind. Kindness was such an irresistible quality. Perhaps that made me trust him.

'I don't know if I should move here.'

'But surely London is terrible these days. It's right on the limit. Violence, no hope, recession, pollution, a terrible government. The Irish problem. Bombs.'

I could see how the French newspapers deflected their own country's problems. 'Stay here,' said Monsieur Nadal. 'We've got our faults but they're liveable with.' He thought he was cheering me up when he added, 'And there's lots of English here.'

'I've never seen one.'

'They're all around. Painters, lots of those, a writer, young people working on the land, builders, retired people. There's a teacher . . .'

Then he listed all the things I could do. Walking, exploring, dancing. Then Marie came in and cut short that list. She'd packed my stuff, which didn't please me, and Monsieur Nadal pretended he didn't understand English during the short spate that followed. She went back to L'Hostellerie to pay the bill. It seemed I had no choice. Monsieur Nadal gave me one.

'You can always stay here. Especially if *that* is too expensive.' He indicated L'Hostellerie. 'They're not from here.' He had a scrupulously clean hotel above the bar. 'I don't have a restaurant any more but you get breakfast. I'll do fresh fruit and yoghurt from the health shop. You'll find so much to do here.'

'And if it rains?'

'You want to learn French. And Spanish. And what about a painting course? You'll get to know people, but I have to say Catalans are hard to know. They're family people, private.'

'Like the Swiss?'

'The family is everything.'

Around his walls hung dozens of paintings, all dedicated to him for his friendship and support. Some from famous artists.

'But you don't know what I do, Monsieur Nadal.'

'No, I don't, Madame.' He went on watching the rain. The privacy was back in place. Then it occurred to me that he thought I was suggesting certain lurid occupations. To cut short any misunderstanding, I said, 'I am a singer. I write songs. I collect songs. I would like to collect old folk songs here.'

'People don't come to Castel just like that. They're drawn here.'

'Who by?'

'The mountain brings them. That's what I was told. So, Madame, I would stay here and find out why.'

He sang a snatch of a cheerful folk song in praise of Canigou and its blessings.

Marie stamped around in the doorway, ready to move, but Monsieur Nadal said that the weather was too bad and the motorway awash. I thought he was making a thing of it so that I didn't have to go. Although Marie was a Viking and fearless, she didn't particularly like the spray flung up from the wheels of other vehicles blinding her view, inhibiting still further her sense of direction. He gave her a sort of calming tea, containing personally picked herbs from the mountains, and told her to wait. Marie thought the wait would be no more than a few hours.

For days the rain fell, straight, noisy and endless, with a rhythm that was unnerving. It was thick, like grass in front of your face. The only thing that didn't change during the deluge was the quality of L'Hostellerie's cooking.

The two brothers-in-law created off-the-menu specialities for us, warming casseroles, *tripes à la Caen*, Lyon sausage in batter, *moules* and chips with green salad. Luckily their business was unaffected by the weather: French gourmets wouldn't let a little thing like a cloudburst or flood dent their style – they came from miles around, in steamed-up cars covered in mud. They ate and drank sumptuously, then glowing with excellence, made the hazardous journey home. I could see there was tremendous snobbery in the food and wine business. Francine, who ate like a fly, had to admit that in this climate she'd rather stay home and dry with a tin opener. She explained that *l'amour* wasn't what the French were about. It was food. They'd risk their lives for their stomachs.

L'Hostellerie had a cheaper section, the brasserie attached to the main restaurant. There was something not quite right about its shape: like a glass mollusc, it clung to the wall and you felt as though only half its shell was there. The space seemed cut in half. But a three-course meal cost 120 francs, and the wine *somme-lier* was always selling off ends of lines cheap.

The vineyards were ruined and the fruit. Farmers rushed to gather in what they could. Village houses leaked. Builders covered roofs with tarpaulin. The newsagent said the storm had carried down bits of the mountain itself. He pointed to lumps of ice and rock in the street: 'In all my life I've never seen anything like it. It's an omen.'

Marie believed it was a climatic change, caused by global imbalance. The farmers and mountain people agreed with her.

'Canigou was in a bad mood for days before the rain,' said the newsagent. 'It had a black face.'

'D'you believe that?'

'No,' he replied, 'but when it looks good, good things happen.'

Yet just as the atmosphere became crucially claustro-phobic, some new person would appear, seeking refuge from the rain, with stories to tell, and I supposed that was how it must have been for centuries. Or Francine would deliver a piece of amusing gossip, or through the dawdling clouds you'd catch sight of Canigou. Its pres-ence *was* out of the ordinary, a living presence, a giant watching over the hills and plains as far as the sea.

'Do you believe the mountain controls the area?' I asked Francine.

'No, but I'm not from this part. We come from Perpignan. That's where we had our previous restaurant. I and my brother come from Tunis. My sister-in-law is Catalan from Spain, and my husband, he's from Alsace. We have nothing to do with the village or the mountain.' And from her tone it was clear they didn't want to. They were just there, the most successful business in Castel by chance, not choice. They rented the building from a cork manufacturer.

After a while, the rain calmed me and the streets had another kind of beauty that was solitary and unequivocal. This is how it is, said the street. Absolute. Bleak. No gaudy allure provided by the sun and a bit of blue sky. Monsieur Nadal said Castel and certain places in the area had resonance, magnetism, and it was here that forces gathered and atmosphere was built up.

'Once you sense that nothing is boring any more, you'll stay.'

The bad weather forced us to relax or go mad, and gradually we lost the frazzled city energy, the need for something to happen, to keep doing something, the fear of losing out. It seemed as though we fizzed over and then were still. No more rushing to the phone making plans. The morning wasn't torn five ways with where to go, what to see. Suddenly we could sit comfortably for more than three minutes, just watching the village. I supposed this was what was meant by taking a true holiday. In the end it came down to where to have lunch and what wine to drink with it. After a while the indolence released deeper untapped energy and space for thought and new desire. I saw that as I no longer tried to control life but flowed with it my security increased. Or, more, I listened to the inside rhythms and acted from that prompting.

Because there was no sun, café life changed. Instead of moving from café to café, sun to shade, the villagers moved according to pastime. In the morning they went to the Pablo for a serious drink and a talk about politics, in the late morning to the Grand Café for placing bets and playing pool. The afternoon was spent in the Grand Café for *belotte*, and the evening in the Café de France for music and dancing. All the cafés had television. Sportsmen celebrated in the Pablo. The rugby team took each café in turn. The girls picked up boys in the Café de France, money was won and lost in the Grand Café, local politics were concluded in the Pablo.

The old quarter had a different atmosphere altogether. The centre was the Place des Neuf Jets, dominated by a medieval fountain with its nine jets of forceful water. Plane trees lined the square and the atmosphere was unspoiled, even by cars. It was a good place to sit in the heat. In one corner a local painter ran the pizzeria and the pizzas and apple pies were cooked on an open fireplace. In the other corner, a cheap restaurant had just opened, Le Chat Qui Rit. There was a painting of Guy, the owner, on an easel on the pavement. It didn't do him any favours: he attempted a Salvador Dali style, which went down well with the tourists. He'd come to Castel from the industrial east of France, opened this small restaurant and learned to cook.

'I want quality of life. It's more important than money,' he said.

He made the best chips and mash in Castel, and sold

cider in small jugs. The rest was a hit-and-miss affair. He had several apartments and was buying more.

'Of course you must invest here,' he said to me. 'I have. Wholeheartedly. I believe in Castel. You can't lose.'

He was certainly a fan of his own cooking. Every time I saw him he was eating and his stomach was huge.

'God put his thumb print on this place. Nowhere is as beautiful as this. Why else did Picasso come here? If you move away to somewhere ugly it's sacrilege, isn't it?'

I agreed with him.

So we moved through the rain from café to restaurant to bar. I longed to play *belotte* but it was their private game and I could only watch.

Chapter Eleven

Once Marie had gone the suite was less light-hearted. I felt a distinct frisson of uncertainty. Tomorrow I would put down the final payment.

As Marie had got in the car, she'd said, 'Wait till it rains.'

'It is.'

'I mean when you're actually living in there. She's got no windows. I hope you noticed. And as for the roof . . .'

I supposed she was angry because I'd killed off her terrace plans, quietly but in front of the pack of assorted enemies upstairs. Marcel had justified all disapproval by claiming it would have been the best apartment Castel had known.

'Leave London and live here?' She still had the car door open. 'Wait till the mountain wind comes. Then make that decision. The *tra montana*. They don't mention that, I notice.' She knew the danger of the beautiful days. 'What will you do here?'

'Live, for a change.'

'You can't live on a beautiful view. Are the people beautiful? You have to ask that.'

As she drove off, she said, 'Don't forget, I fell in love with a village.'

And now I closed the curtains against the rain and longed for the night. I made tea with a travelling kettle. No more trays of anything. The luxuries were over. I'd move into a cheap hotel while JoJo and his brothers did the work. Downstairs I heard Francine shout with excitement at something on television and I remembered it was Monday, her day off, the restaurant and brasserie shut.

Marie had been a close friend for three years so obviously I was very decided to stay in this village if I was prepared to lose her. It wasn't so much a decision as a preference. I understood that something important had happened when I didn't get into the car and go to London via Montpellier.

I drank the tea and hung my clothes over the chairs to dry. And now I didn't feel sure about anything. A cold grey evening, cars sploshed past down the empty streets. I made plans and tried to subdue the unquiet thoughts. And loneliness.

I'd considered the material side of my decision. I'd move from my rented London flat and bring my things to Castel or put them in storage. I'd chuck a lot away. A complete spring-clean. That was the good part. I'd have to take my share of the joint bank account before my ex-partner went through it. And get through it he would, not with premeditated intent but because he was an addict. The hardest thing, I could never help him. Nobody could. They kept telling me that. He had to want to help himself. He'd broken me.

I'd met him at the end of the eighties when his voice was going. He'd tried appearing in movies, mostly in Europe. He didn't go down well in America. Then the drugs took over. He was still reliable about turning up for work — he was too professional to do otherwise — but the heart had gone out of him and you couldn't decline in that business. It was because he couldn't sing any more, he said. But, as I understood it, an addict is an addict. Yet he still had some of that dangerous allure.

Jay Stone — one of the hottest singers of the seventies and eighties. He'd had a real voice. When I met him I believed finally I'd be able to sing, but my job was to find songs for him, then write songs for him. On one album he let me sing in the backing group. From an employee I became an assistant, then a partner. He said I had the minor key, catchy voice he liked. I told him I'd always wanted a career singing. Nothing doing. There was only room for one performer in his organization.

I'd been married for years to an academic and I'd been happy enough. I cooked meals, washed clothes, did his typing, helped with research, soothed his evenings, entertained his guests. We had a son — no, about some things I could not think. During my twenty-five-year marriage there had been no time or occasion for a singing career. He came first. Or survival did. But I promised myself that one day I would live the dream I'd started at fifteen. I would sing. Perhaps that day was now.

My husband had gone to Ireland to teach and, as far as I knew, was still there. Our marriage could take sameness, boredom, symbiotic intimacy, not enough money, repetition, looking after his mother, frustration, but not tragedy. It couldn't take that. I felt he was right just to move off without making any more ripples than there'd been in our marriage. He did say he'd thought

I'd been unfaithful. Those missing hours. So I told him about the singing lessons. He never understood about those.

I was working for Jay before my marriage ended. Then I was living with Jay. I was his partner, then his mistress for a short time, this his nurse, then his unwanted saviour. The last time I had seen him he looked like a shabby tiger, but there were still some claws left. I'd filled the fridge with food he would never eat, left money in his coat – to be spent dangerously, I supposed – had collected his clothes from the cleaners and just left. Just like that. I got on a train. When it got to the end of the line I got on another one. No one would every believe what I'd been through. And no one would ever know. I ended up by a circuitous route at Marie's place and then Castel.

After I'd paid for the flat I'd have about fifteen thousand pounds left. My share of Jay's royalties had given me a bank account. I didn't know if it would continue. I'd have to trust the cunning accountant and get myself a separate lawyer. I must create a financial ... I suppose I meant diet. I hated the word so much I couldn't think it. The good times were over. There would have to be another kind.

I went on sitting in the dank greyness and everything was quiet. I felt quite rinsed out. No hope, not a scrap. And always, underneath, that dynamo of unceasing anxiety. Was Jay frightened, suffering, choking on vomit, lying dying in the street, too alone, needing me? And if I allowed any of this to surface into my thoughts my heart would start up and I'd reach for the phone and, frenzied, call everyone to find out where and how he was. Every time the phone rang I thought he was dead. At least then I'd know where he was.

'He'll kill you off first,' said Marie. 'You have to cut the cord.' They all said that. Tough love.

But I'd stayed. Perhaps because he reminded me of my son.

Walking out of the cleaners with his clothes and leaving were the first odd things. The next was not sending him the clothes. I always did things correctly. I was always responsible. I hated any feeling of guilt.

But now I saw that my departure wasn't such a surprise. Hadn't I wanted to do the same when my husband was teaching in Wales? We lived in a back-street in Swansea. It was the early days and I'd walk along by the sea at a nearby resort – go to the pier, to the end and back – and I was so bored. No, imprisoned. Bored was something else altogether. Imprisoned was when you were doing everything except what you really should be doing. That had been my life. And I always went to the same shop before the Saturday-afternoon film came on and bought the crisps and the cigarettes, and one particular time I thought, 'What if I don't go back? If I just go and keep going? Who knows where? And I left the shop and started up to the road, and there was a sort of freedom. But then came that overwhelming sense of responsibility. And then my son was born and that changed everything.

As I went downstairs I could see Francine, with her shoes off and her feet up, watching television. Her husband, the meat cook, handed her a plate of delicately arranged hors d'oeuvres. And a song started up, one of Jay Stone's. I thought my life had some bizarre ironies.

Monday, and every restaurant was closed. The pizzeria was open but full of young groups. I felt I'd rather starve than go in and sit alone among them. This, I realized, was what having enough inside you, to live alone in a foreign village, was all about. I opened the door and went in. They all looked so unified, sealed off. So I got a takeaway pizza and coffee and ate it back in the suite. I couldn't think of one person to talk to or see. And then I understood you could not be reliant on a place or the people: you had to have a strong and reliable inner world. I'd never been tested in that way.

Marie had met Jay when he was trying to recover from one substance or another in his impresario's home on the Côte d'Azur. He'd discovered her private interest in the workings of the mind, the recovery from trauma, the freeing of the blocked. He'd told her to go for it and do what she'd always wanted to do. He was good at understanding people's unknown sides. He encouraged her to come to London and study. I liked her immediately and we became friends – allies. She lived with us first at the big house, then at the big flat, then at the two rented flats. I told her, what with the subject she was studying, she'd be useful to have around the house.

She replied that Jay's problems were addiction. It had damn all to do with his damaged emotional life. I must cut the cord.

At first she had found him exciting, interesting from a psychotherapeutic point of view. Then she feared and dreaded the chemical change in him. She still stayed in touch with him, perhaps because he'd been a star. Or she tried to put him straight, or make him see he was killing me. Of course, she was a little in love with him.

When I was fifteen I'd hitchhiked through Europe. It wasn't so much leaving as going towards something. My Paris life in Pigalle, singing in a club and then on the Left Bank. That was the alive time. That's when I met the Spaniard.

That last L'Hostellerie night was terrible. I felt I was in a storm. Then I found that the storm was in me. I writhed, restless, from one side to the other on the suddenly unfriendly bed. At one point I thought I should phone my ex-husband in Ireland.

'You block everything off.' It was my own voice. 'To survive,' it said. 'Are you dreaming or fleeing?'

I put on the light and found I was fully dressed. I considered gong to Madame Beaumarchais and waking her up and asking for – wisdom? Valium?

The things that happen to other people around me, whom I love, it's been too much for me lately. Life's choices, too cruel and hard. My inner life. That's there. It has nothing to do with that.

I slipped back into a distressed half-sleep, my mind tossing like a boat on a bad sea. I couldn't get any peace. Then I remembered what I always remembered in the very bad moments. The Spaniard came into my mind, as once he had come into my life, fortuitously, turning on all the lights, making a blaze. 'You've forgotten one thing,' he said.

I dreaded the answer. 'The passion?'

'The humour, of course. You must be down to see it all so bleakly.'

And then I thought about the last time I'd seen him. It was when Jay had done a concert in Barcelona a couple of years ago. I had slipped away for a few hours to see the old city further north, Gerona, home of the Spaniard. It was here that I'd taken on my second identity, perhaps the real one. I'd been with him, that time was blessed. Yet I ended up married to an English academic. So many times in the years that followed I came here to see him, deeply lived, stolen days from the months of sameness. Yet always with that splinter of distrust, a dark splinter in the sunlight. He'd allowed life to take me from him and place me in something unsuitable. Someone, a female friend of his, dared to say it was my karma. I could have done any suffering and learning in a much better and more colourful way, with what was, after all, my true love.

So I'd left the concert in Barcelona and taken a fast train for a hundred kilometres north. Had it changed, Gerona? The ancient part? I didn't think a few additions like Benetton or Yves Rocher, an English pub, could really knock out the soul of this place, which had been substantially there for over two thousand years. I didn't see the Spaniard. I didn't go to his last address. I'd come, after all, to see the city. Again, I walked up the ninth-century street to the cathedral. This time I turned to the left and stopped under some arches looking at the Cal Ros restaurant. It was the first place I'd gone to when I was fifteen. The sign was gold and black. It looked closed. The day was oddly cold. Quite grey. There was no familiar excitement. I felt apart from something that was itself apart. I started towards the Ramblas, at the end of which a taxi would take me back to Jay's world. I passed a painter working at a large canvas on an imposing easel. I would have walked on, but something in the picture made me pause. It was the light. Yes, he'd caught the light, not of now but of that time in the fifties. And I would have walked on but I said, 'That's how it used to be. There was a special light here.'

The painter didn't understand.

And as I hesitated a man came into view, walking quickly down the narrow cobbled street the artist was painting. He walked closer, becoming part of the picture, with fast steps I would recognize anywhere. And then he smiled and said, 'But, of course, I'd meet you. I've thought about you, about nothing else for two days. So it's no surprise.'

And I was suddenly joyous. I couldn't do that for myself. It took him to do that. The only way to express my feeling, to trace my fingers across his face, not as it was now but the memory. I told him about the picture and how I'd hesitated. If I'd gone on I wouldn't have seen him at all.

He said, 'What was it about this picture?'

'The light. It's how it used to be when I was young and had just met you.'

'Oh, come on.' And he pointed to my chest. 'The light was inside you.'

And then I slept, on the skimpy, suddenly unfriendly L'Hostellerie bed.

Chapter Twelve

Maître Aznar put off the signing until the afternoon. I had breakfast in the Pablo. I hardly knew what I ate and kept my dark glasses on. I looked terrible and my hands were shaking. I didn't want any more delay because I was frightened of changing my mind. I didn't want the space to have doubts in. I didn't trust myself enough. And what if some other buyer came along with more money and less delay?

Monsieur Nadal said delay might be caused by the division of the house. The lawyer had to check everyone out.

'Why does it take so long?'

'Because she has Spanish blood. They call her Señora Mañana. You'll get a Spanish bill too. Check it. But you're straight.'

I almost laughed. 'I was married to Mr Straight. I played it straight for years.'

And then I thought, Yes. 'Played'. That says it.

Monsieur Nadal poured me extra coffee. 'Come back when you've signed and we'll open champagne.'

I packed my stuff yet again at L'Hostellerie and paid the bill. Francine was wearing a cherry patterned dress, skimped in at the waist, which emphasized her thinness.

She looked fresh and enviable and *bien dans la peau*. She always looked shimmering, fresh and crisp, like one of her desserts. I'd told her I'd eaten in so many different restaurants, which probably wasn't what she wanted to hear, 'But nothing compared with L'Hostellerie.' I hoped it would never change. The simplicity allowed space for the good things. She promised it wouldn't. We shook hands and the phone rang. It was for me. I answered, believing it was Marie.

Jay, his voice hoarse and rough, said, 'Where are you?'

I told him.

'No, no, no. You're in a chic suite in a four-starrer.' He had obviously talked to Marie. 'You've been there for nearly a month. How can you stay there all that time? How can you pay? Are you fucking mad?'

I told him I'd got my own place. For the first time in my life I had a place that was mine.

'Where?' he said sharply.

'Paradise.'

'I don't know where that is but I hope it's cheap. Joe Tax is knocking at the door and you know what that means.'

I did. I'd have to get my money out of the joint bank account *now*.

Everything was fine between us, so I knew he'd been using drugs, battalions of drugs. Again I told him to go back to the clinic. I got small thanks for that suggestion. Then I told him the French still loved him. He should make a comeback in France and talk about the bad times. A four-page interview for a French magazine. There was nothing the French loved better than a star heading for hell and then making an heroic about-turn. That is, providing they'd accepted you.

Drink, drugs, near suicide, despair, several wives and a superb performer. It ran with their blood. He was now concluding wife three. The first, in America, still gave him problems. He dreaded the alimony. 'Ali knocks on the door every month Stateside and it's taken very seriously over there. If you can't pay they put you away.' He'd left the USA fast. He prayed she would remarry and he'd have peace. The second and third were gone. There'd be a fourth.

Then he told me he needed me back in London to sign the tax papers. He'd sent someone to my rented flat earlier and was surprised to find it empty. He'd had no idea I'd gone away. And he didn't care. I knew that. He'd become hard. The drugs had done that. They'd put him in a cocoon so that nothing got in or out. No ingoing lines. Just thinking about the change in him almost made me sob. Pointless. I had no tears left.

'You're to sign on Tuesday with our lawyer. So I cover this tax bill.'

I said I would not. Distance gave a sort of bravery.

'Do it. You're my partner.'

'Ex.'

He hung up. Total cut-off.

I went straight to the bank.

They gave me a farewell lunch in L'Hostellerie. Afterwards I stayed in the once so pleasurable suite, listening to the breeze, filled to the gills with the old pain. Being away didn't change anything. You took yourself wherever you went. I felt to blame because I hadn't saved him. I'd left, let him down.

And then I saw the plane trees and the sky so clear and Mount Canigou, white and imperious. And I thought, It's beautiful, and I stayed looking out at that and the pain wasn't all there was, after all.

The postman, Monsieur Augustin, and his wife had dressed up for the occasion. The three of us listened respectfully as Maître Aznar talked us through the legal documents – at least, talked two of us through them. I didn't understand a thing. Then she looked at me and said, 'Do you understand, Madame?'

I said I did.

'Now, I want you to listen carefully to what I say about the people who own different parts of the house.' She reeled off a lot of names. Was she talking about one house or a whole block? Who were all these people? I recognised Monsieur Gato: he owned the empty studio next to me and now lived in St Jean – a place that sounded a long way away. How was I to know it was just down the road? A Monsieur Carduso, I'd not heard about him, lived in Montpellier. And the others, miles away.

'They had to sign agreements saying they had no grounds for not wanting you to buy the flat on the second floor comprising . . .' And then she broke into metres, 'Do you understand?'

I did.

'Are you satisfied, Madame Jane, with the property you are about to acquire? Are you happy to live in that house?'

Did the postman's knees jump around a little?

'Is there anything you want to add or dispute?' She laughed. The postman laughed, less gaily. 'Now is the time to say it.'

I said I was satisfied.

'In all, there are eight residents, who form what is called the *copropriété*.'

I didn't pay much attention to it at the time.

I paid the second part to the gorgeous postman, and we shook hands and went for a drink. The rain stopped and the sun came out. It was as though the bad weather had never been. We drank the promised champagne at the Pablo. Maître Aznar looked tired, the shadows under her eyes brown, her skin dry. She said the work was endless, like the rain except it didn't stop. She was beyond exhausted. But there was no one else – she paused – 'With my experience.' Which I took to mean, 'Not good enough.'

'Is that why it took so long?'

'No, I strung it out so you could be sure, Madame.'

I told her she was a very good lawyer.

The postman bought the second bottle, then drove me to the gas company, then to the water supplier. He even helped me keep on the phone. His wife gave me her net curtains and they moved into their new villa for holidays and special occasions.

I moved into a hotel at the edge of the village, the Hôtel Luna, in a street parallel to the main shopping street, running down from the Café de France. Cars sped along in a one-way single line to the new part of town, the Devil's Bridge and the way out to Spain and the north. The hotel was old yet newly owned by an optimistic wife, Natalie, who'd been a nurse, and her husband, Robert, who'd been everything. That included manager of the popular night-club in the old part, Le Zanzibar. That venture had left him out of pocket and he was slightly less than optimistic about the new one.

Natalie, middle-aged, squat, strong and unadorned, had saved her money to buy the hotel. As I walked in, she was unpacking boxes of plates and cutlery and the painters were finishing the dining-room walls.

'I wanted green plates for the salad. Or should they be for the fish?' She picked up a yellow plate, not a shade I'd associate with appetite.

I thought the green plates for everything.

'I want to keep the food simple and cheap. The rooms directly overlook Canigou.' She didn't mention the other side, over the street. She was definitely an optimist. Then she unpacked the cutlery. Her husband Robert didn't do much, I noticed. He just sort of stood about, either inside or out in the street. He was undeniably good-looking, matinée idol good. He didn't appeal to everyone but to enough. Natalie was jealous of any woman, every woman, who even spoke to him. She'd shove herself into any conversation. As he knew most women in Castel she had plenty to do. She showed me the courtyard, in the shade of gentle trees, which was exceptional. There was a terrace of hanging grape-vine. 'I'll put up fairy-lights at night.' Potentially this was the very best location to eat in Castel for miles around.

She gave me room seven, which so far had not been my lucky number. It had a terrace and a direct view of the mountain. The room had been painted soft mauve and pink. There were dramatic cracks, like forked lightning, in the plaster, and the ceiling bulged. A pregnant woman's stomach ceiling. It was her top room. I could have it until the following Friday when a family moved in. Moved in where? The bed took all the space. The floors slid to one side and I could see what they meant about not having surveyors in France. I suspected the building had a problem I'd come across, 'settlement', when the walls moved apart and the floors slid anywhere. The only remedy was underpinning, which cost a fortune. Who was I to darken her joy? Her husband Robert's had been darkened years ago.

As I was walking from L'Hostellerie with my luggage, a French couple stopped me. 'Why did you buy that?' They pointed up in the direction of my freshly acquired apartment. 'And not our house?'

They were the owners of the 'good' house in the rue Pierre Brune. He was a psychiatric nurse and she a schoolteacher. They'd dedicated themselves to their house and would never have moved but their two children were growing up and they needed something bigger. Theirs was a good house but all its qualities were, perhaps, the very reason why I couldn't be there. It was an investment of more than money. It would need time, care, upkeep. You couldn't see all their work disintegrate. It wasn't a part of me but separate to me, and demanded a relationship I couldn't have with it. Whereas the postman's flat was harmonious and made no demands. I couldn't even get the first part of that started, they were too horrified. So I said I needed more a *pied-à-terre*. The husband probably wanted to say, And that's about what you've got.

Politely, he carried my luggage round the corner to the hotel and wished me luck. Then Eliane passed. I soon understood that in a small place we all passed each other all the time. It had nothing to do with magnetism or destiny or the intriguing forces that worked further away in the big cities.

The house-owner sniffed with disapproval as she passed. 'Why on earth didn't you buy *our* house?'

I went to Amélie-les-Bains by taxi to celebrate the purchase of the new flat. I wished Marie was with me. I missed her. In Colette's I drank *blanc sup*, and then more. I even missed JoJo. I'd finally done it, got a place that I'd chosen, that was mine for the first time in my life. I was nearly fifty.

Colette looked tired. There were pouches under her eyes, painted out but still there. She hadn't been run out of town. She looked amazing in her short, tight skirt and awesome heeled shoes. It had worked out in the end because she had become the curists' missing essential – the dream person, the goal, not a synthetic video entertainment but an actual live star. She made them forget their aches and pains. The customers loved her clothes, the variety. She never appeared in the same outfit twice. Where did she keep them all? But the covering was nothing compared with the underneath. She was almost unreal. No vulnerability, no giving in to those excessive heeled shoes and disciplined waist. No letting out belts or undoing buttons.

'She's from outer space,' said one curist.

'She's come off the television screen and just appeared in here,' said another.

I thought, She's been poured into those clothes. A

movie star would have needed time and attention from wardrobe people, pinning and tucking. I could see that the outer-space theory had a point.

The belts, the buttons, the towering shoes, that's where her inevitable lookalikes fell down. As the evening wore on, things were loosened and opened, shoes kicked off and lost. The curists tried to adopt her posture, head held in that elegant, inviting way. They painted lips slippery with gloss, and outlined their eyes above the fringes of false lashes. But they preened themselves while she just was. She was all performance, of course, and after a while I saw it wasn't for us, the customers, but for the mirrors surrounding the bar, so ultimately for herself.

She moved to and fro, seemingly occupied but doing what? All her movements graceful, restrained. She had star quality that many a movie star would have envied. She could make you watch anything, even the business with the kitchen towel and the glass. Her husband and minder pushed through from the kitchen with another beer crate. He looked more than ever like Jean Gabin. She smiled at him. The curists stirred in their places, the movie had begun.

Chapter Thirteen

I changed my appearance in the Hôtel Luna. I put gold streaks in my hair, cut a slight fringe, put it up with combs, did exercises, encouraged my circulation with a primitive spa method – cold water in the bidet, hot in the bath, feet and ankles going between the two. I put on mud packs, plucked my eyebrows, dyed my lashes, relaxed completely, did more exercises. I walked for half an hour, then another. I stopped eating white bread. I started again. I hadn't stopped anything else. Why take it out on the bread?

Because I couldn't drive I stayed in Castel. As things were, I had a little over fifteen thousand pounds for the rest of my life. I had to start making economies. Taxis were out and so was L'Hostellerie. I ate in the Hôtel Luna in the courtyard. Each day Natalie said 'What do you want for lunch? For dinner?' She made sure she had at least one customer. But the courtyard was worth all the culinary let-downs. Natalie was best with omelettes and salads. The other stuff on the menu or in my head took too long. It gave Robert too much time alone in the street. Standing beside him, she could only look ugly. He, the eternal Peter Pan, could only look trapped.

Yet she was arduous, hard-working and deep into life. He, on the surface, was excited about nothing.

And I wondered about my husband. Had he, like me, chosen a complete life change before it was too late? He'd been a senior lecturer for too long, hadn't got the advancement he was due. What next? The last time I saw him the future didn't offer too much. The last I'd heard from him he said he wanted time. I gave him time.

From the start there were difficulties with JoJo. He didn't understand my French, and I didn't have that firm hand. In the end I just walked away. 'Do it like Marie said.'

He came after me. 'That takes money, Madame.'

Was I another Eliane?

I didn't know how much he should have so I gave him half of the total agreed with Marie. I'd opened a French account and wrote a cheque. I told him to lift the floor-covering, strip the walls, paint them white and make the floor tiles good. And throw everything out. I told him to get a new kitchen fitted. To get some brochures.

'What about the bath?'

I considered the bath, wash-basin, bidet and lavatory perfectly adequate.

'Madame Marie didn't think so. Not the bath.'

I said she would not be lying in it so we'd leave it as it was. I went straight to Marcel. He was drawing lines on a plan of a new hotel. It sounded impressive enough but it looked like the same plan he had had on his desk when I first walked into his office. Was it something he unfolded as soon as he heard a would-be client coming in?

'It will be in the old building near the Porte de France.'

It had a beautiful façade, had been empty for years. Five floors, lots of windows, built in the 1800s. I was wrong about that. 'Seventeen-forty,' said Marcel. I was wrong about JoJo too. 'You should never pay them up-front like that.' He chuckled, seriously amused. 'Pay a quarter and something at the end of each week. Otherwise they never do the work. Your friend, Madame Marie, would have known that.'

He approved highly of her plan for building a terrace. He thought highly of the work she'd done on her home in the Côte d'Azur. He wasn't so crazy about her plan to run a property with his partner Juan Pamello.

'What are they making? A rest home? She understands restorations. She should get four million for her Côte d'Azur property. But she won't.' Marcel, with his dreadful honesty, said that properties in France were hard to sell nowadays. He had cause to regret that statement later on.

'You must miss Paris,' I said, having had little to offer in the property discussion.

'I decided when I came here I would make it work. It's a question of attitude.'

I asked him where I could buy a bed. I needed a locksmith: I wanted the locks changed on the flimsy front door.

Madame Beaumarchais caught me on my way

upstairs. 'You have to close the shutters every time you leave. Otherwise they will swing free and fall.'

I asked why.

'Because the mountain wind will come any day. The *tra montana*.'

Was this worse than the rain?

'It can be terrible. It lasts three days or nine days.'

She led me into the kitchen, opened a bottle of white wine. Her cleaning woman was busy with piles of ironing.

'Sit down,' she said politely. 'How's the food at the Luna?'

I said it was too early to tell.

'Then it's too late already. I've known Natalie for years. She's no cook.'

The wine was serious, quite heavy with a roll-back taste. She put some small savoury pastries on the table. Everything was clean and ordered.

'She'll have to try and poach the chef from the Émeraude in Amélie. And someone to do the desserts. There's no good waiting for it to go wrong. People only have one bad meal.'

'I thought Robert could do a little more.'

'He's a night person. He can't even think in daylight.'

A serious-looking ledger waited on the table. She opened it and read, 'The cleaning of the stairs, the cost of the hallway light, the insurance on the building, I am in charge of all that. I have to write to all the owners to remind them to send a cheque. Monsieur Augustin, the owner before you, always paid on time.'

'How much?'

She showed the list of other names; a tick indicated that they'd paid. I got out my cheque book. There was no tick by Eliane van Zoelen.

'She has nothing. She has that child to support. I don't ask her.' She approved of my gold-streaked hair. 'You look better already.'

I wrote the cheque, which was reasonable enough, and had to ask how to spell some of the words. I knew Marie would have challenged the tickless Eliane. Who paid for her? We all did, obviously. I did present a certain resistance. I said I already had insurance.

'For your apartment. Not for the house. Not for the outside. The roof. The upkeep.'

'Doesn't Eliane own that? The outside?'

'You have to pay,' she said, without fuss. 'She can't. Try another piece of pastry. You can get it in the Catalan butcher's opposite. You can trust his cold meats. His pâtés are good.'

On the stove two bones simmered for a broth to be eaten later. A quiche, boiled potatoes and salad waited on a side table for Eliane and the child; a sheet of greaseproof paper partially covered the quiche. Since the break with the croupier Madame Beaumarchais prepared their midday meal.

'You upset the mother,' she said, once she'd got the cheque. 'You can't offer money and then change your mind. You gave false promises.'

'That's the property business, isn't it?' I quoted Marie.

'It's not Castel business. Come to me if you get any other ideas. She's not strong enough.'

'Eliane?'

'The mother. She's got to have an operation. When's your friend coming back?'

I said soon, for something to say.

'I can see she means business. She's never short of an answer.'

I said in my opinion that was fortunate.

She laughed teasingly and didn't pursue it. 'You have to drive if you live in Castel. When are you going to learn?'

'I'll never drive.'

'Not drive? But that's a luxury these days.'

'Do you?'

'I've got a car in a rented garage. If you do learn you can use my car.'

I thanked her. 'But you haven't answered me.'

'Only in an emergency.' She laughed, slightly drunk, and I had an idea why the car stayed in the garage.

'Keep your shutters open during the morning and close the net curtains at night, just in the summer because of the insects.' She was on amicable terms with the seasons.

I stood in the street and saw what Monsieur Nadal meant about the family, all encompassing, Catalans. Strangers came in company. I saw that too. Very occasionally, a person alone. Had I made a mistake? Why live in London? Why be in a city having half a life when I could be fully alive here? Had I said that? And how could I live up to it?

The past year had had some atrocious moments that I needed to heal. I had never had the time. I had covered everything up and moved on, to survive. Now I saw that

that race could stop. I had to trust life. I just had to do better with Castel.

I was the flavour of the month for the first week and everyone wanted to look me over. Who was I? What had I to offer? Then I was part of it, the periphery: more new people had arrived in town and were getting the lookover treatment. That's how it had been in LA on a bigger scale with Jay Stone. He said you had to have staying power, show them you had legs, to be admitted to the central core. It was no different here.

But instead of going to the local film club, or *sardana* lessons or up to the L'Hostellerie brasserie for a modest meal I sat in my room in the Hôtel Luna and faced the past. Always when a painful thought had come up I'd dealt with it by exchanging it with another thought. I'd simply swapped over to something safe and bright. That didn't work here.

So I sat down and, instead of putting on a mud pack, let myself think and clear out the real baggage.

Living with Jay had been hell, more so because I was still very attracted to him. I cared for him, was frightened for him and, finally, of him. Once, he'd been sensitive and fine. There were still times like that. He'd been absolutely sure of himself as a performer, and I'd been so proud of him. About eighteen months ago he'd seemed to lose his way. I asked the manager what he was going to do about it. '*Do*? You don't "do" something to Jay Stone.' And the substances had increased and he was in bad shape, skidding on black ice, staggering on thin ice.

At first he'd loved me in the real sense but that had turned to resentment and often fury. The money was going. I still hung on trying to – save? Maintain? I never thought he'd go over the edge. He was too bright. I tried to claw him back. Finally, I got out. To save myself. Had I? He'd become my child.

And then the really bad stuff happened.

I'd been ill for a year. I'd got a job in a club in Camden Town, singing three nights a week. Then Jay's final film came out. He had the part of a tricky psychopath. He'd done it extraordinarily well. People asked how I managed to live with him while he was playing that part. That was no part. That was Jay. And I'd lived with it for three years.

From a working-class start he'd become international. He was moody, sensual and very kind. In spite of domestic closeness I was always left out of the real thing – his life as a performer. Some of the others were in. The manager for one. But I was kept out, stopped from being able to know and touch the magic. I'd felt excluded and resentful.

And then the next really bad stuff had happened.

Again I found I was looking at the plane trees and the pale clear sky, splayed with stars, spiralling with stars, and Mount Canigou, its face changing like the moon. It wasn't just about pain all the time. There was this majesty also. I was part of that.

I tried to ring Jay, tried all the numbers, then the friends, even the enemies. I wanted desperately to save him as once I'd tried to save my son.

Every morning after breakfast I walked into the country, which was a matter of minutes away. I no longer felt entirely safe or wise. The world had changed a lot since you could do that. I took the winding road up, which quickly gave a view across Castel, the next village, the spa town Le Boulou, the flatland and the sea. Towards Spain, there were high, sharp hills, tree-covered with magnificent views on which the rich lived. I circled round as far as the first signpost, with unpronounceable names, and could see Perpignan to the north and then Narbonne. I turned back along a straight road lined with pleasant houses, mostly owned by Scandinavians. They sat in the sun with their flaxen hair and clean summer dresses. I stopped for some cider at the small café that sold groceries, newspapers and lottery tickets. I always met the same old man with his dog as I turned into Castel. He said he loved nature and it was getting scarcer. But this patch was still untouched. He was the sort of person I used to see in Spain, years ago, solid, sensitive, appreciative of life, gentle, absolutely honest.

'I wish I could be more like you,' I said.

'I wish I had your youth,' he replied. That put him at over eighty.

I always called in on JoJo and his brothers to see if there was anything they needed, but really to see if they were there. The walls had been peeled and the floor half scraped off. JoJo stood in the middle of chaos, talking around his gone-out cigarette. I couldn't understand one word. Something with the door to the lavatory and 'not enough.' He took out his cigarette. It didn't help. I said I'd get Marcel.

'When is your friend coming back?'

I didn't think she was. Could I help?

'There's not enough space to fit the door and have it open and have the electrics running under –'Then he stopped. I didn't know a thing about it and he knew it.

'What do you think, JoJo?'

'It will cost. Very dear.'

'Then do the cheaper thing.'

He looked disappointed.

'Look, I'll get Marcel to –' I gestured 'help'. Then I asked the dreaded question, in my rocky French. 'When?'

'You move in?' He counted on his fingers. 'Three days.'

I didn't believe it.

'Your friend speaks good French. Better than me. Very rare,' I thought he said.

Madame Beaumarchais usually came up to see how the work was going. She didn't approve of JoJo for dropping Eliane in favour of a stranger. I tried to straighten that out but didn't have the words for it. I'd always known that to get their respect, the French, you had to speak the language their way.

I asked Madame Beaumarchais to find out about the door and lack of space. 'I can't understand him.'

'I can't understand him either,' she said.

He led us into the bathroom. Essentially there were some ugly bits, which Marie had found a way to improve. The division between the lavatory and the bathroom would be improved with this old perfectly fitting door, but it meant moving the water cistern a few inches, which would cost money. There were also beams to be uncovered in the ceiling and wall.

I looked at Madame Beaumarchais and she squinted through her bad eye.

'Perhaps we'll do it bit by bit,' I said. '*Petit à petit.*'

'Eh bien,' and JoJo began a voluble outpouring about value, those who understood it and the others who could live with anything.

Madame Beaumarchais shrugged. 'All builders are mad.'

He wanted to know what to do with the door.

'Turn it into a table,' I said.

Madame Beaumarchais was picking at the stone floor around the bath. 'There's a leak somewhere. It leaks into my apartment. I told Monsieur Augustin. He never fixed it but it will have to be fixed.'

The sun was back and everything quite different. It was wonderful just to look at something, to spend time looking, to really see. Chance meetings in the street gave other opportunities. The pharmacist, Pascale, a dark-haired girl with a white wax face and lots of energy, introduced me to a French teacher who lived above the Grand Café. My French, she said immediately, needed a completely new start. 'Forget everything you've picked up. You're going to be a child. We start at the beginning with verbs and grammar.' There was no such thing as a crash course in her world and to get on quickly I'd need a class a day and an hour's homework. We chose the hour after lunch.

Maître Aznar introduced me to the *sardana* master, who gave classes in the Catalan centre on Mondays and Wednesdays. Madame Beaumarchais's cleaning woman introduced me to the local choir, who rehearsed every Friday evening. They did concerts in the church and occasionally in other villages. It was absolutely French with no Catalan influence.

That week, the restaurant at the Luna was packed at both mealtimes. Everyone wanted to sit in the courtyard. At night Natalie turned on the fairy-lights and put candles on the tables. If only she could have put food there as well. With the help of the cleaning girl she served soup, bread and salad. The omelette orders were jammed up. There was no one to open the wine. Earlier she'd made a very good cheesecake and fruit tart. Robert still stood in the hotel foyer, doing nothing that I could see. I went into the kitchen and put pieces of chicken on plates. The microwave was on full force. Natalie was sweating till it dropped into her eyes. The cleaning girl was running in and out on the edge of panic. The guests were hungry and becoming impatient. Natalie kept her head. 'Give them all chicken, cover it with a lot of sauce and blow out the candles. Tell them the vegetables are served afterwards.'

And she started a speedy serving that a canteen would have been proud of. I saw her cut some corners in the kitchen department that might have put me off eating out. Marcel joined us and started opening wine.

At the end of the evening Natalie sat half collapsed, her feet up on a chair, her legs so swollen they looked like a prehistoric animal's. 'I'll have to get a chef.'

I told her about the one Madame Beaumarchais had recommended.

'No, I prefer to keep the control. I know a young man who'd be excellent. I like helping the young.'

And keeping her overheads down.

Chapter Fourteen

On the third day JoJo kept his promise. The apartment was ready. There was just the matter of the door, which could be solved if I agreed to a sliding one. I said we'd think about that. Then I noticed a space where the kitchen should be.

'Of course,' he said. 'You haven't chosen one.'

'But you should get the brochures.'

He spat his cigarette on to the floor, then picked it up neatly. 'You don't need brochures. You get it from a friend of mine.' He rubbed his fingers, 'Cheap.' What sort did I want?

'Electric.'

He shook his head. 'Everyone has gas. Electricity is too expensive.' And he went into a quick burst, an outpouring of which I could understand not one word.

Again I said 'Electric.'

I went to get Marcel to interpret for me. He was out. Juan Pamello came along and looked around and said he quite admired the work. He didn't believe in a mason or builder getting too much praise so emphasized the 'quite'.

JoJo pointed to a corner in the ceiling. For once I understood him. 'Mushroom.'

'Is there wet rot or dry rot up there?' I kept myself steady.

'No, no, no,' said Juan Pamello generously, calming me, soothing me with everything he had. 'They always find something to panic about, handymen. Especially when they're working black and it's coming to an end.'

'Why?'

'Obviously to make more money.'

JoJo obviously protested.

Juan Pamello turned on him in very fast French. I went on to the terrace and looked up at what was above. Eliane's terrace with a dark crack in it. I heard Juan Pamello say, 'You tried to do me over before the contract was signed. I have to make my living too. Stirring up all that Eliane van Zoelen shit. Why bring her into it? Madame Jane is the one unique person in this entire world who would buy this place and you tried to fuck it up.'

I wished I hadn't heard that.

Juan Pamello came smiling on to the terrace and said, 'What a beautiful day. The sun — a present from God.' The sun took away the shadows.

'So what is the mushroom?'

'A shadow.' He smiled, and was gone.

So I took JoJo into the trouble corner and asked what he'd seen.

'When she gets her place upstairs done there will be no problem. I'll do it next.'

'Can she afford it?'

'Put it this way, she can't not afford it.'

He said he'd fit the kitchen the following day. He

kept using a word I'd never heard. Slang was a big part of his conversation anyway. So he held up two hands.

'Oh, a second-hand kitchen.'

The Luna was full and I had to move to a smaller room. Natalie said she didn't like me walking in the country too long on my own.

'Danger?'

'Heat,' said Robert, cutting in. 'You're not used to it.'

'I've found you a very good companion. His girl-friend is helping me in the kitchen.'

Jean-Pierre was a mountain climber and took groups up Canigou. He was young, open-faced, working hard, saving to go to China. He'd be happy to walk with me on the flat. I would pay him whatever I felt. We agreed three afternoons a week.

Natalie was pleased. 'You can't be too careful. Because –'

'There's no crime in Castel,' said Robert curtly.

'No,' she agreed. 'But there are mad people every-where.'

Francine phoned from L'Hostellerie and said that an Englishman was going to phone me in ten minutes. I could see Natalie was hurt that such a grand place should seek me out. I explained I had stayed there to begin with. She seemed more agitated. Robert made it worse with too many soothing comments: 'It's the obvious place to stay. It's right in the centre.'

'But it's a restaurant not an hotel,' she said.

'But we weren't open then,' he concluded.

What they really wanted to ask was, 'D'you like it

better here? How's the food over there? How much did they charge you?'

Natalie managed to slide in, as I went to the street door, 'They obviously gave you a special price.'

They hadn't. Where had Marie been on that one?

Francine was pleased to see me. They were changing the menu as they did every month. 'So how is your new hotel?'

I told her it was fine but different.

She said, 'I don't think I've ever seen it.'

I described the street.

'I never go over there.'

She didn't ask how the food was and I was grateful for that.

Today she was wearing a tight-fitting suit patterned with huge red poppies. Her hair was newly styled and glossy. She looked as though she might take either hours to get herself together or three minutes.

She showed me the new menu. 'We have *dorade* in *sauce estragon*, red mullet done our way.' And there was another fish beginning with F, which was more expensive. 'We've got pancakes with sour cream and berries. And a very good champagne. A hundred francs a carafe. And we're going to do a champagne evening. And then an Alsace –'

The phone rang. She said quickly, urgently, 'Does the mayor eat at the Luna?'

'Why ask that?' said her husband, angry.

'Because he doesn't eat here.'

Jay said, 'How you doing?' He sounded thin-voiced and weak. 'I don't want you to worry about me. I'm fine.'

'I do.'

'I hope it all goes OK for you.'

'I do worry about you. You've broken my fucking heart.'

'And you got a new kickstart –'

'Jay, listen to me –'

'The dealer got himself dead. Over where you used to live with your husband. I thought you'd like to know.'

'How do you know?'

'It was in the papers. I would have told you earlier but you'd left the country.'

'Why tell me?'

'I thought you'd be relieved. Wasn't he the one who supplied your son?'

'I have no idea.' I sounded icy.

'I just thought it would be hard to live in Paradise if that snake was still around.'

There was a long pause.

'It says in the Bible an eye for an eye. Are you still there, Jane? But I don't think anyone should take justice into their own hands. Leave it to God.'

'What has all this to do with me?'

'Nothing. Anyway, he deserved to kick off.'

Another long pause. Behind me, the restaurant was filling up.

'Marie tells me you loved a man and now you love a place. Will that be less deceiving?'

'I'm sorry I left the way I did.'

'Stories end.'

I wanted to say I'd do anything for him, even come back, but he'd hung up. I rang back. He knew not to be there. The day looked a little less bright. But he was right. I couldn't live in Paradise unless my son's death was avenged.

I went to my first French lesson and learned about verbs that behave irregularly called 'false friends'.

In the morning I walked into the country and did yoga exercises, breathing, singing exercises. Then I ran up the hill to the signpost and did aerobic exercises. I was glad the dealer was dead. Apparently he'd overdosed on something but it didn't bring back the past.

I'd lost a couple of kilos but I was far too heavy. When I'd arrived in Castel I was nearly thirteen stone. It was another thing I'd avoided thinking about. The sun, the fresh air and doing things for myself had all increased my energy. Even I could see I looked better. Now and then there was an inner glow, a bit like a faulty light-bulb on and off. Then I drank a cider in the small café, said hello to the old man walking out of Castel as I walked in. I bought fruit and fresh vegetables from the Casino grocery. Then I went to the flat, and at that point all autonomy was taken away from me.

JoJo had put in the new kitchen, an electric stove, a washing-machine, the noisiest fridge I'd ever heard and a sink. None of it matched. He said, 'The stove is in good nick. The washing-machine perfect. The fridge has a defrosting problem but it's in working order. It's all very clean and good and second-hand but better than an all-in-one flashy range.' Then he told me the price of each item new and how what I had cost less than one new cooker. I was confused: because it didn't quite fit, he had had to cut something – the wall? And then push the sink and the stove nearer the – I thought he said mountain. I said yes to all of it. I could see he was a perfectionist. The inconvenient door was being turned into a table. He had to find some legs. The five brothers, I'd never seen all five, had been reduced to one. He was mending a fault on the terrace.

I went to the peace of my French lesson and learned about the infinitive and how to avoid the subjunctive, the perfect and the conditional. With my tape switched on I read from a book and was corrected. Then I read again. No one could ever say 'rue'. Well, I knew that. And I was one of those who couldn't say *fauteuil* or *mille-feuilles* either.

Then out with Jean-Pierre for a walk on the flat, two hours of it. He was passionate about the environment, protecting it. Jacques Cousteau, the underwater film-maker, was his hero. He didn't want money for walking with me. 'Give it to Greenpeace.'

After dinner in the courtyard, off to the *sardana* lesson, where I learned the long and the short.

I fell asleep effortlessly, truly exhausted.

Monsieur Garcia came back from his house on the Spanish coast. I could hear him giving Madame Beaumarchais some Spanish ham, olives, salt anchovies – the best – and a bottle or two of her favourite sparkling white. He was full of sound and warmth. He made everyone's day. I asked him into the apartment to see the progress. JoJo was screwing iron legs to the old doorway.

'But it's *merveilleux*, Madame.' He, of course, made '*merveilleux*' sound like it should. He brought in a bottle of Banyuls aperitif wine, and we all had a *verre*. He invited me for lunch. 'You'll like the Can Mora.' He was surprised I'd not been there: it was two kilometres out of town.

Then there was a light tapping on the open door and a laughing 'Coo-ee.' JoJo saw her first and looked overjoyed. I wasn't surprised she'd come back. Jay would have sent her with the papers to sign so he could get Joe Tax off his back.

Chapter Fifteen

 Marie had a lot of presence and the men were no problem. She wasn't sure about me. 'I've got papers from Jay —'

'To sign,' I said.

'He needs them now.' Then she saw the stone floor and frowned. 'Why haven't the stones been oiled and treated and polished as we agreed?'

She was cross enough, the way JoJo liked it.

He broke into his rattling French, which only she understood.

Then she had a real turn. 'What's that?' She pointed with horror at the kitchen. I turned, terrified, expecting to see one of those huge flying things with the long snout. A hornet?

'No! No! No! No!' She shook her head.

JoJo smiled, with genuine pleasure. Of course, she, the real Madame, would not accept a kitchen range like that.

'She wanted it cheap.' He lost no time in blaming me.

'Get it out and get a proper kitchen range.' She named the manufacturer.

I said it was all OK for now.

'You can't have all those stray bits. And that fridge.

That noise. It's going to blow up. You can't live like this. You're not a student.'

I felt I was losing ground and said we'd discuss it over lunch.

JoJo had already got his stone-oiling equipment. 'It will take a few hours and cost —'

'We've agreed the cost,' said Marie, looking into the bedroom, then across to the bathroom. They had a lively discussion about the non-fitting door. Monsieur Garcia loved it. The drama of turning the modest into the unique.

She came out on to the terrace, where I sat in the sun trying to keep some dignity. 'I've told him you can't have those beams exposed. I'm not sure they're in good condition. I hope you're not disappointed.'

As I hadn't known about them I was not.

We went for lunch in the Luna's courtyard. Garcia, Marie and me. JoJo had lunch at home. Obligatory. His mother liked him where she could see him.

Natalie had had the walls painted a sturdy green, bushes planted just in front of them. On the end walls, a *trompe-l'œil*, very popular with the French, a painting on the stone in good, bright colours of a window opening out on to a view of Canigou. It depicted exactly the views from the hotel rooms that faced the mountain. We praised her for the excellence of the artwork. She was dressed up in a bright green dress with some corseting underneath. Her hair was done, the village black, and she wore makeup and shoes with heels. She was in a very good mood, and I supposed immediately it had something to do with Robert.

'I've got a chef,' she said proudly, and opened a new

and considerable menu in stiff covers. 'The young man I told you about.'

The menu was impressive but offered too many choices. I was always happier with few. Smart local people sat at the other tables: the mayor and his secretary – he'd left the bright-yellow-haired wife and the dog at home – a doctor and his receptionist, some bank staff and a travelling salesman. There was no longer the curious rush or the impatient diners. These people had an hour to spend.

Marie liked to take over and soon had the table laid and arranged with the sun umbrella giving us shade and the chairs right for the view of Canigou. She picked a flower and put it in a glass, stuck it in the middle. Sometimes I thought she went too far, but she seemed to get away with it.

Quickly I asked about Jay.

'Terrible.'

A wince of fear, the usual one.

'How?'

'You don't want to hear.'

'I do.'

She indicated Garcia. 'I'll tell you later.'

I wanted to know now.

'He won't last at this rate. Physically. He's in terrible shape. Can't even walk up the road.'

'Shall I go back?'

'If you want to suffer.'

Sometimes Marie could look hard. She disguised it with her smile. She did a lot of smiling, these days. 'I'm glad you didn't see it,' she said. 'He's been on drugs for ten years, you know.'

'Twenty,' I said. The shelf life of the average drug addict wasn't eighteen years so he was on overtime.

I asked what his friends were going to do, and she said they couldn't do anything.

'He has to do it. He has to go to the bottom and then want to come up.'

In my experience, when they went to the bottom they couldn't always come up. My son couldn't. So I wasn't a fan of her suggestion. It seemed unfair – I had to go through it twice.

With a heavy heart I looked at the mountain. The courtyard offered the best view, unobstructed from base to top. Nothing in the way. Not even a washing-line.

'He wanted you to know the dealer's dead.'

I shrugged. 'Not before time.'

She looked at me searchingly. 'You cut off beautifully.'

I looked at Garcia, his air of complete life enjoyment. What had he to do with this conversation? I talked about the courtyard and the view.

'She's got it made here,' said Marie.

Garcia said he'd never even noticed this hotel. This was a lovely surprise. There was so much choice he didn't know what to pick. Neither did I. We looked at the other tables. Meat with a sauce, spaghetti, salad.

Marie introduced him to Natalie, and they agreed they'd passed each other in the street a hundred times. Of course he knew Robert, who ran Le Zanzibar. What times he'd had in there. Natalie's expression made it clear she didn't want to hear about them. Her moments of happiness were as fragile as everyone else's.

I chose the soup of the day, lentil and tomato, and a

pizza with salad. Marie chose *moules* and *coq au vin*. There was a big discussion about the vegetables.

'Let's have them all,' said Marie.

'What about Monsieur?'

Garcia chose the terrine, the dish of the day, which was the meat with sauce, and a salad. We picked a local rosé, *pétillant*, and local spa water.

Natalie clattered towards the kitchen. A transformation had occurred in a mere twenty-four hours.

Garcia told us about Spain and his house right on the sea. When he learned I was a singer he invited me to use his piano any time. He'd even accompany me. He'd give me some of the old French songs. He sang a chorus of 'La Vie en Rose'. He stopped singing when he saw the hors d'oeuvres. The terrine didn't usually come with red sauce.

Marie suspected it was blood.

'It looks a little raw,' I said.

He poked his fork into its midst and discovered some bumpy things that could have been anything.

Natalie came with the soup and the *moules*. She was smiling, so happy. It had all taken off. 'I've got a booking for ten tonight.'

The *moules* were not in hot white sauce, after all, but out of their shells and cold, in a small pile in the middle of a huge wilderness of vast green salad leaves, which covered one of the huge green plates. The *moules* looked a little lonely, as though they were lost in a dark wood. Marie didn't like the way they clung together. Were they stale? The soup was just soup until I tasted it.

'Madame.' Garcia lifted the plate of terrine towards Natalie. 'I think I'd prefer the soup.'

'You wouldn't,' I said swiftly. The soup had had salt added to it. It was salty beyond sanity, and I liked salt. An accident had obviously befallen it.

'No, I'll have . . .' He paused. '*Jambon*,' he said quickly. He couldn't go wrong with ham of the region. He thought.

Marie said the *moules* were all right but the salad had sand in it. 'It doesn't matter,' she said. 'It's freshly picked.' She held up a leaf. It was big enough for a part in a Cleopatra movie. Slaves could have waved that leaf and cooled down the Egyptian queen and her court for ever. Marie bit into it with her good teeth and chewed and chewed. I poured plain water into the soup. Along came the local ham. Enormous thick slices, with dry, rough edges.

Softly I said to Natalie, 'Too much salt.' I winked.

Natalie lifted the soup plate and peered into it. 'That's the style here.'

'I'll have a – a–' I looked around desperately. 'What do you suggest?'

'It's what you like.' She was getting a little frosty.

'D'you know? I'll have an omelette.' I added helplessly, 'One of yours.'

I heard a shout in the kitchen. The chef? Burned himself?

Garcia was also chewing. The ham would not change its texture. Marie got down the lettuce leaf and took a piece of his ham. 'Uneatable,' she said. 'And it's curled at the edges.'

'Not a good sign,' he said.

There was nothing wrong with the wine and we poured it.

Natalie came out quickly with a plate of melon and ham and put it in front of me.

'But I asked for an omelette.'

She shook her head, just one shake. She'd done that so often as a nurse. The patient's dead, I'm afraid, said the shake. 'Omelette's not on the menu,' and she lifted her large black eyebrows meaning, Get it?

She cleared the hors d'oeuvres and I noticed she threw Garcia's uneaten ham into a flower-pot.

Robert took a stroll and asked if everything was all right. He shook a few hands and agreed it was a splendid day.

Natalie and the cleaning girl brought the main course. The *coq au vin* sat in the centre of the plate surrounded by a lake, a sea of sauce, and I recognized one or two of the original lettuce leaves. I thought that these huge green plates were a mistake with the 'local style'. The dish of the day for Garcia looked reasonable and the pizza not bad at all. We got another bottle of wine.

Marie couldn't get the knife through the chicken so Natalie brought her a sharp one. The pizza was fine until I got to the centre. That was burned underneath and tasted that way. On the far side it was undercooked, raw dough. The vegetables were fine, but too much grease, and the parsnips, if that's what they were, were shrivelled and hard from being too long in the hot oven.

I left most of the pizza and Garcia gave up on the vegetables. 'But you aren't hungry.' Natalie was disappointed. 'Eric will be upset.'

Marie had had enough. 'It's not good enough. This meat is impossible. Try it yourself.'

Natalie picked up the offending plates and went towards the kitchen.

'And I'm not paying for it,' said Marie angrily.

'I agree,' said Garcia. 'It's a shame because it's such a lovely location.'

The cleaning girl brought out the cheesecake. Then she took a bill to the mayor. He was still alive.

There was a horrible shout in the kitchen and the door flew open. Out came a thick-set young man with long hair tied back and the usual chef's outfit. 'What do you mean you don't want to eat my food? Why do you keep sending it back?'

I let Marie give this one all she'd got. She told him, in fierce French, what his food looked like, tasted like, and how she would never pay for it.

'You should ask for it underdone,' he shouted. 'And I'll do it underdone.'

'I'll have dessert,' she said.

'You won't,' he said.

She couldn't believe her ears.

'You'll eat the *coq au vin*. I'm not slaving away cooking for you.'

The mayor had stood up. Robert was in the doorway but not actually in the courtyard. Natalie hovered beside her choice of chef. She managed to get in, 'Eric has just started. Give him a chance.'

The chef rushed back to the kitchen.

'Thank God,' said Marie. 'If there's one thing I don't like it's an angry chef.'

He came out straight away with the plate of *coq au vin*. He smacked it on the table, lifted the meat in his hands and ate it, glaring at her with terrible eyes.

Everyone had to watch. No one seemed able to move. Then he swiped his hands together as though to clean the grease. It sounded like bizarre applause. He went into the kitchen and the door swung shut.

Natalie and Robert had a hurried conversation. They both looked strained.

Robert, smiling, came to our table. 'Would you like anything else?

'Absolutely not.' Marie got up.

'It's on the house.' Robert waved a hand at the table.

'Of course it is,' Marie said.

Garcia didn't like any of this. 'I'll pay. Another time we'll choose something lighter.' He put a two-hundred-franc note on the table.

'Have a coffee and cognac,' said Robert. 'On me.'

Garcia stood up. 'It's a little too hot for that. But good luck with the new –'

'Venture,' Marie found the word he wasn't looking for.

I was still sitting. Perhaps that was unwise. I got to my feet.

Marie was entangled in a dispute with Natalie because Natalie wouldn't do the smart thing. She was still defending the chef.

He came out as we tried to leave and stared at us, one at a time. 'Don't ever eat here again.'

'You didn't need to say that,' said Garcia drily.

The chef looked as though he'd head-butt him, but Robert cut in quickly. With great charm he said, 'Eric, the mayor enjoyed the duck.'

'Oh, was that what it was?' said Garcia.

Marie dared to laugh.

The chef looked her up and down. If he had had his way she'd be the next corpse on the plate.

'Psychopathic,' she said to me.

I thought she'd said psychic.

'He's crazy,' she said.

That's what I thought.

As I crept back into the hotel to get my French-lesson notebook, Natalie came out of the dining room. She'd been waiting for me.

'I don't think your friend is familiar with the food down here. It's a meat area. Chicken-liver pâté, ham, lamb, chicken, duck. And that gentleman isn't from here either. He's Spanish.'

So they were going to hang it on the 'foreigner' tag.

Robert was agreeing with her in soft, charmingly chosen phrases that I almost understood.

'We're not L'Hostellerie here,' she said. 'We serve plain food the locals of Castel eat. Eric wouldn't work at L'Hostellerie for that lot. Whatever they paid.'

I was going to disagree with her but I remembered I had to spend another night on the premises and that Eric was mad. Also he might find out where I lived.

Deviously, I said, 'I think it's the brightness of the day and those large green plates. It makes the food look different. A bit distorted. You were right. You should have had the yellow ones.' And, trying to steer a course between my conscience and the mad chef, I said I wouldn't be dining that night as I'd be in Spain.

Amazingly the chef didn't go. He served up some horrendous meals apparently among quite normal ones. Never anything special – in the good sense.

On the last morning I asked, as usual, for an egg for breakfast.

'No eggs left,' Natalie said quietly.

'Then I'll buy one if you'll boil it.'

'I can't use his kitchen,' she whispered. 'He won't let me in.'

Chapter Sixteen

'Put the door on as we agreed.' Marie's cheeks were scarlet, fiery, her mood inflamed.

JoJo mumbled around the cigarette.

'We measured the door and it fitted — at least, when I was here.' She was getting steamed up and all set for a row.

I put in my share and said the door was fine as a table. Neither of them listened.

JoJo waved his arms and said something else incomprehensible.

'Then take the legs off.' She was exasperated.

His eyes flicked to me, then back to her, and there they stayed. She had the clout.

She got hold of one end of the door, which had been a table for a day, he the other, and they carried it into the lavatory.

'Of course you can do it,' she said. 'You can make it fit. Take this ghastly door off.'

'Will this take long?' I said, trying for some proprietorial rights.

She was in a fierce mood. 'Go out and sing or something. Don't hang around in here.' She'd become controlling and worse. If I opposed her, there'd be a row.

I didn't want discord, disagreements in this new place, charging the atmosphere, leaving bad memories. I'd be living here when she was gone. I thought about opposing the new door but he'd got the old one off. That one would never make a table. I decided on a wise retreat.

Monsieur Nadal passed me as I sat outside the Grand Café. I felt embarrassed that I wasn't sitting outside his café. But I felt so much else, all painful and bad, that I didn't bother for long with embarrassment.

'I'm waiting for someone,' I said.

He asked how the apartment was coming along. I said he must come and see it. I had about one minute of social brightness left. I wished he'd leave.

'I heard Madame Marie is back.'

'Only temporarily.' I realized Castel was like Colette's mirrors: even the most insignificant happening was reflected a dozen times. Of course, the play with Marie was not altogether a surprise: my mother had had some terrible episodes, controlling and angry. But I had been wiser then: I didn't think I could change things or make her better. I'd simply left as soon as I could.

Marie had been all charm at the start. Then I'd thought I could avoid the scenes, the rivalry, the power struggles. I *wanted* to avoid them because for the rest of the time we got on well. I made the mistake of thinking that they were something separate and shouldn't happen, that I could change things so that the niceness was all there was. But I was now beginning to see that there would be blackness and sunlight. Marie hadn't just rampaged in and taken over. At some point I'd made over my power to her. At some point I'd given up.

I'd come here to change. I thought she would, too. Another mistake. I was in no mood to see anyone, talk to anyone, especially strangers, so the one at the next table leaned across and said, in perfect English, 'Have you bought a property here?'

He was English, from Manchester, and he'd come to Castel via Madame Beaumarchais at about the same time I had. 'I drove her down from Toulouse. I must say, I like it here. I bought a house immediately.'

I thought it must be an epidemic, this buying immediately. He looked elegant, a professional man in his fifties, with an attractive, strong face, very good eyes. A cleft chin, well-shaped sensitive lips. A hat perched rakishly on his thick, greying hair.

'What would you like to drink?'

I stayed with dry white wine and he rum and Coke. His hair was long enough to show that he had confidence in his style.

He described his new house, and it sounded for a moment like the good house in the rue Pierre Brune but the price was all wrong – at least, I hoped so. He said he'd paid the equivalent of 28,000 pounds.

'Which agency?'

'Marcel.'

We wrestled with the exact location: his description meant nothing to me. Then he said, 'Pizzeria.'

'It's further down. There's a sort of impasse. I can hear the fountain from my windows. Marcel was going to build a roof terrace.'

He introduced himself – Herbert Dunn, solicitor. I vaguely remembered dancing with him at Colette's.

His wife had fallen in love with Castel too. This

would be their third property. In England he had a town-house, a place in the country. 'Now I just want to retire and live here.'

He epitomized substance, satisfaction, success. He had got things the way he wanted.

Was I a good judge of character?

Back in the flat, I found Marie and JoJo still in the lavatory struggling with the door. An electric saw was at work. I heard her say, 'You can do it. You will do it.'

I decided to go to my French lesson. I gave my teacher a list of the words and phrases with which JoJo puzzled me. She said to forget them. No respectable woman even knew them.

Monsieur Garcia had his car right up at the door. 'Get in,' he said. 'I'm just waiting for Madame Marie. I'm taking you to a real restaurant for dinner.'

I was about to rush upstairs to have a conservative talk with her but she came down, just as cool and stylish-looking as ever. Not even a speck of dirt.

'Is the door on?' I hoped it wasn't.

'Of course.' She was about to walk past. Her bad mood was over, and she was more than prepared to forget it.

'I don't like the way you take over.'

'Someone has to or they walk all over you.' She patted my stomach. 'Too fat. And you actually let him turn the door into something with legs. A table? Was that what you called it?' She laughed and flipped my cheek. 'Come on. We're going to the sea. I should have gone back on the evening plane from Toulouse with

Jay's papers but I'll have to stay. I can't leave you alone. I'll have to sort out the furniture.'

'I want you to go.'

She didn't reply immediately. When she did her voice was ice. 'Oh, well, that's nice. After all I do for you. And for Jay. I came out so you didn't have to go back there. I *will* go. But I'll choose when. Right now I'm going to eat.' And she walked past me coolly and got into Garcia's car.

I was stuck in my second worst state – no, third. Wounded was the second. The third was ambivalence. I wanted it to be all right between us because she was some quasi-Mummy. And I could never bear the guilt of a falling-out. I did not want an unpleasant departure. I wanted her as my friend.

We passed the beautiful building that Marcel was turning into a hotel. A part of the ground floor was occupied. Next to one door I saw a bronze plate, on it 'Psychiatrist'. I thought I should really speed up the French so I could get in there.

Before we left Castel, she said, 'He'll need those papers.' She stopped at Marcel's office and faxed them.

We ate a wonderful fish meal by the sea at the next bay down from Collioure.

It became clear that when she said she'd sort out the furniture she'd meant she'd do it in an antique shop. She made enquiries at L'Hostellerie and heard about a substantial shop at the entrance to Castel near the Devil's Bridge. She was smiling and charming on this exquisite morning. No reminders of the unpleasantness of the day before. That wasn't mentioned. It didn't exist. Life just went on. That was the usual pattern. And the light and the beauty did discourage the sorting-out that I knew would have to come. It was Saturday, market day, and the stalls stretched from the town hall, past L'Hostellerie, up around by the rue Pierre Brune and straight on to the last road of the village.

I met Robert, then Natalie, then the dark-haired pharmacist, who introduced herself as Pascale and invited me for a drink one evening. Then the bookshop owner, Juan Pamello's wife and a lot of people I didn't know but I would know. I joined the charity that ran the animals-in-distress refuge. I met Marie somewhere in the middle by the shoe stall. She'd bought local wine and natural soap for the apartment, and olive oil and garlic. She'd met a Canadian who'd retired to Le Boulou and he had invited us for lunch. I didn't like him: he was all over her, staring at her with a fixity of purpose I found disquieting. He had nothing to do with Castel and I wished I hadn't seen him.

'He knows all the places around here.' She thought this would excuse him for whatever I didn't like. She went on walking between the market stalls like a galleon in full sail, proud, head held effortlessly high. She was full of gold, the sound of coins, that's how she seemed. And the traders vied for her attention and the Canadian limped on behind her – he had trouble with his legs. I told him he was lucky. I had trouble with my whole life. He went on staring at her profile, as though she had some secret she was about to impart that would change his sad state. He was like a lost dog, but mean. He got the best chair at the lunch table. He chose the wine. He ended up not paying for anything. He'd never been in L'Hostellerie brasserie but dared criticize the food. He lived in one of those rich people's houses on the sharp hills.

Francine, then her brother Vincent, the fish chef, her husband, the meat chef, and later on her sister-in-law, the *sommelier*, came to greet us. Both the brasserie and the restaurant were full.

The Canadian looked at Marie as though her brightness, smile, gold energy would solve his problems, as though she was a quick-working anti-depressant. Suddenly she was sick of him. She could get a man's attention without all that dreariness. I think she'd thought he was richer than he was. She said she'd take care of our part of the bill and that made him sadder than ever. I couldn't bear it, and left and waited for her under the plane trees.

'How can he be in love with me?' she asked. 'I've only known him half an hour.'

What had time to do with it? I thought I would have to spruce up my appearance 100 per cent. Perhaps a perm, so that my hair was fuller and my face less so.

We went to the antique shop and she spent the rest of the afternoon choosing tables, chairs and cupboards, a bed. I liked a grandfather clock until I heard the price. Then, just as we were leaving, she saw a wood stove. Then a better bed, and it was evening. Marie had absolute certainty in her choices and taste. They could see that in the shop. Finally, they showed her a special collection kept for a special client, a bedroom suite, a few hundred years old, named after one of the French kings. The name went completely out of my mind because I'd heard the price.

'Marie, that's crazy. I can't.'

'Of course you can't and you won't. I'll get them down. I want the flounce thrown in, too, and the washing bowl and stand.' The owner of the shop came hurrying along in his Italian sports car. He'd been told he had a real client. He shook hands, then sped into the cellar to get a couple of bottles of good stuff. We sat around the table. Marie had already dropped the price. I had to give it to her: she was good. She got the whole lot, the apartment furnished, for half of what they had asked. She'd learned how to do this being married to a wealthy businessman. She'd accompanied him around the world and learned the art of negotiating. But the table I was immodestly leaning on – the wine was heady – cost three thousand pounds.

The owner opened a third bottle and Marie saw a mirror, a rectangular one that would fit in along the middle of my wall. It had come from a famous brasserie in Lyon.

'A gift,' said the owner.

'Done,' said Marie, and got up. 'They'll deliver at the end of the week.'

Fortunately I was not so full of wine that I wrote a cheque. I said my cheque book was back at the flat. My cheeks felt anaesthetized I'd drunk so much. I was having trouble with English now as well as French.

I didn't think I was going to sort out the imbalance of our relationship without a scene. I thought we should eat first and we went to a much applauded Catalan restaurant in Vives, a village near Castel where the food was '*typique*' and came in vast portions. The dining room was upstairs and the tables tight together and crowded. Tourists liked it here. The food was very good, too good to leave. Everybody looked flushed and stuffed. You could spend a couple of hours there, what with all the courses and different wines.

We ordered the Catalan speciality, bread smeared with tomato, olive oil and garlic, then salt anchovies and a salad and a portion of radishes and tortilla to start with. That was before we knew about the portions. They could hardly get the spread on to the table. We laughed, couldn't stop, until the tears ran, and the quarrel had quite dissolved. Bread with tomato. Twelve large slices of it on a huge platter. Tortilla enough for twenty. A mountain of salad. Then the meat balls in gravy, the squid in sauce which could only be tasted. We were embarrassed by our over-ordering. We saw the desserts going to other tables like showgirls in a club, mountain peaks of frothy cream on huge pastries decorated with ice-cream. The dessert wine in the glass decanter, which you tipped at a distance and poured straight into your mouth. That didn't happen at our table. I didn't suppose many people left entirely sober and we weren't two of them. We sat outside in the full moonlight in the absolute quiet of the country road and had a huge row. The antique-choosing had all been for nothing. I had enough money for two, three years, although I chose not to think like that.

She said simply, 'Rent a couple of hundred metres of pavement in Perpignan. I'm sure that's how Eliane gets her *fric*.'

I was insulted. 'I don't need a couple of hundred metres.' It wasn't that she thought I was capable of turning tricks in doorways but that I needed a whole boulevard to do it. I could still attract men. I was creeping up to fifty but –

'Name two.'

'Two what?'

'Men who are attracted to you.'

Ludicrously I said Monsieur Nadal and Jay.

'You don't know about men any more than you know about furnishing a place.'

But I was going to know. She made sure of that.

I got up and walked around. A dog started barking and then another. All she seemed to do was to take everything out of my life and then fill it with furniture.

I paid JoJo the second half of the money. I told Marie calmly I would buy the furniture for my apartment myself. I would definitely make mistakes but it would be a learning process. And the kitchen furnishings stayed.

She blamed it on my husband. Called him a 'cloth'. I happened to think the good stuff wasn't laid out in the room but inside yourself. But the king bedroom suite – she was right. It did belong to my apartment. Had for years. Eliane's mother had sold it to the dealer when she hit hard times.

Marie reduced antique to what she called *brocante*, good second-hand. I wanted first-hand from the modern furniture store on the edge of Le Boulou.

'How can you do this place up?' she sighed. 'You've been a housewife all your life. How can you know about refurbishing an old, valuable apartment –'

'Actually, I'm a singer.'

'Well, yes. You can be anything here.'

Furious, I went to Monsieur Nadal. 'She wants a perfect apartment. I want a place that expresses me. What I am.'

'Who owns it?'

I said I did.

'Let her go and find her perfect apartment.'

I walked up into the country and supposed, with my luck, I'd meet one of those madmen Natalie was so worried about. Maybe Eric, the chef. I knew Marie was better than me. I knew she'd had some kind of relationship with Jay. She'd obviously wanted him. I was second best. She'd caught me at the very worst time. I'd needed a friend. She was the friend. She made sure of that. She had classy looks, a well-boned, ageless face, wholehearted winning smile. She had a good carriage; the way she held herself made heads turn. She looked like one of the boys and wasn't afraid of anything. Her hair was cut boyishly. She dressed in a tomboy style. But she was someone to watch.

My attraction, which I was still convinced I had, was more female and receptive. I knew that good energy and radiance was the real turn-on, and occasionally I had it. Here, with my life in Castel, I would have it more than occasionally. Eyes bright, physical self glowing. I could feel light and bright and my body effortless, legs strong.

Of course, her extrovert fearlessness could turn to controlling invasion and my receptiveness became pulp. It wasn't that she was after Jay but she needed to control him, contain him. Yet he was naturally self-protective because he could only bear to hear a lecture once.

Repetition meant cut-off. He had the self-defence capability of an eel.

After her gibe about my standing unsuccessfully on street corners I decided to keep my financial prospects to myself. If the worst happened, I'd rent the apartment.

I prowled around outside the building and didn't relish going in. It was as though a dangerous animal had got into my home. All her furniture greed seemed to go to her jaws.

Then I remembered the Spaniard just an hour over the border. At least I had him in my heart. He was there like a secret bank account, magic money. Marie didn't know everything.

And then she quietened down and was a good friend, and in spite of my earlier decision I started confiding in her again. I was one of those who fell out with someone and hours later forgot all about it. And I'd see him or her in the street and treat them like a friend and I'd think, There's something I should remember here. And the same with my actual friends. I preferred to trust them and be close to them and not have no-go areas. But I came to realize that that was my need and not some superior quality.

With great pleasure I furnished the apartment. I bought a round French zinc coffee table and a larger rectangular one, which I put in the kitchen, and four café chairs to match. It gave me real pleasure to look at this brand new evocative furniture. Then an ordinary double-bed and a Provençal-style sofa-bed. Finally a small wooden chest to keep everything in and a brown bedside cupboard, which stood in the corner of the room with a china jug and bowl on top. The rest was space, longed-for clarity. The only addition was a small fountain running over ceramic rocks.

It said a lot for Marie that she accompanied me throughout these buying trips and said nothing. I think she saw that the simplicity of it pleased me. She bought, as a present, the rectangular mirror from the antique dealer, and placed it midway on the wall behind the café table. It gave a brasserie effect. She designed lights from old tiles, which JoJo bent and formed into a spouting oval that stuck on the wall, the light behind. Madame Beaumarchais brought me *sardana* cassettes. It was amazing, the peace of the apartment. Lying in bed in the indisputably clean room gave such pleasure. I'd never imagined a place could do that.

Chapter Seventeen

I had become aware of Rennes-le-Château because in the sixties my husband had found a book published in French by Gerard de Sède. My husband disliked the mystical but he was intrigued by the story of the poor priest who became a multi-millionaire overnight. That was the fact. Whether it was through black magic, the Holy Grail or finding treasure was a matter of speculation. The money the priest spent was not. My husband translated the French text effortlessly as he read to me, a section every night. His voice had soporific rhythm and it could put the most entrenched insomniac to sleep. He used to test if I was awake or not by inserting the word 'baboon' into his reading. If I didn't object – 'Why did you say baboon like that?' or 'What has baboon to do with it?' – I was asleep, and the book snapped shut. Rennes-le-Château. I decided that one day I'd go there.

Monsieur Garcia was bending in the sun on the side of our terrace, sorting among a crate of freshly picked Spanish vegetables. 'I'm going to Rennes-le-Château,' he said.

'The Holy Grail place? Where is it?'

'Just to the north. Come with me.'

He didn't go that day, after all, because friends from Paris arrived to take the cure. I discovered Castel was one of the stopping places for Rennes-le-Château. Coming from the south or the west, people stayed the night or for a meal, and then went north to Quillan or Couixa, then up the circling hill to the still unsolved mystery site. Some from the north, from England, also stopped in Castel. Two were standing at the Pablo bar discussing their journey: they'd taken the night train from Calais to Montpellier and wanted to hire a car. Monsieur Nadal was trying to find a garage.

'So many go up there,' he said. 'And then they come back.'

'Meaning what?' said the English boy.

'They think they're going to find the secret of the universe.'

The English boy didn't think much of that. 'You obviously didn't look in the right places.'

'Oh, I haven't been,' said Monsieur Nadal.

'Why not?'

'I don't need to,' he said sharply.

The English boy looked at his girlfriend and muttered something not altogether friendly.

'Lots of people from Castel go up there,' said a young guy I'd seen around a lot. He was dark and very good-looking. I had thought he was French, but his accent put him further afield. He came from the Ukraine and worked as a labourer. He said if they'd put petrol in his car and pay for his time he'd drive them up.

Monsieur Nadal wasn't crazy about that idea, and when I saw the Russian's drinking habits I could see why. He bought a round of beers and then settled into the shorts. His name was Sergei, but some called him Serge. He was a painter but did what he could to get by to keep his Russian wife and children, his French mistress and child, and another one on the way by a young local girl. He even found time to fit in Eliane.

The English couple agreed a price and bought another round. Serge said he'd get the car and they'd start right away. It would take two hours.

And then the English boy seemed nervous. 'It's a funny place. It's one of those places you can't just go to. If you're not meant to you don't get there.'

'What does that mean?' said Serge. 'It's just a place.'

'A friend of mine set out for Rennes-le-Château and his car broke down. So he got it fixed and a girder fell off a building site and went through his windscreen. Right between him and his girlfriend. The car was smashed up but they weren't touched. And they hadn't even left Newcastle.'

'Newcastle?' said Serge. 'Well, that sounds like a helluva unlucky place. We're talking about Rennes-le-Château.'

'My friend took the plane to Toulouse and hired a car and got caught in a storm and was stranded. In the end he hitched a lift. A coach full of tourists. And something happened to that.'

'A wheel came off,' said the girl.

'And he never got there.'

Serge said that was crazy. Thousands of people set off for Rennes-le-Château every year. By the law of averages a few wouldn't make it.

Juan Pamello had joined us and I asked what he thought. 'You hear all sorts of things, but I don't like the place.'

'Why not?'

For once he didn't know.

Serge had another drink and then another, while the English told more horror stories of those who had tried to get there and failed.

Monsieur Nadal said, 'If you get the Russian behind the wheel you'll be two more.'

The best-selling books in the eighties about the Holy Grail had attracted the visitors. Before then, Rennes-le-Château had been known only to a few interested in history and myth.

'The French always knew about it,' said Monsieur Nadal. 'Especially the locals. Why should anyone else? It's a dark story.' And he refused to talk about it again.

Marcel was fascinated by the place because of its architecture. He had a cut-and-dried approach and told the story. There was no darkness or light for him.

The priest, the Abbé Berenger Saunier, born in the Aude district of the south of France in 1852, took over Rennes-le-Château, a poor parish with its run-down church, in 1885. His income was just sufficient for survival but he had strength, energy, was handsome and educated, and he set to improving his church and parish. He hired a maid, a young hat-maker, Marie Denarnaud, aged twenty. No one would have heard of Saunier, and possibly Rennes-le-Château, if in 1891 he hadn't found two scrolls that changed his life. From this point on he was wealthy beyond belief, building extravagant follies: a neo-Gothic tower housing a vast library, the Renaissance-style Villa Bethania, stuffed with treasures, an extensive park with fountains and exotic animals. He led a grand life and people were curious.

He entertained cultivated friends from Paris, including the opera singer Emma Calvé and composer Claude Debussy. Marie Denarnaud wore the latest Paris fashions and the locals called her, cynically, 'Madonna'. She told them, 'I know a secret that could turn your streets to gold.'

Saunier restored his church lavishly, and in a tantalizing fashion that many believed is a code, the solving of which would lead to cosmic secrets, the Holy Grail, the Cathar gold. Saunier had certainly discovered secrets that disturbed the Vatican: it was rumoured his wealth came from blackmailing the Vatican. He allowed them only a certain part of what he'd found: to give all, he knew, would end in his death.

Saunier was a monarchist who wanted the return of a Bourbon king to France. He sold masses by post, which was illegal. There was some conjecture that that was how he had made his money. He took constant short journeys, sometimes with his maid, often returning with sacks of stones and rocks. He visited famous artists and possibly a supernatural circle in Paris. He was on close terms with the Archduke of Austro-Hungary.

In 1909 Saunier was called to account for his wealth and its source by the Bishop of Carcassonne. He would not answer and was removed from the pulpit. Strangely, the Vatican reinstated him. Another priest, a Father Gélis in the next village, was murdered and the crime never solved. Saunier died in 1917; a priest hearing his last confession fled white-faced from the house. After his death, Marie Denarnaud burned his private papers. She believed he had been murdered. Some years later, she was seen burning stacks of banknotes. The villagers stared: why had she done such a mad thing? The money was in old francs. Some time after Saunier's death the currency was changed and old money was supposed to have been handed in in exchange for new. But she preferred to destroy it rather than declare its source. Every day she sat by Saunier's grave. Fearing the devil, she never revealed his secret and died, aged eighty-five, in 1953. Saunier and the mystery of Rennes-le-Château had always intrigued a small number of people, and after the best-selling accounts in the eighties, in which the secret was connected with the blood of Christ, thousands had flocked to the hilltop village in search of the meaning of the universe, the Holy Grail, the secret of Jesus and Mary Magdalene. It was rumoured that there existed a master plan for human life on this planet, drawn up by extraterrestrial beings, the discovery of which would make the finder master of the world.

After Marcel had told the story, there was some discussion.

'There's obviously a secret that still hasn't been solved,' said Juan Pamello.

'The Vatican bought it from him,' said Marcel.

'So what is it?' said Juan Pamello.

'Well, they haven't told me.'

'It's in the scrolls,' said Marcel's wife. 'Details of a hidden treasure.'

Marcel gave a mirthless little laugh. 'I shouldn't think so. Otherwise the priest would have hopped it and lived somewhere a little more worldly. He had exotic tastes.'

'Meaning?' I asked.

'He had to stay there. In his parish. That was the condition. He fed them a little bit now and then, and they paid a lot now and then. But he was trapped. What could he do with the money? So in a way he mocked the whole thing. He built a strange tower, made a bizarre church interior that people will be puzzled by. Is it really a treasure trail or –'

'I don't think it was even money he found,' said Juan Pamello. 'I think it was the Holy Grail.'

'I think it's time you took that train journey,' said Marcel. 'Use up all that romanticism.'

And so they discussed it to and fro but whatever anyone said the poor priest had got rich and no one knew how.

There was hardly anyone in Castel who didn't have a view on Rennes-le-Château. Their grandparents, considering themselves neighbours of that parish, had passed down stories of the priest, the maid and their short journeys, of the treasure, whether coins or information. The treasure was either a master plan, which showed, among other things, how to transcend death, how to become invisible, how to pass from this planet to other realms, transcending time, or the Cathar treasure, which had never been found. Whatever was secreted in Rennes-le-Château would be dangerous in the wrong hands. The Vatican knew that, Saunier had known that, and apparently, the Prieuré de Sion, a secret society that had existed for hundreds of years also knew it.

Garcia loved the idea of being invisible. 'That could be very useful. That would be enough for me.'

Juan Pamello was struck by the Holy Grail notion.

'Of course something exists. Every culture had a Grail. It's appeared in mythology over and over again.'

'What did the Grail do?'

'Gave eternal life. The Celts, the Druids knew about it. You should know about them. That's in your language. Read "King Arthur". What else is that about?'

And now that I knew where Rennes-le-Château was, I also knew that many of the visitors passing through Castel were off to this hilltop to search for life's purpose. Saunier in his extraordinary church with its challenging imagery, may have found it. Had it helped him?

I asked about the English couple. They hadn't been sure about going. Had they come back?

'They never got there,' said Juan Pamello.

'Well, of course they wouldn't,' said Monsieur Nadal. 'They went with Serge. He was drunk before Le Boulou. There's no mystery about that.'

I wouldn't have thought anything of it but a few days later a biker told a tale.

Chapter Eighteen

A sign told us we were now in Cathar country. Monsieur Garcia overtook the car ahead as though it was a rock on the roadside, and the one in front of that. He just snipped through space. Even now he loved going from one *département* to another, saw the excitement of it. The landscape already looked different. Canigou was now behind us and, seen from this northern aspect, was one mountain in a range. It was still the most important, the sacred, in fact the first one, but it had plenty of company behind it.

Garcia took what he described as the panoramic route and almost sang his praise to the view. Effortlessly he spun around rock formations, under tunnels of rock, between great sculpted traps of rock, whole banks of it going sheer downwards to the ravine, where thinner, sharper rock jagged upwards like a hundred open sharks' mouths. This ocean of dry violence, waiting down there for us if we should make one unlucky move, made the journey a little less than 'superb', and what the travellers had to say about not getting to Rennes-le-Château or, more precisely, being stopped *en route*, passed through my mind. The road became too narrow, with tortuous turns, but Garcia avoided all oncoming cars with a magnificent arrogance. He handled hairpin bends and any other surprises with aplomb. A Parisian taxi-driver for forty years, he didn't get surprised. It was as though he knew the road or what was coming. He had the radar of a bat.

I asked what he thought about the travellers' tales and how they thought that either the time or they themselves had to be right to get there.

'My dear Madame, they just want to make their journey interesting. Make more of it than it is. If only someone could do the same for the Costa Brava, tourists would flock back there again and my property on the seashore would go up.'

I told him about the English couple who didn't get there because their driver was drunk.

'I've been driving people all my life, and getting drunk never stopped anyone going anywhere.' Then he added, 'If they want to go.'

The rocks in all their dramatic configuration pleased Garcia. 'They're ancient, the oldest known thing in the region.' He pointed at the sudden view, the immensity of which made him praise God. All I could see was the unfenced road, the sheer drop.

Nervously I asked why people made such a mystery of Rennes-le-Château, the experience and the journey.

'My dear Madame, it was special long before the priest started digging up treasure. Thousands of people, a whole empire, lived there at one time. The Visigoths.'

'Why?' I didn't want to know. I wanted to scream with fear.

'Because it's very high. It was strategic.' He turned and laughed. 'Are you nervous? Not with me.' He swept a hand off the wheel and waved at the rocks. 'That's the treasure.'

I agreed they were beautiful.

'I love rocks, Madame. But I tell you, that is the treasure of Rennes-le-Château. There is no mystery.'

I nodded. I'd heard quite a few treasure theories. This was no worse.

'From these rocks and certain stones, the Cathars made white gold. It's called radium, I think. Saunier found out how to do it.'

'Is it that simple?'

'Why shouldn't it be? Why did he drag bags of rocks and stones back to the church late at night? Everyone worries because he didn't leave. How could he? It had nothing to do with blackmail, the Vatican, his treasure was *sur place*. The Vatican bought some of his gold. How could he leave? Other people would come sniffing among those rocks.'

'The scrolls had the formula?'

'Of course. The Cathars knew how to do it. The alchemist's gold. Find out if it's radium. You're cleverer than me.'

'I doubt it.'

'So they've got the story the wrong way round,' he explained.

'He didn't find it, he made it.'

'And people bought it. Always look for the obvious. I'm a taxi-driver and the obvious is what I trade in. When you hear that a priest and his maid carry sacks of rocks and stones, you have to pay attention. There is no point in talking about plans and outer-space people and living for ever. What part do bags of rocks play in that?'

We swept on to a normal road; the precipice was gone.

'Have you tried to find these rocks?'

'I haven't time. I live my life,' he said simply.

He stopped in Quillan for lunch, rather than Couixa further along because he especially liked the Hôtel Centrale. 'It's ordinary. Here everyone eats.' Before I got out of the car he said, 'I hope you didn't think I made light of what you had to say. People are always saying the place is cursed, damned, spiritually robbed, unlucky. There's a society very high up.' He flicked his fingers indicating wealth. 'They have meetings there. Ceremonies to try to find special knowledge and advantage. They're like Freemasons.'

'Who are they?'

'I've never seen them. But I will say this. You get to a place if you want to. You don't get drunk.'

And with old-fashioned charm he led me to a spacious table in the cool dining room with a view of the courtyard. I thought of Serge's estimate, two hours. Monsieur Garcia had done it in less than one.

The wine region had also changed and we were now in the Limoux, with its Blanquette, its Crémant – Madame Beaumarchais had asked him to bring back a dozen bottles. Of each? She had left that open to interpretation.

The table wine was immediately different, light, fresh and irresistible. Garcia certainly wasn't going to resist anything. 'Let's have another bottle. It's quite inoffensive.' He ordered a huge local dish with cabbage, sausage, potatoes, meat, akin to *choucroûte*, enough for a whole family, and he mopped it up with wedges of bread. Away from all Catalan influences, we were looking at French peasant food, hefty and sustaining. With the local cheese and salad he chose a bottle of red. 'They say these Limoux wines are not important. They're wonderful. Look at the colour. There is so much snobbery with wine. This is *cru*, a young wine.' It went down as fast as the older ones. With the home-baked apple flan he chose a bitter-sweet orange-coloured glowing dessert wine, tangy, almost medicinal. He selected the year. A real pedigree, this one. 'It came out of the right bottle.' He poured another glass. With coffee, a substantial liqueur and I thought, Here are two more who are never going to arrive in Rennes-le-Château. I was feeling less than clear-headed and didn't know how I was going to get on my feet, leave alone out of the door. Then along came the proprietor with two glasses of champagne. Garcia loved its 'chocolate' taste. I realized he'd been known to be soberer. '*Blanc et noir*. White and black,' he said. And it was true: in the heart of its taste the champagne had something reminiscent of dark chocolate.

I wanted to pay something. He wouldn't hear of it. He was flushed with the pleasure of it all and told the proprietor that although he loved Bordeaux wines, as did everyone, those of the Limoux had their place, the younger brother and sister, young being the operative word. And we had to remember that the region was small. This talk was as a red rag to the bull. To my horror, up came another bottle of something special.

'Try a glass of this, and then we'll talk about Bordeaux.'

Young, old, it still contained alcohol, and I could see that my driver was not very different from the English couple's driver, and that our journey to Rennes-le-Château would have the same ending. I said we should go.

'Of course we'll go,' Garcia said expansively, 'but I have to buy a round. The *patron* and his wife – she does the cooking, superb – are coming to join us. And the wine manufacturer wants us to sample one or two of his new vintages.'

We sat in the courtyard for a final and necessary cup of coffee, and Garcia explained that we were going on to Rennes-le-Château.

'But the best of the day's gone,' said the proprietor. 'Go up in the morning. Stay here tonight. Dinner on the house.'

'No. No.' I was adamant. Garcia understood immediately and asked for the bill. Then up jumped a customer who knew him from Paris, and I dreaded that in the pleasure of this meeting another bottle would be offered.

Some hours later, several bottles later, when we left the restaurant Garcia seemed as clear-headed as when he'd gone in. It was now five o'clock and a wind had got up. Wisely he suggested a short walk – as he put it, 'To get the feel of a new place.'

And I realized, almost laughingly, that in the old days we'd have lingered even longer. It was quite probable, in the orgy of drink and life-love, that we'd have gone to bed. And he said, 'If I was a younger man, Madame . . .' He looked at me and laughed. Then he held my hand.

'But then we'd never get there,' I said. 'We'd be like all the others.'

His eyes were melting warm and brown, his hand lovely to hold. It was a nice little moment. A bit later he said, 'And then it would ruin our friendship.'

He said lunch was his best meal. He owed it to himself to live well. 'I don't get fat because for days I drink nothing but water. Mineral water, boiled water, water from the spring. I call them white days. I walk a lot and sunbathe a little. And I take all the massage and mineral treatments. I look after my feet. Very important. Look after your feet, Madame, and they look after you.' Of course he was tight. And he talked about his grooming and beauty treatments with pride. He looked after himself like a woman.

'I make as much of myself as my wife. People might say I was homosexual.

'That is, until they know me.'

He bought Madame Beaumarchais's supply of Crémant and got into the car. 'I was born in the street, brought up in the worst quarters of Malaga. That's in Spain.'

'Yes, I know where Spain is but I don't know where we are.'

'We are five minutes from our destination,' and he shot up the nearest hill.

'In the back-streets I learned to fight. I had no choice, and I was small. Otherwise I would not have survived. Now I don't have to survive. I live.'

We circled around the high hill on a narrow, unwel-coming road, which perhaps accounted for some of those travellers not having finished their journey. What took most people twenty minutes, Garcia did in five. The car shook to a stop and I arrived at the summit with shivering legs.

The buildings seemed to wait in the light, syrupy sun, while a cool breeze sent a tree-rustling swell and fall of summer sound across this strange territory. Whatever should be happening wasn't. That's the feeling I got. Visitors swarmed between the presbytery, the church and the Villa Bethania, the graveyard, expecting what? They didn't know. They left empty. On the most superficial level, there was no bar, no café, no lavatory, no restaurant. It was simply the priest's business up here. There was one concession, the bookshop opposite the church, run by two Englishwomen, Susan and Clare. They seemed to be in charge of the site. People asked them questions and they gave answers generously. They could tell the story of Rennes-le-Château in at least two languages. Problems began when they were coaxed into a discussion. Tourists circulated, looking for a place to stay, a coffee, a drink. The Tower Magdala was stuck up on the edge of a sharp hill. That's the first thing I saw. The second was that everything seemed to be in decline, which was surprising in view of the attention it all received.

Garcia pointed at the tower. 'It's mock medieval. Why he should choose that I can't imagine.'

'Why did he build it at all?'

'Marcel says to get rid of all that money. Some people think it's a landmark.'

'And you?' I asked. Where did it fit in with the Cathar gold?

'It gave him power. Why not? He could see in every

direction for miles. It could also have been a deception.'

And the trees almost sang in the breeze. I'd seen a building like it, in Spain, in the old days, when the Spaniard had lived behind the cathedral.

'Who runs this place? How?'

Clare explained there was a diversion of opinion on that.

'Why isn't there some provision made for the tourists, Madame?' Garcia sounded accusatory.

'They don't want tourists here,' she said. 'It's the journalists who started all that.'

'Everyone starts something,' said Garcia. 'But people pay taxes. Why doesn't the municipality –'

Clare explained that the Tower Magdala and the Villa Bethania were not municipality business but privately owned.

Who by? had to be the next question, so I asked it.

Discreetly she said, 'Monsieur Privat.'

'He must have *des frics*,' said Garcia, rubbing his hands.

In spite of herself, Clare laughed. 'That's what he hasn't got.'

Monsieur Privat had bought the properties eighteen years before, intending to turn them into a hotel. He was now desperate to sell both and get out.

'Cursed?' I couldn't keep the eagerness out. 'It's what I've heard. The place.'

'He can't afford to keep them and do them up. And now he owes money.'

Monsieur Privat was financially and spiritually exhausted.

Just to keep his hand in, Garcia asked the price. He

hungered after available property in beautiful places. On being told, he clicked his teeth, neighed with alarm. 'My dear lady,' he said to Clare, 'not even the Abbé Saunier himself could afford that.'

The inside of the small wooden church was startling in its clear bright colours and imagery, the wide use of sky blue, almost hypnotic. Ste Germaine held a luxuriantly embroidered cloth, with white fluffy creatures I took to be lambs, jumping at her legs. It looked energetic for the depiction of a saint. Saunier had been definite about colour. The decorative colourful journey to the Cross. The devil crouched in the doorway with an unforgettable face. Saunier's message, '*Par ce signe tu le vaincras*,' and his initials on a red circle below. 'Why did he leave this?' said Garcia. 'It isn't a Bible text.'

It was a treacherous, beautiful church on the edge of something that was not safe or even divine. It wasn't a joke or a trick.

The church worried Garcia. 'Did you see the message above the doorway?' he whispered.

I had not.

' "Beware, all ye who enter here." What sort of priest was he?'

I thought Garcia must have got it wrong. Too much to drink. Not wearing glasses? Back in the sun, I joined the other visitors trekking from one much-questioned spot to another. Saunier's grave, at the far end of the cemetery, was surprisingly unadorned. That church disturbed me. It was unfinished business. Another coach was unloading eager Japanese tourists, and Clare was asked to take them on a tour of the church. Who would look after the bookshop?

'I will,' said Garcia practically. 'I can speak a bit of everything.' He stood behind the till.

Thousands of visitors climbed the hill every year and looked around Monsieur Privat's property but it didn't help him at the bank. Where was the centre, the pulse? The Englishwomen could not say who ran the place or what was happening. A buyer had to be found for the property owned by the unhappy Frenchman, then order could be established. They explained that every facet of the place was contradictory. No one got on. Nothing happened. Tourists clambered over everything and left empty. The villagers were resentful of the intrusion in their lives. They disliked, especially, the journalists who had descended on their world, written best-selling books, made documentary films, made plenty of money, yet not one had given so much as a *sou* in thanks to the village.

A bearded intellectual Frenchman dug, or rather excavated, outside the presbytery door. Garcia laughed. 'Looking for treasure?'

'Could be.'

'Monsieur Privat?' I asked.

He pointed to the tower. 'He's getting ready to give his tour and talk. He does it on the hour.'

'If he can,' said Clare. 'He's been very depressed.'

While Garcia sold postcards and books as though he'd never done anything else all his life, I watched the Frenchman sifting the earth with care. He was Raoul, the grandson of Saunier's verger. He ran a Rennes-le-Château association from Carcassonne, the legendary walled Cathar town to the north. The Englishwomen were also starting an organization. There was a French one already in the village and another in Quillan.

'There's a lot of organizations but no organization,' said Raoul. He planned to excavate under the presbytery house. Who owned it? He said the municipality. Then he said it was actually his grandfather who found the scrolls that had changed Saunier's life. They had been secreted in the altar – I thought he said 'tubes'. Raoul didn't say whether his grandfather was rewarded for his find. Or what was on the scrolls.

He expected to uncover a flight of stairs going into a second cellar but the mayor was giving him trouble: he was not eager for more discovery leading to yet more speculation. He had looked at Raoul's digging and said, 'Cement it up.' But Raoul's organization in Carcassonne had applied for the rights to the new excavation. Raoul did not intend to stop. He expected another visit from the mayor, an unfriendly one, before nightfall. His digging got faster. It was now seven o'clock.

He pointed to a depressed middle-aged man in a clean shirt walking mournfully towards him. This was Monsieur Privat. I was happy to go on his tour of the tower. There were ten or eleven or us, listening to a talk on Saunier's life, which took half an hour. Most of it had been culled from the best-selling books: there was nothing new. Like the church, the inside of the tower was vividly painted, disturbing, exotic. Also very run down. 'Who was Saunier?' asked an American. 'A madman? A dangerous megalomaniac?' He was disturbed by the place and wanted to leave. Monsieur Privat, eyes red-rimmed after nights of economy-worry, spoke slowly. We were now in the tower, with uninterrupted views in every direction. The wind carried off his words, and he waited for calm to say that a financial contribution was not obligatory but would be welcome for the upkeep. He left the amount open and the offerings were sparse.

Monsieur Privat jangled the coins and joined Garcia in the bookshop, drawn to him as though to a warm fireplace. One thing Garcia exuded was luck.

After the lunchtime folly, Garcia and I were thirsty. I could see one of his water-only white days coming up. I went to look for mineral water or beer, but the bar further down the hill was shut. So was a restaurant. It seemed I'd have to go as far as Quillan. Then Clare rounded the side of the church with her second group and offered to make tea. Unlike, or perhaps like, Monsieur Privat, she worked for nothing.

'That's crazy,' said Garcia. 'How are you supposed to survive?'

'That's what we're working on,' said Clare. 'We're not officially here yet. We're not allowed to run it as a business or a charity.' She explained she'd visited Rennes-le-Château some years earlier and that it had made a great impression on her. She wasn't satisfied until she'd come back and made it her home. She felt she lived on the pulse, or the centre, that it was mysterious and exciting. She wouldn't change her life for anything. She had an apartment in Rennes-les-Bains, a spa village a few kilometres away on the plain. Either she or Susan must have been emotionally involved with Raoul. The organization they planned would not hinder his. It would rectify the obvious difficulties and she named some of them: proper guides to look after the visitors and get the history right, gate money from the tourists and entrance fees for the tower.

'You must,' insisted Garcia. 'You can't even entertain the word "optional". Charge a fixed price for each thing and everyone knows where they are.' Including the municipality who, it seemed, might own some of the territory, and would not be enchanted by two foreign women pocketing the take. As it was, everyone did everything free, straying over private and municipal property alike. Clare intended to draw up a proposal that she become an accredited director of the site. She would arrange talks, try to pay off the debts incurred by everything going out and nothing coming in, organize a further excavation. So what was wrong? We knew we'd get to that. Raoul and the English were unified but others were not. The village did not run smoothly: there were rivalrous factions.

'It's a funny place,' said Clare. 'It's obvious what needs to be done but we go one step forward and the rest back. With eighty thousand people paying a hundred francs a time, we could afford full-scale excavation of the entire area, staff wages, the upkeep and restoration of Monsieur Privat's properties. A café would be opened, a restaurant, even a hotel. And lavatories.' She said there were some on the field where people parked.

It sounded sensible. The only problem, nobody got on with anyone else. The local people were against the tourist invasion of their village. The churchgoers hate their old priest being under the gaze of the world. The mayor was against all of it. The priest who presided over Sunday services hadn't given clear instructions so the church seemed to be in the hands of anybody. The other organizations were mystical, historical, in essence, and were not keen on tourism.

Garcia and I paid a subscription, which made us immediate members of the English organization. As he said, they sounded sincere and energetic. We would receive a twice-yearly bulletin.

I thought they all looked as though someone was missing: they were waiting for that person to climb the hill with ideas and the will to save them.

Garcia was thoughtful. 'Anyone could come up here and be anything. We could all have our organizations. What's to stop us?' he looked at Raoul, then at the Englishwomen. 'We've as much right as they have. We could start a Castel Friends of Rennes-le-Château and charge something.'

He'd enjoyed running the bookshop and handed over the till. Monsieur Privat watched with interest as Garcia counted the money. He was as neat about that as everything else.

'You've made more in one hour than they do all day.' Monsieur Privat was loath to let him go. 'Come and have something with me. I haven't got much but I can give you a drink.'

Garcia was unsure. He could see that the Frenchman was desperate and Garcia was kind. But since leaving the Malaga mean-streets, he was also kind to himself. He wanted to go to the nearest of his homes, which was in Castel, and have a peaceful and restorative evening.

'A clairvoyant came up here in the spring and told me I'd be saved by a man from Spain. The description fits you.'

Garcia almost crossed himself.

'So please let me tell you my story.'

'My dear Monsieur. I love a coincidence the same as anyone else, but I have to tell you immediately I am not that man.'

Chapter Nineteen

Garcia said that if we accepted the Frenchman's invitation it would be too dark to return by the panoramic route. Not having got over the outward journey, all those rocks, I said we should not put ourselves first. After all, Monsieur Privat was the master of Rennes-le-Château. Garcia said we'd take the motorway from Rivesaltes, cutting the journey time by half.

Monsieur Privat stood between a reproduction of Poussin's painting of a tomb, *Et in Arcadia Ego*, which had been strongly linked with the Abbé Saunier mystery, and a coded plan of buried treasure from older times, when the area was known as Reddae. The plan was inked out on parchment and would thrill the Americans. It had signs and incomprehensible words – Cellis, Arcis, Regis, Etina. We were still in the tower. All around, the sky turned mauve against distant hills and rocky inclines.

'Why did he build this?' asked Garcia.

'To hold his book collection.'

'No. Really.'

'I have no idea.' Monsieur Privat showed us the estimates for the work as given to the priest by his architect Eli Bot. 'And here are his household accounts kept by the maid. You can see a sharp difference before the scrolls and after. The same can be found in my household accounts but the other way round.'

It was still hard to understand exactly what had brought Monsieur Privat, self-described as a French businessman from North Africa, to this uncommercial hilltop. If it had been for treasure he didn't look as though he'd found it.

He wasn't over-keen to entertain us in the Villa Bethania, but that's where the drink was. The villa was kept private. He was somewhere between moving in, moving out and sinking down. Old books in piles in a corner. Saunier's? 'No. They're from the thirties.' They were damp and covered in mould. They may have been the maid's books. Some of Abbé Saunier's original lavish wallpaper, with hand-painted landscapes, young trees, inlaid with gold, birds, butterflies and large white flowers, still existed. In front of these creations Monsieur Privat had laid out his own. In what resembled a shrine, stood tinted photographs of a lovely woman, the same woman at different ages in different locations.

'My wife.' The way he said it indicated she wasn't any longer.

'Is she deceased?' said Garcia respectfully.

'I don't know.' He opened an embossed book which contained more photographs. She was undeniably alluring. More, unfathomable. An Algerian film star?

Monsieur Privat wrenched the cork off a bottle of white wine and looked around for some glasses. There was a certain amount of chaos. The kitchen had got the better of him and he tried to keep that door shut and us out.

'I would like you to help me.' He looked at both of us.

I said, 'We're not together. We're –'

'Neighbours,' said Garcia. 'Our combined resources are probably not equal to what you require. You must wait for the right man from Spain.'

'What exactly do you need?' I asked to be polite.

'The treasure.'

Garcia's eyes swivelled towards the door. He needed to be off. The Frenchman correctly interpreting his reaction said, 'I'm not mad. I should be. I came to this place with that beautiful woman and our three children. With the money from the sale of my business I bought this villa and then the tower. I wanted to turn it into a hotel. Come and look.'

He took us further into Saunier's villa and here and there sumptuous reminders and then unused rooms with unused beds and hotel furniture and half a bathroom.

'I would have made a fortune here.'

Garcia could see that.

'How did you know about this place?' I asked.

He paused prudently and told me what was probably a lie. 'From books. I was fascinated. My wife and I should work on the place. Renovating. Then one day a woman appeared at the door. This was in the mid seventies. She was from a mystical cult. She took my wife away. I never saw her or my children again. Naturally I went to search for them and I even found where the cult was located but the woman had me arrested for trying, as she described it, to kidnap my wife and my children. I was in prison for four years. When I came back here my life was in ruins. And this place too. I need the treasure, just one small part of it you understand, to make up for some of what I've endured. And the treasure is here. Every night when I lie in my bed I feel it below me, below this house and it has a presence, it mocks me. And I too unknown to them, out there, have started digging.'

Garcia groaned and sighed to do justice to the terrible story. 'You should get away from here. It's too obsessional.'

'Chance would be a fine thing. I have debts and loans and –'

Garcia waved his arms dismissing them. 'Your life is more important –'

'The treasure gives off a greenish glow.'

'Leave it all to those energetic English women and start afresh Monsieur.'

'What you suggest is normal, ordinary. My predicament is worse.'

'Can it be?' said Garcia. He was losing his voice. His life charm didn't work in here and he sagged and sighed. The wine was dying and he felt ragged. I could see the unlucky owner depressed him.

'Couldn't the clairvoyant tell you anything about your wife?' I asked. The light was fading, becoming if anything greenish. Perhaps the treasure was all around us.

'I don't believe in clairvoyants particularly but one does what one can.'

The atmosphere made Garcia nervous. He looked more than ever like a bird, eyes bright and watchful, mouth tired and closed up for the night, a beak, his hands unhappy, one wringing the other, talons, his hair stuck out at the back of his head likes birds feathers. He wasn't the same man who had left Castel, not by twenty drinks and too many unlucky stories.

'The place has brought me bad luck,' said Monsieur Privat, somewhat unnecessarily, 'but I'm scared to leave. The owner before me sold up and left. He'd got only a few kilometres before dying in a car crash. The owner before him got away but soon died of a heart attack. There is a curse on this place. You can't just leave.'

Garcia was incensed. 'Some can't get here. Some can't get out. I'll drive you.' He hopped to the door, got it open, breathed the fresh, evening air. 'Come on, Monsieur. No one has ever died while I'm at the wheel.' A forceful wind bent back the cypress trees. Lightning flared on the horizon. 'After all, you've been told I've come here to – was it save you?'

Monsieur Privat got as far as the door. Then he looked back at the photographs of his wife. It seemed that the unknown he knew was preferable to the unknown Garcia offered.

Going down the hill circling and turning, spinning with small stones hissing beneath the car's tyres, I felt oppressed. Then the storm broke. Garcia thought nothing of it. 'Clears the air.'

He was glad to get back to the normality of Quillan and its hospitable bar.

Back in Castel, in the sunlight in the morning with the Saturday market full of gaiety and noise, the hilltop village seemed nothing more than an unresolved community, unresolved in the modern way – no direction, no unanimous spirit. 'It was,' said Garcia, 'a few obsessional people in a deadlock.'

But I kept remembering the villager bringing in his flock of sheep, his face as he turned and looked at us, taciturn under the weathered hat, the expression beyond hostile, annihilating. That's how he looked at us, two sightseers, as we waited in the car to go down the hill, waited rightly for his animals to pass. Why such a look? And what had his pastoral life to do with that extraordinary church up the hill?

'They've ransacked the place, the journalists, the treasure-hunters,' said Garcia. 'They've dug up this and that, broken and lifted and stolen and taken away. Of course the villagers are upset. I felt rinsed out up there last night but in the light of day I can see it's an enterprise all right. Turning the villa into a hotel.'

'That was his cover,' I said. 'He went there for the treasure.'

'Store not your treasure on earth. He should read his Bible. But what he also should do, poor man, is allow a miracle to happen. Touch the Tower Magdala stone and a little later say you're suddenly richer. The treasure has affected you. Turn the place into a Lourdes for the financially distressed. Instead of candles, coins.'

I wanted to ask him whether, if he had the money, he would buy the place. But I wasn't sure about the 'if'. Madame Beaumarchais had said taxi-drivers worked all the hours they wanted, declared as little as possible to the tax man and made a fortune. And Juan Pamello had added, 'Garcia loves quality of life. He'd spend absolutely nothing if that's the way to get it.'

The two bikers stood in the doorway of a small bar next to the Hôtel Luna. I'd passed it often enough and not really noticed it. The owner, a student from Thailand, sold oriental tapas, spring rolls, spiced fish-cakes, squid, duck and ginger, hot noodles, and the customers, unobserved from the street, stood at the scrupulously clean marble counter, ate from small dishes with chopsticks and drank Chinese beer.

The bikers were eating their tapas at the open door with the bead curtains held back so allowing a view of the inside. An electric storm had stopped them going to Rennes-le-Château and they were waiting until it was less sultry. One English, the other American, they discussed the enigma of Saunier's tower.

'It's mathematical,' said the English boy. 'It follows an exact meridian. Understand that and you understand the lot. It's all to do with –'

'Ley lines?' said the other.

'What are those?' asked Natalie. She'd stopped by to ask if they wanted to keep their hotel room.

'They hold the earth's energy.'

'Perhaps the priest found something there,' she said. 'It has to be more than simple treasure. Turning energy into light. Maybe that's why we have such bad storms.'

'The tower points deliberately in a certain direction,' said the American.

'To connect with –'

'Intelligent sources in outer space,' said the American.

'I don't like it up there,' said Natalie.

'Outer space?'

'Rennes-le-Château.'

'Why not?' asked the English boy.

'Everyone's out for themselves,' Natalie decided.

'Haven't they always been?' said the American. 'What did Saunier do that was so beneficent?'

She wasn't having that. 'He put in a water system, he looked after his parish. You don't know the half of it.'

I mentioned the difficulty some people said they had in getting there. The bikers had never heard that. Then another English boy, younger and rougher, joined them at the door. 'It's a dead scary place,' he said. 'I met a guy on my way up there the last time. He was in a terrible state. On his way to the airport. He'd gone all the way from Hull on a really great bike, his girlfriend passenger –'

'A Harley Davidson?'

'Yes, it was. And they were on that curving road to the top when a dog suddenly ran out in front and he tried to avoid it, couldn't, crashed. The girl fell off and hurt her back badly. The dog was in terrible pain, the bike a write-off. And then the owner appeared through the hedge, looked at all this and didn't say anything. The English guy thought he'd come to help and started to ask for an ambulance. But the man didn't say a thing. Not a word. He looked at the dog, then the girl. He was carrying a farmer's gun. He levelled it and my friend thought he was going to put the dog out of its pain. But he shot the girl, put the gun up, walked back through the hedge and disappeared. My friend screamed for help and eventually someone came and they got the ambulance and the police shot the dog. The girl was put in hospital, nearly didn't make it. And this guy, my friend, d'you know what happened to him? The police didn't believe him. They said he'd shot the girl. He'd made the story up. There was no man with a gun. They put him inside. He got a lawyer who said they'd trace the man through the dog. All dogs have to have a number tattooed on them by law. This dog did not have a tattoo.'

Natalie said that was impossible.

'So the man could not be traced. He must have been local. He couldn't just appear like that otherwise. The lawyer said the whole thing was weird. The guy was on an attempted murder charge but the girl got out of hospital and he finally got out of prison. They'd never try to go there again. But who was this man?'

'He shot the girl in revenge for his dog,' I said.

'But he wouldn't leave his dog like that,' said the boy.

'He got confused and shot the wrong one,' said the American.

'He was dead calm. And why wasn't the dog tattooed?'

'Must have been if he was a farmer's dog. Any dog,' said Natalie.

'They must have removed the tattoo from the dog so the man couldn't be traced,' said Robert, who'd been listening from his doorway.

That solved some of it.

To cheer things up, Natalie asked what I had thought of Rennes-le-Château. The modern-day dramas took the attention. I had not found the key to the universe either.

Chapter Twenty

Marie hadn't got her way in persuading me to buy the granary. She hadn't chosen the furniture.

Perhaps that was why she turned her attention laterally and asked to view the adjoining studio.

'Get that and you've got an apartment.'

It belonged to Monsieur Gato, who lived in a place I thought was miles away. It turned out he was just up the road in a neat little village with modern villas, St Jean-de-Corts. She asked Juan Pamello to get the key.

'But it's not for sale,' I said.

'Everything has its price. It's empty and he won't live there with you in here permanently. And vice versa.'

It so happened that the studio was for sale. Juan Pamello played it down. 'It's on the market but he's not hurrying.'

The price was high. We got the key, also Monsieur Gato, a tough introvert-looking type, with one dramatically inward-turning eye. In his thirties, he had cropped hair, tough jeans, meaningful boots with studs, a jacket with studs, and so that we didn't doubt he could take care of himself, he was accompanied by a large, restless Alsatian dog.

Juan Pamello said he was reasonable and good to

deal with. I instantly stopped trusting Juan Pamello's judgement. Monsieur Gato was rude, impatient and unreasonable. He started off on the wrong foot with Marie by saying, 'My price is my price.'

'Everything's negotiable in this life,' she said.

'Not me.'

'Everyone negotiates –'

'Let them. I get the asking price.' He snapped up his wrist so we could see his imitation Rolex watch. 'I haven't got long.'

Because of frequent lessons, my French was coming along, but was still not good enough for this encounter. Marie retaliated with some adequate arguments. 'It might have been all right with Monsieur Augustin because he was only here for holidays. But Madame Jane is a permanent resident and how will you like it? The walls aren't that good.'

Gato smacked the wall and upset the dog. 'Not that good, but I'm never here. My tenants are.'

'You let?' I asked, trying not to sound the way I felt.

The dog panted and its breath filled the room.

Juan Pamello cut in but Marie shut him up. She said she would come up with an offer.

The studio was not in great shape: it was empty and dirty and musty, and hadn't been properly cleaned or decorated for years. Gato had wisely opened the shutters and windows but too many unclean things had happened in here. The bathroom was partitioned off and one look was enough. A stove, sink, a broken cupboard against one wall comprised the kitchen. The studio, one medium-sized room with greasy lino, could only be improved. A large stain in the ceiling had my attention: since having become a property owner I was always looking at things I'd never before noticed. Gato said it was nothing. The result of some accident upstairs.

'It's quite dry,' agreed Juan Pamello.

But I kept looking at the dark stain. It did not bode well. It was not dissimilar to the one on Garcia's ceiling.

Gato strode to the door; his boots clicked and clanked and his muscles bulged and rippled. He obviously spent time working out. 'Let me know what you intend to do before the end of the month because I've got a lodger who wants it in the autumn.'

'Some lodger,' said Marie.

And a chill shot through me. 'Some lodger' was probably what he got. Why think the best?

Madame Beaumarchais tapped on the door and came in to look round. Then she shook Gato down for upkeep money and light-bulb expense, which subdued him momentarily. He made up for it with his abrasive departure. 'Take it or leave it. It's all the same to me.'

Marie spoke for some of us when she said he wasn't someone she'd like to meet again.

'Not sympathetic,' said Madame Beaumarchais.

I thought he must be into EST or Scientology, one of those groups in which you're trained to be decisive and knock out any opposition. A yes meant nothing but yes. He'd certainly worked on his no.

The two windows were old and lovely, and looked out directly on to the hills, the shrine of St Ferréol. They looked over Madame Beaumarchais's courtyard and garden.

'It's a wonderful addition,' said Madame Beaumarchais. 'You can put your guests here.' She looked at

Marie and laughed, and the laugh teetered off balance. She'd been at the Pernod. Marie was saying again what a terrible man Gato was. I thought the same about the studio. It didn't have the charm of my apartment.

'But you can make it what you want,' said Juan Pamello.

'The structure is sound,' said Marie.

I said I'd think about it.

'It won't need much doing,' said Marie. 'A new bathroom obviously and get that filthy stove out.'

Juan Pamello said that, as a friend, he would forgo his commission. 'You mustn't mind Monsieur Gato. It's just his way. He works in the post. He's married to a nurse. Nothing fancy. Just getting by.'

As I came up the stairs after a modest dinner in the pizzeria, Garcia's door opened slightly and I saw one beady eye. On seeing me alone, he waved for me to come in. He took me into the music room and I thought he'd found a new old song. After I'd sat down he said, 'I speak to you as a friend. That studio is not worth fifteen thousand.'

'It's sixteen.'

'It's been on the market at fifteen. He's been trying to sell it for years. He got it for eight. Don't buy it, Madame. It's too dear.' Then he ushered me back on to the landing. Advice, although free, was quick.

'But why does he want to get rid of it?'

Garcia gave a wonderful shrug and winked. His eyelid came down slowly, fluttered then lifted. His eye looked like a flying insect about to take off. The shrug could have meant, 'Who knows?' or 'Gato's stupid.' It could have meant a lot of things.

Chapter Twenty-one

When I first arrived in Gerona they were lighting fires at the edge of the old quarter. I was fifteen. The sky was violet, flashing with huge flat stars. The sun was up there too, taking its time setting in a blaze of scarlet rage. Dogs loped in front of the fires and music started. Church bells chimed as though for a celebration and all the lights of the town came on, hundreds of yellow eyes. It was a true welcome. And yet, as I stood on the bank of the modern sector across the river, I must have known I was approaching a definitive territory. Once over there, I would not be the same again. Yet I crossed the river that ran through the centre of Gerona. I climbed the iron-canopied bridge and I began to feel strong and clear and the exhaustion of the day had no place. The atmosphere was something I could never forget and have never again experienced.

In the last light of the evening the local craftsmen were working by the fires. I asked a man shoeing a horse the way to a cheap hotel. As I stood by his fire I became weightless, without needs or fears.

The sun finally sank until it was so low it was caught in the river, its reflection coloured the water like blood. Men hammered metal and softened it in the flames.

Meat was cooked on charcoal. Street cries, singing. That's all gone now. It is a polite town, these days.

Then the smart restaurant, Cal Ros, was already filling up. It had been a clamorous night and everyone was on the streets, the bars full. There was a definite feeling of *fiesta* and yet for them it was just another day.

I'd met the Spaniard, Luis Santina, immediately. He was articulate, had a persuasive voice, an easy smile; his eyes brightened as he spoke. Even then, on so slight an occasion, his speech was salted with irony. They said he was political. Even then, they said he was no good for a woman.

Gerona is a pre-Roman town forty miles inland from the Costa Brava. It has a vast old quarter with a much-visited cathedral, Arab baths, monumental churches. Bells ring across the town every fifteen minutes, day and night. The cobbled alleys, sharp stairways, deep arches , courtyards, are all of stone, most of it medieval, some from earlier times. The buildings, huge buttresses of stone, lean together across the strip of street leaving only a shine of brilliant sky. Parts of the original city wall still remain, clumps of stones, almost covered with weed, supposedly four thousand years old, from when the Iberians ruled. The stone makes the town echo and enhances every sound. Only the bells are free, as they toll high above the buildings. The stone makes the town very cold in winter. It holds on to atmosphere. It makes sure that the past is there, always solid, unconquered by decay. It's said that the stones have a magnetism that draws certain people back, time and time again, to the city. I believe it.

Again I crossed the iron-canopied bridge, many

years later, many kilos heavier, but with the same expectations. I hoped – no, I longed to see Luis Santina. I described some of my first arrival in Gerona to Marie as we neared the edge of the old quarter. I did not describe Luis.

A perfect music was sung in the rooms where he lived, out of reach of most ears. He, the poet, discerned even its high notes and tried to keep up with it by laughter and joy and creation, his day a hymn to life. The music played for him, in those days. The birds heard it too. They were lucky. And the geraniums on his balcony throbbed with light. The jealous ones heard nothing. They saw only the earthly pleasures as they unfolded each day. He was the first warm person I'd ever known.

I showed Marie some of the places I'd so loved, that had been there during the best part of my life and were still there. This was my home that I presented as proudly as she had shown me her Côte d'Azur village, her Viking cottage, her ex-husband's estate.

She went back across the iron-canopied bridge, stood in the middle and looked across the river to the cathedral, the Arab baths, the lopsided colourful houses at the water's edge, and gave it her best compliment. 'Better than Florence.' She was impressed to the point of silence.

In the midst of refurbishing she was like a hen with her chicks, impossibly controlling, dominating, on guard. But as soon as she was away from the smell of the house paint she cooled down.

We had a late lunch in the Café Antigua, opposite the town hall which had been there for nearly two hundred years. Cheap, friendly, famous for its traditional snacks, tortilla between hunks of bread smeared with tomato and garlic, hot sausage spiked with a dark brown mustard, a small fresh salad, a simple dish of the day, often kidneys or roasted peppers and beans cooked in mint. Slim toasted sandwiches for the ladies who came from the hairdresser in the mid-afternoon, wearing fur coats and good shoes and carrying expensive handbags. Later, the mothers and children ate crème Catalan, with a toasted brittle top, or a pot of whipped cream piled with sugar. Men came in singly, almost furtively, and devoured a dish of thick hot chocolate topped with a mountain of cream and sugar, or a pile of assorted ice-creams festooned with biscuits, chocolate syrup. They ate these puddings of their childhood with more gusto than any child. They'd longed all day for these.

In the early evening the students crowded in to drink Coke and coffee, filling the place with smoke, noise, discussion. The café was run by a good-hearted, good-humoured man, who'd been there as long as I remembered. He was proud because recently he'd changed the decoration from peeling pale green, which I'd loved, to a yellow brown. Did I like it? Suddenly everything was about interior decoration. Luckily he'd kept the old mirrors and art-deco wall design. He was always keen to give you the food you wanted, whatever your caprice. He'd even send out for it. He wasn't on stage about his food or his place: he just wanted everyone to be content; happy was too big a demand.

Discreetly I asked if he'd seen Luis? He shook his head. Not for days, weeks. I'd already left Luis a message, with a friend of his who ran a bookshop, to say I was in

Castel. I'd heard nothing, so I left a new one with the café owner, and he put it away with his banking papers, private.

We walked up the narrow Calle Forsa, the main artery of the old quarter, sloping up to the cathedral with shadowed doorways, hidden courtyards, stairways, scarcely seen, on either side. Parts of the street were eighth century, and along here had walked participants of all the religions and cults that had been housed in this city, the Druids, worshippers of the Mithra, the cabbalists, the Muslims, the sun-worshippers, the Jews. Some of these devotees had climbed up this street before even the cathedral had existed. Gerona had been generous to new beliefs and, for some often described magnetism, it seemed the place for these beliefs to flourish. The Mithra followers had discovered huge sun stones, Catholic saints had performed miracles in the fields, the cabbalists had attempted spiritual journeys to the furthest outposts of consciousness. Charlemagne had conquered Gerona, so had the Romans. The Moors had tried. Conquerors invariably became the city's lovers, but were always kept on the outside: their blood was not allowed to mix with that of the true inheritors.

The dark street burst open into a high square surrounded by stone buttresses. To the right, dozens of steps led up to the cathedral, which stood in its vastness, courtesy of some miracle in the thirteenth century. The Gothic builder had designed the nave and the walls in such a way that nothing should have been able to stand up. It was like a house of cards that must tumble. Yet it is still there seven centuries later, having survived wars and geometry.

The old quarter, heady, sensual, smelling of wood-smoke and the eau-de-Cologne its inhabitants still used in their hair, olive oil cooking, frying garlic. A Spanish ballad I remembered from the fifties swelled out from behind the bead curtains of a forbidden café. Around the next corner, out of an open window, a snatch of melody I'd always loved and thought epitomized Spain. It turned out to be the radio advertising tune for the popular Torres chocolate. On the balconies birds sang in cages among brilliant geraniums. It was a place of intrigues, illicit encounters, passion, the unattainable. No one could step into the area without being changed in some way. And Marie, in turn, was reminded of passion. On this particular evening, the atmosphere was so persuasive and sultry that I quite expected to see Luis Santina coming out of the next doorway, turning the next corner. But I knew he was not around, that I would not see him, and in a way I was relieved because I didn't want to introduce him to Marie, for her to have knowledge of any part of my relationship with him. But I asked in the second-hand bookshop if the owner had seen him.

'He's here and then he's not here. When has that changed?'

I couldn't have described him better.

I bought some fifties postcards, which showed the old house with a strange tower that Luis used to own or visit. I was never sure which. It had been torn down in the sixties to make way for the new gardens and exca-vation area. I always used to come to this bookshop when I was unhappy, and the moment the owner understood my love, he said, 'It's a pity he's a priest.'

'Not any more,' I'd said.

He'd laughed. 'He'll always be a priest. He can't take that off like an old coat that no longer suits him.'

The atmosphere deepened, was as tangible as the weather, and Marie was affected soon enough because she started talking about her rotten husband, his wealth, his meanness, and how his one fix, 'pure profit', reduced everything else in his life. She was saddened by that marriage. Then she talked of her one love, a beautiful Danish boy, a millionaire's son, related to royalty, who went from riches to rags and back again, someone who skidded to the very edge, every day of his life. Was he bad? Good? She didn't know. He was bright as hell, fun, sophisticated, witty. He behaved so impossibly that in the end he could only justify his actions by becoming an artist. They got on wonderfully, had been made for each other. But her marriage had got in the way and she saw that she'd made the wrong sacrifices for the wrong security.

Shadows were literally carved into the stones, coal black, eternal, and the blinding sunlight split them up, forming patterns on walls and buildings, mystical messages, a secret language.

'He would have loved this place,' said Marie. 'It's grand and huge enough. He hates compromise.'

She'd lived with him in the South of France, then he fell in love with a man. That didn't matter particularly: he was promiscuous – but his lover wanted absolute fidelity.

'I never met anyone as impossible and funny as he was. And never will.'

I'd never heard her so emotional. 'You might,' I said, with polite optimism, 'meet someone else.'

'I never will because I don't want to. I want peace.'

That surprised me.

At the junction of several stairways and alleys, I heard the hiss of water, and there in the gloom, stood a stone lion, upright on its back legs, with water trickling from its open mouth. Marie felt the stone body of this strange fountain and asked if it was drinking-water. I doubted it. She drank some anyway. Like her love, she was reckless, daring, stylish, graceful. He sounded like a reflection of her. I hadn't thought she'd let herself be hurt. She didn't let things go that deep. An elegant defence was essential. But the persuasive atmosphere had seduced this story out of her, which no person could have done. She'd supported his art career and then him, but he'd slipped through her fingers like a piece of wet soap.

I opened the gate of the old hotel where Luis and I used to meet. I crossed the overgrown courtyard, dotted with statues, and its atmosphere was immediately healing. I pulled open the heavy outer door and stood, not moving, because it seemed at first sight that I was in another century altogether. The ceilings were high and moulded with angels, the lights, magnificent chandeliers, the staircase made at a time when people could handle splendour. The smell was as I'd remembered. The door closing made the usual sound.

But there was something else, a rearrangement of the present. I'd disturbed this place, caught it in its true and preferred state – another time altogether. I stood waiting for reality as I knew it. Of course, the long skirts and high-piled hair were not what they seemed but ghosts created by real objects, the way the light clawed through the dust in golden shafts. The lace curtains did their share. The rustling of the long skirts was only the sound of breezes in the garden. Yet I'd heard laughter, an echo, perhaps, of a gayer time.

The hotel had always seemed empty. I approached the woman at the reception desk, who recognized me immediately but did a good job hiding it. I asked if she knew where Luis Santina was. The woman said she did not know the name.

This was the last real old hotel left. It had lofty rooms with peeling paint, bathrooms with pedestal wash-basins and cupids, marble-topped tables. The hotel had rejoiced in my passion for Luis, soothed my pain, occasionally given hope.

And yet more modern people stayed here often enough. They seemed to be absorbed into the real atmosphere, made anonymous. They weren't strong enough to do otherwise. And I in my turn must have seemed invisible.

'I used to stay here. Don't you remember?'

The woman hadn't changed. Her hair was dyed a uniform black. The spoilt, spiteful plant in the tub beside her had grown sharper. It had given up trying to flower years ago. The fading map of the province dated 1840 was still on the wall beside her.

'What do you want?' The woman spoke sharply.

I looked into the breakfast room, still full of dark oily paintings. The tablecloths were bleached by sunlight, the big china cups gave off a milky pale glow. Mostly the rooms were unoccupied, their blinds closed, doors slightly open, and in the vacancy there was a definite sense of the past, of romance, heady but undeniably gone. And it made me sad because wherever I went in the town it would not be found, or in the country, or perhaps in whatever place I visited. And if I should find it, could I hold it again? Could this sense of the past ever be more than a sweet, tantalizing fragrance in an out-of-date hotel?

The building had been preserved either by accident or through lack of money. Every time I'd come back I'd dreaded finding some modernization. I'd been made happy here and that happiness still existed, an obstinate, solid thing. I always felt a thrill as I pushed open the entrance door. There was nowhere in the world I'd prefer to be.

Long, winding corridors, old clocks, a large, still dining room, 1920s posters and timetables. Sun pouring in through a high window could transform a gloomy passage into an illustration for *The Arabian Nights*. The hotel had a smell: I sniffed deeply for it immediately. Musty, slightly scented, old Maja soap. In winter, wind howled around the ends of corridors, banging shutters, and the hotel sign creaked and swung.

To look for ecstasy was useless. It was a gift, an impossible quality.

Then I remembered that Marie was not with me. I'd simply forgotten all about her.

'I'm looking for a friend,' I told the woman.

Of course, it would never have worked out with the Spaniard. He was a priest, yes. But, worse, a political activist.

Chapter Twenty-two

I'm free. I can do what I want, anything. There's nowhere I have to be. I don't have to go straight back to Castel or back at all. There is absolutely nothing in this world that I have to do except keep breathing. It was a strange feeling, this abundance of freedom. On impulse I took a room at the hotel.

I stood before the grandfather clock that tapped out the minutes, whirred out the quarters, wheezed the hours, and asked for my usual room, the one with the balcony that looked on to the sloping street hardly wide enough for one car, leave alone two. But in those days when I used to look out there were hardly any cars. I wanted that room with the embroidered net curtains and half-closed shutters that used to give glimpses of Luis as he came from his mother's apartment or the town hall on his way to make love to me. She said that was taken, that room. I had to have one at the back where the balcony wasn't high enough and I could hardly see the sky. Everything was ordinary and dull. And then I understood why. Luis wasn't in the room. Was he even in Gerona? Even alive? I dreaded seeing some serious change in him – old age, illness, marriage. Or, worse than that, Luis without his uniqueness, charisma. The walls were pale green and the lace curtains made the light soft. For a moment there was the cold, thrilling, damp atmosphere I remembered, then it was gone. I could have been anywhere. The trouble was, nothing had quite equalled Luis Santina and the early years. They were too bright and everything else wasn't even half bright. Then I remembered I had Castel.

Marie was in the street, surrounded by attentive men, and she wanted us to go with them to a smart place in the modern part of the city. We crossed the river and arrived at a sparkling neon-lit restaurant I'd never heard of. 'It's better here,' she said. 'That old part is too emotional.'

We had red mullet, aubergine, pepper and onion, fried, then octopus with mint. We could have been in any town in the world. If it wasn't for the chiming of the cathedral bell, I'd have doubted that the old quarter existed.

I didn't go with them to Playa de Aro, to the clubs on the coast. Instead I walked back to the river and on the way found the original railway station, still standing desolate, still lit by gas lamps. Nineteen-fifties posters were visible on the walls. A sudden gust of mountain wind all the way from Canigou made the lamps rattle and swing and cast huge shadows, and among them I thought I could see myself again, young and arriving on the train from the frontier, and he on the platform, dark winter coat, white scarf, beautiful face, eyes so alive, and our souls reached out to touch before our hands were able to meet and hold. I used to have to see him with an urgency that made my usual life impossible. To say I dreamed about him would not be correct. In those days he would come into my dreams but he wasn't confusing or insubstantial. His appearances always made sense. At the moment of his arrival the dream would be flooded with colour and it became more vivid than any wakeful state. I could still recall those dreams. The sea would be there and the yellow stoned, pre-Roman part of the city. And I knew that if I didn't get back to him I'd lose him. Over the years I sometimes lost a great deal by going on that journey but I never really lost him.

They said Luis had a fatal charm and, from what had happened to some of the people involved with him, the adjective was not too strong. During the Franco regime he'd kept the province alive: he had organized the cultural events, restored the fiestas, protected the language, the medieval buildings, guarded the legends. Also, he kept Madrid out. If I was asked what he really did I'd say he enchanted people. Why didn't I know the rest? Was it merely a language difficulty or did the rest not matter? Or did he withhold it from me?

Back in the hotel room, I turned on the lamp and a stream of mixed and rather showy insects rushed through the window, like women going into a Harrods' sale. I looked out at the street, little more than an alley, seething with starving cats, their eyes more brilliant than the street-lights. Being here was like the dream but less substantial because, as I heard the cathedral bell chime the quarter, I experienced the punishing solitude that belonged to my present life. It had nothing to do with those years with Luis. It was a secret, unrelenting loneliness because I'd been torn from that which I loved and to which I belonged. Like other people who existed in a state of ruptured perfection, I made the best of it.

After lunch I strayed up behind the cathedral along the stone passageway with gardens, which had been created in the sixties. Before that, the house with the tower had stood on the then dusty track. Of course, the tower was the same as Abbé Saunier's at Rennes-le-Château. Because I knew Luis wasn't there and that I wouldn't see him, I took Marie further, to a garden surrounded by a broken wall which looked across to Canigou. It was called the Garden of the Frenchwoman, and was partially restored. As I climbed the steps up to it I could see the whole of the city. It was too hot, a burning, sweltering, sickly heat that would melt the surface on the roads, and the black fumes would sting our eyes and nostrils. I said we should get back to Castel. I helped her climb down to the pathway because, for once, the climate affected her worse than me. I would have carried her back along the *paseo* to the cathedral and down the shaded alleyways, if it hadn't been for a little breeze that was so delightful I turned to check its direction. 'A wind from the south,' I said. And then I saw him coming up towards the Garden of the Frenchwoman, carrying a bag of oranges and a bottle of water he'd got from the spring. For a moment he was insubstantial, ghostly. Was it the heat?

'How are you here?' He was amazed.

He became no less insubstantial with sound.

'To get back my past.' It was the only thing that came to mind.

Then he laughed and the past was now in place, the ghostly impression quite gone. He tapped my chest. 'The past is inside you. There's no good looking here.'

'What are you doing?'

'Restoring the past.' He gestured at the garden. Fleshless, sun-scorched workmen gathered at a distance like dangerous birds, their teeth full of gold. They watched Marie and me lasciviously. Then Luis introduced them, and that made them polite. I introduced Marie and everyone shook hands.

'Come and sit in the shade,' he said, 'and have some water.' He had an edgy charm. He was the one person I'd met who was not confused and didn't waste life. His voice could seduce just by its sound. Luis was seductive. Sex and death were his influences: he understood them and seemed to carry them inside him. He was intuitive and as sensitive as a weathervane, eyes beautiful and, these days, cold, but they could heat up dramatically. He was sun on snow, nothing much in between. I'd come to understand that he was manipulative and secretive, like other charismatic people. He was in the Catalan government and had refused the key job that would have led to leadership of the province. He'd said, 'I prefer not to be in a fixed position, labelled. I'm more dangerous when they don't own me.' He'd written some prize-winning books on politics and the church. He was at the top of his own tree.

Marie was silenced by the onslaught of his beauty. Age couldn't change it. Agile as a cat, he sat in one smooth enviable movement on the earth of the garden.

'So why are you here?'

Once again, I said the first thing that came into my

head. 'I'm on my way to Rennes-le-Château.' I didn't want him to think I had been looking for him.

Excited, he said, 'Then you've come to the right place. Rennes-le-Château is here.'

And he poured us the cool spring water and broke up the oranges. 'It's here, part of it, in this garden.'

'Did Saunier know?'

'But of course, he came here. Here is the birthplace of Jewish mysticism and cabbala. The magnetism here allowed those medieval spiritual discoveries and experiments. The caballists constructed them and left accounts. Saunier came partially for those.'

Marie wanted to know about the experiments.

'Transcending time and space, to the very furthest states possible for a human being.'

'Did they?'

'There were four of them. One died during the experiment, another went mad, the third ran away, denying all faith, and the fourth returned and wrote the account.'

'Which Saunier wanted?'

'That and other things. In those days, Gerona had a direct link with the Cathar area and Rennes-le-Château. Saunier came to see what there was to find and to leave certain documents for safety. Here in the Garden of the Frenchwoman. The house with the tower. You must remember?' he said to me. 'That was hers. Saunier's friend. Madame Matthieu.' He said the name again.

I didn't know it. 'A Frenchwoman. That's why the garden is named after her,' I said.

'She lived here for years. She must have been quite

a surprise with her elegance and sophistication because the inhabitants of this town had hardly seen a foreigner.'

'Did you know her?'

He hesitated. 'No.' And I knew it was untrue.

'So she was Saunier's friend?' said Marie.

'He came here to see her,' he agreed.

'And built the tower,' I said.

Wrong. That was built years before. In the last century, he thought. 'She was so cultured and cultivated and sophisticated. No one had ever seen anyone like her. She always dressed in the latest fashion. Had it sent from France.'

He walked us to Marie's car and told her some of the history of his beloved city. She was quite captivated by him. I'd never seen her so receptive.

He let her unlock and cool the car while he spoke to me privately. 'Politically I shouldn't be seen with you. A married woman. They'd get anything, even that, on me right now. Let me contact you.'

I gave him the phone number and address in Castel. Then I said, 'Let's meet before you finally get there. Life's too short.'

'Somewhere else?' he said.

'In another place. In between.'

'Figueras,' he said.

We agreed on the restaurant.

He said Thursday. I said tomorrow. He half smiled and looked at me, and I could believe he still loved me.

'And I'll try and find you a photograph of her,' he said. 'My family has them.' He looked at me again and smiled in spite of himself. I got into the car, feeling full to the brim with happiness and more.

Marie started the engine. I turned and said to him, 'Have you been there? Rennes-le-Château?'

'No,' he laughed.

As we drove north she said, 'I think he's the most tactile man I've seen.'

I kept thinking of his friend, who had been killed in the sixties, a Catalan exile fighting for separation from Madrid. He'd said, 'I should think Luis' way of being alive prevents a domestic life with anyone.' I should have handled the past differently. But I only saw part of the truth, the part Luis Santina wanted me to see.

Chapter Twenty-three

The Hotel Ampurdan, Figueras, one of the best restaurants in Spain, perhaps anywhere, with a battalion of well-trained staff, friendly and deft, who'd been there for years. The atmosphere was lively, ironic and absolutely secure. The main dining room was large and could absorb Catalan groups, sometimes ten or more at a table. Equally it was quite acceptable to eat alone. The interior was surprisingly modern and unadorned.

I hadn't wanted to come here. I didn't want to see him again. After the evening before, when I'd felt so high – ecstatic, more like – I'd realized how vulnerable I was, how easily I could fall into that all-absorbing love for him, which would overwhelm my life. I needed to become myself and had that chance. I must have discipline and self-resource. I hoped he would not show up. How I distrusted ecstasy.

After the champagne, the *vina sol* white, the aubergine mousse, the onion bread and olive paste, after the fish soup, the luxuriant salad, the baked cod with olives, exactly cooked, the mint beans, the lemon sorbet, the red wine specially from Perelada, the lamb, after the Manchega cheese and white grapes, I said, 'He won't come. Politics is only part of it.'

'A woman?'

'Oh, no. He really does change things. Protecting old buildings, the old ways, taking care of people.'

A dessert of mixed cake and puddings, and a strong reviving wine.

And then he came in and sat down. 'I'm sorry. I took the train. I don't drive.' He ordered the white beans, sausage and bacon. And then they came, one after the other, men to shake his hand. He ate his lunch invisibly, while talking to these associates and acquaintances. The manager had his turn and said that lunch was on the house. He produced a bottle of his best red dessert wine.

I didn't get to speak to him uninterrupted until we were in the car going towards the sea.

'Where are we going?' said Marie.

'But you are driving.'

'I've no idea,' she said.

'Keep going,' he said. 'And never stop. Why should we?'

Then he produced two photographs of Madame Matthieu, in the garden behind the house with the tower. I thought she was enigmatic, stylish.

'She was there in that house. No one knew where she came from or how. She was suddenly there and she had nothing to do with the people of Gerona. Only one. My uncle, who was a priest.'

'And you,' I said.

'How old do you think I am?' he teased. 'This was before the First World War, and she entertained important guests from France, cultured people, artists. From Paris. Dancers, singers, musicians. She always made a fuss of the local priests and, I believe, taught them French. She had gatherings in her garden under the royal palm tree, which you should remember,' he said to me. I remembered the tower and the shuttered windows and him going in through the main door, which was right on the common path. 'And it was said she had a special friend, the Abbé Saunier, who would visit her quite openly. After all, the place was full of priests,' he said. 'Who would notice him?'

'Was she married?'

He didn't think so.

'Did she have a relationship with Saunier?'

He paused enough for doubt. 'My uncle had various letters and photographs. She was quite an inspiration to the local society.'

'But how did you know the priest left something there from Rennes-le-Château? What is it?' said Marie. She had trouble saying, 'The Holy Grail?'

'He left what couldn't be found in his parish. It was the perfect hiding place. She always denied that treasure was buried there but she said visitors came from time to time, looking under stones, swinging pendulums.'

'So you did know her?'

He was stuck behind the ease of a lie and an uneasy truth. 'Oh, look, I knew her but I didn't know her. And I was too young.'

'But you knew she loved Saunier?' I said.

'I believe so.'

'And he?'

'I've no idea. Possibly. The letters suggest a certain proper relationship between them. Nothing more.'

Marie changed the subject and I could have

strangled her. 'Why did he build the tower? A copy of the one here?'

'He sent his architect Eli Bot to look at it. That's all I know.'

He didn't say anything for a while and we arrived at the coast. He said, 'I haven't really thought about all this before.' He produced another document. 'I checked the house. It was built in the early nineteenth century, an ordinary countryside dwelling. Nothing special. Then a wealthy Señor Massaguer added the tower in eighteen fifty-two.' He looked at the document. 'Paying for it out of his own pocket.' He paused. 'Eighteen fifty-two. That was the date of Saunier's birth. And then Saunier copied the tower. I must say, it was never successful here. It stuck up incongruously next to the Gothic cathedral.' He turned over more pages of the document. 'The property, tower and garden, was left to Massaguer's maid after his death in eighteen seventy. With one condition. She must remain celibate.'

Luis remembered when the Frenchwoman's house was bought by order of the mayor in 1962. 'The place was ransacked. Even the palm tree chopped down, its root dug up. The tower was taken apart stone by stone. Someone was searching for something.'

'Where was Madame Matthieu?'

'After the Second World War, the day after it ended, she went to Paris to sort out her affairs and never came back. She said she'd return in a month. My family nego-tiated the sale of the house to the town hall. She didn't want to sell but it was done by official order and she received money. I think she was frightened to sell.'

He opened a letter. 'This was sent from Paris to my

uncle just before she died. It's in Spanish. "I am ill, my dear friend, and haven't long. Why didn't I sell earlier? Perhaps it was there in that garden I'd once been happy. If only I could see the priest once more. Even as I lie dying." I thought she must mean one of the Spanish priests. She knew enough. But she writes "priest" in the French way.'

After a few wrong turns we ended up in Palamos. Marie still couldn't handle crossroads and Luis had no sense of where he was going.

'Are you interested,' said Marie, 'in solving the mystery?'

'As far as I'm concerned, there isn't one,' he said.

We tried to ask what that meant but he wasn't saying any more. He did say, 'For me it's amazing that that Frenchwoman lived alone in that house all those years. He died in January nineteen seventeen. She left in nineteen forty-six.'

'Why did you stop being a priest?' asked Marie.

'Oh, that's for another time.' He never talked about that.

'I think you should go to Rennes-le-Château,' I said. I thought suddenly that Luis might be the Spaniard who would save Monsieur Privat.

It was certainly a day for the past. Under an arcade in Palamos, there were posters from the previous year for a concert Jay had not been able to do. It gave me quite a shock to see his face: he had a danger, an impact, an immediate sexuality. He would, promised the face, take you where it was perhaps unwise to go but thrilling none the less. He had a superb surface. Underneath, it was another story. That was the one I knew.

Chapter Twenty-four

Once the apartment felt finished, I asked people I'd met to come and see it. I thought the hour before dinner was best and they came at seven sharp, Marcel and his wife, Juan Pamello, Garcia, Maître Aznar. Because we all lived in such a resplendent wine and food area, we always drank and ate the same things. Garcia agreed that it was dull to place a Cazes wine on the table when the guests would be drinking it at home an hour later, and he went across into Spain and brought back some good rosé Ampurdan wine, a silky, splendid white Rioja and *vina sol*, sharp white and directly from the vineyard. He brought tins of olives stuffed with anchovies from Collioure, a Spanish ice-cream and *dolces*. He swept and washed the terrace and put out a tub of red flowers and some chairs.

Madame Beaumarchais came up, but not Eliane. 'She's very upset.' I asked why. She wasn't saying, but looked at Marie with a certain impertinence. We were all dressed up, except for Marie who'd just driven back from her house on the Côte d'Azur. She was covered in dust and flower-petals, which provoked Madame Beaumarchais to make a few pointed comments. 'Well, you don't get so much of the landscape sticking to you if you're just sitting in a car.' Garcia said that Marie was beautiful – Madame Beaumarchais didn't doubt it, but since when had that been a reason for not making love out of doors? Marie changed, brushed, combed in a minute flat. Marie did everything in a minute flat, and looked as good as if she'd spent hours. I opened the locally bought crisps and arranged the assorted local sausage. A little later, JoJo arrived and the French teacher, and it soon became clear that I was short of places to sit. I was very soon short of wine. There were three serious drinkers present, and the rest were not hesitant. Marie hurried over to the late-closing Catalan shop and bought a couple of bottles, and Madame Beaumarchais went to get a Crémant de Limoux.

Francine from L'Hostellerie popped in just to wish me luck and admire the apartment. It couldn't have looked better: everything gleaming and glowing and shimmering, and very precise and defined. JoJo and Marie between them had made it what it was intended to be – its full personality had been brought out.

I'd heated tiny cheese rolls and chicken wings. The oven worked perfectly – it was the first and last time it did. Garcia brought in more chairs from his apartment and the guests sat formally along the walls. They approved of the place, all of them, loved the rich shine of the oiled stone floor. They weren't so sure about the space. Marcel's wife said she liked it. Then they started to gossip. How could Gato dream up a figure like sixteen for that shit-hole next door?

Juan Pamello shut them up with a terse retort that I did not catch. Even if I had, would I have understood it? But he had to go home. He had a wife who did not like to be kept waiting. He washed his glass ready to give to the next visitor, and said, 'Don't take any notice of anything they say.' He meant Garcia, Madame Beaumarchais and JoJo. The minute he'd left I said, 'So tell me about Gato.'

'Just getting by' – as described by Juan Pamello – far from it. Gato owned property, lots of it, all around Castel, which he let at stiff rents. He liked to get his rent on time. He had, courtesy of his karate instructor, a physical presence that made tenants pay up. If he needed anything extra he had the dog. They didn't dislike him. They disliked the wife. I hoped I didn't get to meet her.

I would have been perfectly content in the apartment – it was everything I'd wanted – if it hadn't been for the nagging uncertainty about buying the studio. The guests were all for it.

'You can knock down the adjoining wall and make it all open-plan,' said Marcel's wife.

'You can take down both front doors and have another one in front of them, flush with the hallway. That's how it used to be,' said JoJo. 'All one apartment.'

'You can let the studio,' said Francine. 'Just during the day for a professional person. A beauty therapist, a psychiatrist. You can't lose.'

'You'll never lose here,' said Marcel. '*Plein centre ville*.'

Marie considered hiring it as a consulting room when she'd finished her studies. 'I would take short-term clients.'

'You certainly could,' said Madame Beaumarchais enigmatically. Seeing that Marie was about to challenge that remark, Madame Beaumarchais said to me sweetly,

'If you intend having more than five guests again, you'll have to buy another sofa and more glasses.'

Monsieur Nadal pushed open the door and two of his waiters carried in an old juke-box. Surprised, pleased, we all gathered around it. 'No one could have given me anything better.' I wanted to kiss him. The discs were fifties and sixties, rock and roll, ballads, Tamla Motown. While the waiters plugged it in, Monsieur Nadal had a look round. Then he saw the kitchen. 'Oh, that's where that got to.' He seemed to recognize the stove. 'That's Eric's. The chef from the Hôtel Luna. I'd heard it had gone missing. And that's his fridge.'

Eric? The psychopathic chef? 'How did it get here?' I asked.

'From the person who nicked it from Eric. You'd better not let him see it. He's inclined to be touchy.'

Madame Beaumarchais had first turn at the juke-box: 'Only You' by the Platters. Natalie and Robert arrived with champagne. I told Marie to cover the stove but Natalie was already looking at the washing-machine as though she recognized it.

Marie danced with Garcia. His guests, the curists, came in and put on tango music. They danced, then JoJo, and it became, for a brief while, a real party. In this mood there was only one place to go. Colette's.

She was standing – or, more correctly, appearing – behind her bar wearing a scarlet suit, which few women could carry off, and gold jewellery and a gold pin in her hair, and lashes so long they looked like insect's legs. They were her own and between them her eyes, languid and blue. Her mouth was half smiling and sensuous. She was experienced in the ways that mattered, the places that mattered, far away from this little-known resort for the ailing and elderly. She nodded at JoJo, but had little to do with anyone else. She skilfully avoided our eyes and there were plenty watching her. Madame Beaumarchais was thrilled. 'She's everything people say. But they don't say what she really is.'

'And that is?'

'A whore.' She laughed, truly amused. 'She must be paying good money to someone to be allowed to stay here just like this.'

Garcia thought she'd worked at the Lido in Paris.

'Not tall enough,' said Madame Beaumarchais promptly.

Garcia was sure he'd seen her.

I just stared at her. She was the one I would have loved to invite. I wanted to tell her about my apartment, my new life, how I couldn't sing with Jay. He had to come first. Now it's my time, my turn. But she stood, eyes on the street, looking at people passing but seeing . . . who knew what? And then it occurred to me that she, in that cocoon of glamour and magic, isolated from everything, could be waiting for someone. That person would come, who knew when. But she was always ready.

On the way home when the sky was lighting up for dawn, Madame Beaumarchais said, 'Eliane's upset because you didn't buy her place and now you're buying someone else's.'

'I haven't decided.'

'You shouldn't raise her hopes and then back out. You shouldn't do that.'

'But her mother —'

'Her mother's got nothing to do with it. Now they're not even speaking. Because of you.'

I couldn't buy both. I didn't have the money. But I wasn't going to tell her that.

The Grand Café was just opening and we went in for a very early breakfast. JoJo went to the baker for the first croissants. Madame Beaumarchais was thrilled by the night out. She had such an organized life: dinner at eight, television, bed at ten, up at six. This night had been 'Like Christmas. Or, rather, like Christmas should be.'

JoJo said he knew nothing about my kitchen or its pedigree. Was it Eric's? Maybe once. Who knows? He, JoJo, did not spend his time knocking off disturbed chefs' private kitchens.

'He probably flogged it and hasn't told Monsieur Nadal because he owes him money.' Drugs came into it. JoJo put a complete camouflage over my kitchen and its past.

Once again I longed to be back in the bar at Amélie.

'But it's not such an innocent place,' said Madame Beaumarchais. 'The waiter does it for money and the girls dance for money. They're all professional.'

It had every kind of person in there. That's what made it what it was.

Marcel kissed me goodbye. He was off to get an hour's sleep. 'Your French is good. It was good before but now I can understand you.'

And the sun came up against the café windows, immense, inescapable, and I was filled with a high, holy happiness.

Chapter Twenty-five

I'd talked so much about the house, the apartment, the people and what had been done, that Luis, when we actually got there, had high expectations. I opened the front door and led him through the perfect oval, washed with pale light, to the kitchen.

'Oh, is this all?' he said, and choked back the rest.

Marie was quick to describe the original plan.

'A terrace facing Canigou?' He frowned.

Nobody could say that the Spaniard and I didn't think alike.

'Yes, exactly,' she said, not a jot put out. 'A terrace!'

And he frowned deeper and said, 'But that's wonderful. A terrace facing the mountain.'

Disappointment never did me any good. I sat on one of the café chairs, which obviously wouldn't be good enough either. Did I know him at all?

'An uninterrupted view.'

'Why didn't you go ahead with it?' he said.

'She was frightened.'

They looked at me, these renovating perfectionists, as though I'd killed something.

'Was it the price?' he asked softly.

'Oh, no,' said Marie.

I knew she was enjoying all this. Later I would kill her.

'I got it down to . . .' And she mentioned some heroic figure.

'It would have been . . .' he chose, '. . . fabulous.' He stood in awe of her inventiveness.

'But I want it like this, Luis,' I said. 'Simple. Not fabulous.'

'But you could have a marvellous apartment,' he said, trying not to sound impatient. 'A small sum like that and –'

I didn't want to hear any more, opened the fridge, got out the first bottle of wine I touched and poured a glass shakily for each of us. He didn't like it. I didn't blame him. It turned out that the bottle was a cherry cordial, with iron supplement, to give energy. A present from my mountain-walking guide. I wasn't going to get anything right this visit, and I was right about that.

'She's lived too long with that cloth of a husband who never had any taste.' Marie was vehement.

'Any choice, you mean. I didn't marry the first average-rich guy I could get my hands on whatever he was like. We were poor and I'm proud of it.'

'Rich guy?' She mocked. 'You'd be so lucky.'

'Whore,' I said, and underneath the fury, deep down, I was laughing. Everyone was calling everyone else a whore in this place. Was it an epidemic?

'All right, you two,' laughed Luis uneasily. 'You're good friends. You have the same virtues. Marie, on reflection, has more vices.'

'I hope so,' she said. 'What amazes me is that she knows you and yet lives like this. She's come here to change her very skin and yet she's still got that dusty husband's ideas.'

Over-patiently, I explained the awful truth of an academic life with perhaps a grace-and-favour house, but otherwise you got a mortgage like anyone else and lived accordingly. I explained how we'd moved with our son from rented to bought to bigger to near what we wanted. We lived according to our taste, which was not spending a great deal of time or money on the place. We spent that on what went inside it.

'You've always been inside,' she said, deliberately misunderstanding. 'You've just had to fit in with that dull husband and too many dusty ideas. But I must say you're a paradox. You know him,' she brought Luis into it, 'and yet you don't let him influence you.'

We were beginning to get on too sticky ground for him and he remembered he had to get back to Spain.

'Couldn't you have influenced her?' Marie asked.

He fenced that off and got his bag. 'You like it,' he said to me. 'That's the important thing, surely. But I just think you should put a door here.' And he indicated the hallway where it started to flow into the main room, cutting off all the glorious space.

'Why?' I asked.

'To keep out the draughts in winter.'

He had changed. I never thought him capable of such a consideration. Winter. I sat down on the bed and had to admit that we all got older.

His eyes were now drawn to the bed. Another mistake. 'You can't have it like that. It's north-south. It has to be east-west.'

'But this way she has a marvellous view,' said Marie. 'You can't lie looking at a wall.'

'You can't lie at the wrong angle in a magnetic area like this, near a mountain especially. You won't sleep. Head points to the east, feet to the west. Any Oriental will tell you that.' He laughed at her expression. 'Don't you English know anything?'

'I'm not English,' she said, sniffy as hell. But she helped him move round the bed until it faced the desired direction.

I took him to meet Madame Beaumarchais because I thought that hers was one apartment he couldn't fail to like. She was charming and worldly and took him round all the walls, showing the painting collection: paintings from the last century, Spanish, German, French. She had several by Eliane's father. There was a small Picasso but, worried about thieves, she denied it.

I whispered to him not to say that I knew Jay Stone. He dismissed that with a brief nod.

'I don't want them knowing here.'

Madame Beaumarchais took me into the kitchen to help with the drinks. 'He's so graceful. A cat. I love a good-looking man.'

He said she should have an exhibition. The paintings were worth it. He loved the ones by Vila and had known him in the old days. He was unsure about the Dali. 'At the end he used to sign a piece of paper or canvas and tell his apprentices and friends to go and do a drawing in his style. I think that's what you've got.'

She wasn't having that. She'd got the work on good

authority from the artist himself. She got so angry, steam seemed to come out of her and she looked quite dangerous.

So he admired the furniture, the fireplace, the beams, and that quietened her down.

'Who is he?' she asked me.

'Just a friend,' I said offhand. 'Of Marie's.'

Juan Pamello was waiting with the key to the studio. Marie had gone urgently to get him so that Luis could have a look and give his opinion.

Luis slapped walls and jumped on the floor and didn't miss the dark stain on the ceiling. 'What's up there?'

'A mess,' I said.

'But she's redoing it,' said Juan Pamello.

'Slowly,' I said. 'She's got no money. JoJo doesn't work for her any more.'

'And that's your fault,' said Madame Beaumarchais, suddenly at the door. 'You let her think she was saved. So she didn't accept other options.'

I suppose she meant the fat suitor. He had looked like an option. Eliane didn't have a family: they were a gang, and fought and cheated each other, but fell back into a hostile loyalty as soon as an outsider intruded.

'What state is it in up there?' asked Luis.

'Dubious' which was the best I could say.

'Then I'd buy up there so you have the control,' he said.

'Exactly,' said Marie.

'But then I have to buy here for the same reason. He'll put tenants in. This wall is –'

'It's just a partition, not a real wall,' said Marie.

'Then I might as well buy the whole house.' I was irritated, and just wanted to get back into the peace of my apartment and listen to music.

'Then you must rent this from him,' said Luis. 'So he can't put anyone in. And buy upstairs and make the terrace and then you can sell it, if you care to, at an advantage. You can't sell that in there,' pointing to my apartment.

So I asked why not, knowing I'd get bad news.

'For the same reason you should buy upstairs and rent this. Neighbours. Anyone looking at your apartment will know that.' He laughed, flicked my hair. 'Except you.'

'She's a Bohemian,' said Marie. 'She doesn't see things the way we do.'

I was angry with both of them. And I remembered Juan Pamello being angry with JoJo, saying, 'Why tell her all this? She's the one person in the whole world who will buy this fucking place.' And I felt cold.

Juan Pamello, intrigued by the Spaniard, did an unprecedented thing: he invited us to his home for a drink. By then Marie and I were no longer at each other's throats but terminally quarrelling. This amused both men, which made it worse.

I told her in fast English, so that perhaps they'd miss some of it, that she'd taken control when she met me because of my poor circumstances. My son's death, Jay's illness. Otherwise it would have been a different story. She'd tried to control my husband, she'd certainly controlled Jay. She was even trying it on the Spaniard. Why didn't she keep her advice to herself? *She* could certainly do with some.

'They're bound to fight over that flat,' Juan Pamello said, man to man. 'It's only natural. You can't have two cooks in the same kitchen.'

I thought Luis replied, 'You can't have two queens in the hive.' I hoped he hadn't said that.

'But it keeps them young,' laughed Juan Pamello, as he stuck a newly filled pipe in his mouth.

I nudged Marie. 'They're just making fun of us. Let's talk this over privately.'

Marie became very calm and I thought she'd agreed. She said to Luis, 'It's just some menopausal thing. All of it.'

I shouted at her and she lunged at me, and we had the full attention of the rugby club, who were having a losers' drink in the Grand Café. This made up for some of their disappointment and they ran to the door cheering. Luis dealt with it: in perfect French he said we were practising for the next fiesta, the one in which the children threw eggs and flour at everybody foolish enough to be out. Then he walked along the street calmly, an arm around each of us.

Juan Pamello said, 'I've never seen a cat fight outside of a brothel.'

'Remind me to tell your wife,' snapped Marie.

I told her to come into the Pablo and sort it out. They could go and laugh at something else. She didn't sit down but came up with some comment about my being an only child. I'd never been teased and was far too touchy. I told her that that was unacceptable and that I hated all that shrink talk. And we fought our way from her professional aim, to my desire to sing, and then arrived at the real problem. The apartment.

'It's simple, harmonious and I want it that way,' I said.

'Why be selfish? Instead of a Bohemian hovel with bits of café interior, you could have a wonderful place, part of Castel's history and culture. Bigger than you and your small existentialist ideas. The apartment will live on after you.'

'Then let the town hall pay for it.'

This was the first big row we'd had.

'And I'm doing you another favour. Turning that crazy menopausal impulse into something safe. I know all about this. You don't,' she said.

'Then let me learn and make my own mistakes.'

She was horrendous back, so I told her she was obsessional and should get treatment.

'You don't know the meaning of the word.'

'About old stones you are,' I said. 'You lurk around them like a toad.'

'You were a bohemian once for about five minutes and it was the best time of your life and you can't let it go. You keep harking back to that style, that look.'

'And you can't bear to leave things as they are. Those old houses, old stones. You have to control even them. They frighten you.'

'Why?'

I knew I'd touched something. 'Because you're in Paradise here and you can't take it. You can't just be.'

And, for all her charm and not inconsiderable beauty and energy and reliability, she could not stand Paradise. Because she felt excluded. If it was flawed, she could get busy with it. But superb scenery, that life just flowed through blessed, she couldn't take.

'Well, old fat nightingale, I'll leave you here to warble in Paradise. Let's see if it can take you.'

And she walked away.

I shouted her name and she half turned.

'There's an expression in French grammar, "false friends". That's what you are.'

'You're not really going,' Juan Pamello said to her.

'Stories come to an end.' She looked at me as she said it, and sounded exactly like Jay. You couldn't manage that unless you'd been really close to him. It's what he'd said to me by way of goodbye. 'Stories end.'

I looked back at her. 'False friends' just about said it.

I didn't pay much attention to the evening at Juan Pamello's because I was upset about the break with Marie. She'd packed and loaded the car but needed, it seemed, to keep face with Luis and the village, so here she was having a formal drink in Juan Pamello's wife's home. On the way in, Juan Pamello had opened some surprisingly glamorous electrical controlled gates. He'd said that the little joke about the brothel was nothing to worry about. 'I wasn't in one. Only selling one. I want to put that right.'

'Yes, I bet you do,' she'd replied coldly.

Juan Pamello's wife was all done up, shimmering, static, electric, acrylic that didn't let her skin breathe, and hair all sprayed and Carmen-rolled, emergency-curled, and jewellery that jangled in spasms as though an electric current was passing through it. The house was done up in the same way: super-modern, cheap fabrics and coverings, and resistant surfaces. If you touched anything or the hostess, you'd get a minor electric shock. It was the last place on earth in which I had expected to find Juan Pamello.

His wife offered an aperitif. The smile she gave Luis was genuine. He found something to admire in all this. I think it was the kitchen windows, which darkened like sunglasses to keep out the worst glare. There was no need to struggle with small-talk. Juan Pamello presented my predicament as though he'd come back from a hunt and laid the prey at her feet. She loved it.

'It's like marrying in passion, then getting to know the family,' she said. She had a good laugh at that. Marie gave her a baleful look but left her alone.

It was decided that it wasn't just a choice as to whether or not I bought the studio. I didn't have a choice. I had to buy it. Luis had decided that for me. The next question was, how?

'I can get you a mortgage,' said Juan Pamello. 'It's better than paying rent.'

'And if I don't need the studio?'

'Resell. *Plein centre*. You can always sell there.'

'Gato can't,' I said.

Juan Pamello couldn't dismiss that fast enough. 'He's asking too much.' He realized that that wasn't much of an answer. 'We'll get him down a thousand. He'll see reason. I'll drop the price on another property he's interested in. And you'll do it up. Or Madame Marie will.'

Madame Marie looked as though she certainly would not.

He said, 'So the value will level out with the price. You pay something down, the mortgage payments are less than paying the rent and you come out with something.'

All I could see was the stain on the ceiling getting bigger, like a dark cloud. I was so confused I almost asked Marie what she thought, but she looked into space, unapproachable. Had Monsieur Augustin experienced these problems, I asked? It had all looked so happy and full of life that first day.

Juan Pamello took a deep steadying breath before he replied, which allowed his wife to get in first. She said, 'Take the studio. I'm sure you can afford it. After all, you're committed to the apartment. You've decided to live here and, as my husband says, you can't be more in the centre. Then, in a little while, you'll be glad you're there. It will be easier for you to get your shopping and go to the hairdresser.'

'Easier?' I wasn't sure what that meant.

'Easier to get to the chemist, the doctor, or for the doctor to visit. You're right there. It's no good living far away. How will you manage stairs, get to the shops?'

I still didn't understand her. 'When's this?'

'When you're old. None of us is getting any younger. And you're no spring chicken. Who is, in here?'

And she gave a laugh, the shrill kind that her tight, narrow mouth would allow. I could feel Marie actually physically change. I could feel the heat in her face. She was one year older than me. She had never felt old. It didn't belong in her thinking. She hated the lemon-haired midwife so much that she actually considered running off with Juan Pamello.

Before we left, we watched the electric gate open and swish shut. 'Just like Hollywood,' said Marie. The wife took it as a compliment. Another switch turned on a fountain and sprinkler. 'I'm not the only one who controls,' Marie said, once we were outside. 'It's the last place he'd live in. It's all her doing. Even the wine was sickly.'

Luis took her arm. 'One thing I didn't understand. You take the granary upstairs and you make a room and a terrace. But how do you get up there? As I see it, you have to leave the present apartment and go up the common stairs.'

'No,' said Marie. 'It's a spiral staircase that would go from the hallway cupboard in the present flat up to the granary.'

She hadn't let him down.

She decided to drive off immediately.

As a final and half-friendly sign to her, I said, 'Should I buy it?'

'Why don't you ask Colette?' And she was gone.

Chapter Twenty-six

Autumn was the best season. There were days when the atmosphere was beyond anything I'd known. Yes, I could remember mornings like this in the past when I'd vowed never to forget this beauty. Always keep it a part of you. And I forgot it soon enough. It was only reawakened when the same morning presented itself, years later, a golden morning, blue, endless blue sky, air with a haze and dazzling brilliance as though it was filled with diamond droplets. I turned into the cobbled passageway and even the sound of my shoes seemed different, important and exciting, and the sunshine was golden. God had put out all his best colours. He'd not stinted on these mornings. When two women left the bakery, chattering in Catalan, I was so joyous I wanted to kiss them. And then the figure came towards me as though embalmed in gold. And that walk. I'd know it anywhere. Nearer, the hair a little greyer. It was Luis. And nearer and beside me, and it wasn't him but it could have been. It was that kind of day, so beautiful it could even bring him to me.

There were many days like that. They all said it was exceptional. Day after day of golden light, cool mountain breezes, the nostalgic smell of woodsmoke, and the village recovering from the days of intense heat and the tourist season, getting back to its own rhythm and drama. There was nothing sad about it, this autumn. In fact, it had all the promise of spring.

Every week there was a different fiesta – they always had something to celebrate. In the street Monsieur Nadal put on Catalan plays and the bank put on concerts, and there were always invitations to art exhibitions and wine tastings. That was taken very seriously, not only at L'Hostellerie. And there were lots of dances in the street or at the Salle des Unions and a flamenco group every Friday in the Café de France.

I became friendly with Pascale, the dark-haired pharmacist, in the shop whose green cross shone in my terrace window. She said, 'I'm a neighbour of yours. The owner Monsieur Roux is tired of night duty so I do it and he's let me have his flat in return. I'm wall-to-wall with you. I hear you doing your musical exercises.' She said it didn't bother her and invited me for a drink. In return I took her to Amélie-les-Bains, to the Café des Arcades, and for the first time she saw Colette.

Pascale had energy for five clapped-out pharmacists. She did her night duty twice a week, 'on guard', without flicking an eye, with the old and pregnant and stomach-sick banging on the door through the night for medicine. Then she did a full day's work. Then, in the early evening, her cultural work – she ran the cinema club, arranged talks on cinema, invited prestigious French *auteurs*, then went on to Le Zanzibar for a few drinks and a dance. She slept the minimum, she ate the minimum.

'She's a minimalist,' said Madame Beaumarchais.

I did wonder if she was also a speed user, and there was nothing minimal about that. She was pale-skinned and never sat still. Did she dip into the medicinal boxes piled just inside the front door? We became friendly enough for me to ask her. 'No. My family are all like this. Hyper. It must be the thyroid gland. But I would take pills or anything else if it helped me. Why not?'

Medicine was made to be used and she approved of it. The boundary came with the degree. If it was a government-controlled, prescribed drug, it was treated accordingly. The serious life-sustaining chemicals were treated with respect, but medicine, for her, was relative. Madame Beaumarchais's 'heart pills' were 'not serious', her 'blood pills' were 'nothing to worry about'. She could measure a person's state by the importance of the drug given. The mayor's wife with the over-peroxided hair: 'She's ill. I can see by what she's on.'

Pascale responded to most ailments with, 'Oh, that's nothing. It's not serious.'

She trusted doctors, perhaps, but she always checked the prescription, its function and side-effects, in her large pharmaceutical ledger. The clients loved her and she loved their needs. She was one of the most popular people in Castel.

It was the best autumn I'd known. I danced *sardanas*, learned French, walked with the idealistic young guide in the hills. I wished, how I did, that the planet could become the way he deserved it. He and his friends protected wildlife and nature, ran a refuge for animals, lectured in schools. He was right on the pulse with global changes and he wanted the young to be there with him. He believed they were the only hope. What he said was disquieting: it was the one shadow in the sunlight of that autumn.

In Perpignan I found a singing teacher who had performed in French opera companies. She got me working on operatic scores, practising the mezzo-soprano roles as well as French and Spanish folk songs. I started singing in the local choir. Madame Beaumarchais and I took excursions in the Monsieur Rey coaches opposite to Lourdes, Nîmes and Montserrat, near Barcelona. We were the youngest passengers. The old, I saw immediately, had a good laugh at everything. 'Perhaps that's how they get old,' said Madame Beaumarchais.

When Garcia came to stay – he divided his life between Spain, Toulouse, Paris and Castel – we'd have afternoons singing in his music room in the lovely autumn light, he at the piano, the old French songs, then some standards, 'Careless Love', 'Love for Sale', 'Smoke Gets in Your Eyes'. He could just get his vowel sounds around those. We split the range, he took the higher and I the lower, and now we had duets. He said that if we ever got that broke we could always make a living. The French liked street-singers and so for that rainy day, which wouldn't come to him but might to me, he threw in some Piaf and Freya. And then we'd have English tea with delicate cucumber sandwiches and cakes from the best shop in the rue St Ferréol.

'I'm fat,' I said.

'But no, Madame, you are curvaceous and worldly.'

When his wife arrived, there were no duets of any kind. She was elegant, slim and very French, and made the best of herself. I took in a bottle of champagne by way of a greeting. She said, 'Oh, no. My husband doesn't drink.'

Garcia coughed and tried to find my eyes.

Delicately I said, 'But for you, Madame.' And using Madame Beaumarchais's argument, 'It's really medicine.'

She wore designer clothes that Madame Beaumarchais said had not been purchased at source. These were seconds, sold at reduced prices via an outlet in Paris. Her shoes were as elevated as Colette's, her body almost as good, but she didn't have the allure. Nothing in Castel matched her ambitions and she was glad to get out. After a quick three-day *remise en forme* at the spa, she was gone. And the piano lid lifted and the bottles came out, and the English teas and the excursions. He loved new things as much as I did. By chance, he found the village where they produced the aperitif Byrrh, which I'd seen advertised on walls in northern France for years, but had never tasted.

We drove several times to Toulouse to hear the opera from visiting companies, and afterwards would sit in the brasserie of the famous Hôtel Opéra with its theatrical style and simple food. All the *vedettes* of theatre and the musical touring companies had passed through this brasserie for generations and some of their photographs lined the walls. Colette, in her days as a music hall artist, had apparently lodged there.

When he'd gone I missed him. The landing was quiet. Madame Beaumarchais and I were the only occupants. I was having a good time, my days were so full that I wasn't lonely. When the bad moments came I'd go down to the cafés or to the square with the fountain of nine jets. If it happened at night, I'd sit at the open window and look at the mountain, often snow-covered, and the busy star-strewn sky. A lot of stars seemed to whiz around like wasps. 'Meteorites,' said Madame Beaumarchais. 'Or shooting stars. Or the lights around Canigou that I've told you about. They're either souls departing or visitors from another life system. You don't seem to have anyone in your life,' she continued quickly. 'You do all that fast walking and improving yourself but who for? A woman needs a friend.' She chortled into her Spanish linen handkerchief.

'I've had my share.'

'That doesn't do a thing about now,' she said, quite precisely. 'Memories are hardly companions. But, of course, there's more to you. You wouldn't just come and live in this backwater –'

'Oh, I would.' And I meant it. 'And so does *la patronne* Colette –'

'Yes, but she had her reason just as you have yours.' And then, realizing that I might start occupying myself with the little secrets in *her* life, she said, 'Anyway, it's your business. You're in the right house. Everyone living here is mysterious, one way or another.'

I did my singing practice daily, having first asked Garcia and then Madame Beaumarchais if they minded. 'But of course not,' Madame Beaumarchais said, and came out with the equivalent of live and let live.

I took a bus to Perpignan twice a week, which took forty-five minutes each way. I couldn't get to Colette's often because the buses didn't run after a certain time and that did not correspond with any timetable. Garcia was the only person who would go. JoJo would be compromised I felt, if I asked him to drive me. Pascale, surprisingly, offered once or twice.

I didn't say yes or no to buying the studio, and Gato didn't let it. Marie phoned several times to ask if the floor was being polished in the right way, and told me to lift falling leaves from the drains on the terrace and use a certain chemical in the pipes and to get the waiter in the Grand Café to clean the windows. She told me how much to pay him. She asked if I had seen Luis and if I'd decided to rent or buy the studio. She was finishing her last year of study and when she talked about psychotherapy, psychoanalysis and all the rest, I realized how young it was. Nothing much had happened before Freud. I missed her. I talked to Monsieur Nadal about the relative youth of the discipline. What had they done before Freud?

'They drank,' he said, promptly.

Eliane got no further with her apartment and spent most days with Madame Beaumarchais and I'd see her on the stairs, either taking the child to school or bringing home some shopping. She said she'd finish the work on the whole attic before Christmas. She was soft-voiced and pleasant, and obviously intelligent, and I wondered what she did with her life, apart from fixing drinks for Madame Beaumarchais and herself and tea for the little girl. Pascale said, 'Nothing. She does the minimum. She doesn't know from one hour to the next how her life will be. It's called living in the hour.' Madame Beaumarchais said Eliane had a new lover, a German businessman who was very keen on her and was going to pay for all the renovation upstairs. Every second weekend he flew from Germany to see her and stayed in the super-smart Résidence du Soleil. Eliane was quite grand about this lover, and the days before he was due to arrive she cut down on drinking and the nights out, and bought new clothes. She was one of those rare people who, whatever she did, couldn't kill off her beauty.

As Marie discerned, I had spontaneously gone back to an earlier and happier time and tried to re-create the style I'd adopted then. Hair up in a chignon, a fringe, strands of hair hanging down at the sides, long chandelier earrings in marcasite. Going back to the old days – the perfume, Guerlain's Shalimar, Houbigant's Chantilly, Pagan by Picot, and the tight-waisted skirts and wasp belts that nearly killed me. Even the music, the Ink Spots, Johnny Ray's 'Destiny', 'Dragnet', all early fifties before Elvis, before it all went in the wrong direction and became the sixties, which I'd considered shallow and overblown. I re-created this time because it had been my most successful.

The French teacher tried to get me to converse about this period. Most of the language I picked up outside was unacceptable. '*J'en ai raslbol.* Who is this Général Bol?'

'That's slang, Madame Jane, and whoever says that you want to avoid them.'

'*C'est foutu.*

'Equally.'

'*Draguer les filles?*'

'Forget it. Go back to the fifties.'

Whatever I did, in honesty, I could not.

For a week I went every day to Amélie-les-Bains on the early-morning bus for the cure. I did *remise en forme*, which was less severe and more toning. I was massaged under water, pummelled by water, my feet were planted in wax. I was wrapped in seaweed paste and covered in foil. My legs were strapped in two boots for a lymph-drainage treatment. My face was steamed and cleaned and massaged and oiled and then I lay in a dark room, full of violet light containing certain molecules, which was good for stress and 'the nerves'. Then I went to London and sorted out my practical affairs. I gave up my rented flat, threw out most of my belongings and put the essentials in store. I didn't want to see friends, or Jay or Marie. As I locked the storage container I felt I'd said goodbye to the first part of my life. I couldn't wait to get back to Castel and flew directly to Perpignan. After that I had to do another session in the violet light.

I now lived simply, with a certain frugality. Money was not a problem but it might be. Mentally I kept apart the sixteen thousand francs to buy Gato's studio. I started giving singing lessons to Francine, who found that the breathing relaxed her and the voice-work made her enjoy speaking, using the newly discovered tones. She said it gave her an added attractiveness and people listened to *her*, whereas before they had listened only to the words. I didn't know how much to charge so, in the eagerness to see my pupil, asked too little. She paid by cheque. 'Don't tell my sister-in-law.' Francine sent me the daughter of one of her regular clients and Garcia let me use his music room. Then I got the fat owner of the Catalan food shop who really wanted to learn English.

But it was all subterfuge. I longed to see Luis, waited for him, and occasionally went to Spain to see if he was there. I went down from the mountains into the plains and along the river into the dark, secret streets of Gerona, and if I didn't find him, reached him with my thoughts until our souls joined and then I was truly alive. And I never told one person.

Chapter Twenty-seven

Fleur, a film agent from Paris, came to stay. She was unmarried, nearing fifty, childless, travelled constantly, had a free and, on the face of it, exciting life. Born in Brittany, she'd worked in various aspects of the entertainment business, and that's all I knew about her. She was visiting Castel because she'd reasoned that if she went to enough new places she would find Mr Right. I didn't know what he looked like, but I didn't think he was in Castel. I was wrong.

Fleur spent a lot of time and money hiding 'fifty'. She had all the usual regimes, treatments, tucks, and was now travelling inwards into herself and beyond. Tai chi, meditation, chanting, yoga. She wore yellow and gold clothes, and they were exactly right for her. Pale gold jewellery, gold touches in her hair, gold-flecked makeup over a sturdy tan. Oddly, she wasn't extrovert; she was dreamy and had the ease and self-containment of a cat.

I'd met her during one of Jay's tours, and she'd been helpful during the inevitable rough patch. I'd liked her, probably because she was sane. Also, she had the knack of dropping trouble and getting on with the next bit of life or, more, recovering herself and then returning to the *status quo*, which was essentially happy. She had no false self, as Marie would say. Yet obviously there was room for her to make some mistakes because she was looking for Mr Right.

She had a quick, professional, theatrical-agent look around the three principal bars – it was called having a drink but even Mr Wrong wasn't on show tonight. The rugby team destroyed whatever little elegance there might have been, along with peace and, at moments, sanity. I was prepared to make soup and buy ham and salad from the Catalan shop, but she preferred L'Hostellerie. She wasn't at all keen to spend time shut away with a woman in a private flat out of sight. So we made a weekend plan: restaurants, clubs, bars, sea, mountains, Spain, dancing. She didn't bother too much with sleep. She could do that in her grave. She hired a car, which secretly delighted me. I was no longer grounded and I prepared to show her the places Garcia had shown me.

The locals were interested in Fleur and called her 'La Parisienne'. She was invited for a drink with Madame Beaumarchais, Monsieur Nadal – even the mayor came out for a look – but she was restless, in hunting mood. It seemed to me she would know him if she saw him. I was well aware of the crisis in female life, these days, the lack of men and how women who once would have been sought after now advertised or joined dating agencies or sat at home on their own. As she put it, Fleur had wasted her best years on married men. Nowadays unattached men weren't interested. 'They're either homosexual or want very young girls.' She admitted she didn't stray far from the film business. Where else could she go? I suggested late-night supermarkets, launderettes, art galleries, health clubs. She thought I was laughing at her expense and accused me of being lonely. I supposed I was. I supposed I hid it from myself.

After a superb meal in the main L'Hostellerie restaurant – they'd changed the menu to include winter dishes – she confided that an astrologer in Paris had predicted she'd meet the man of her life now. Mountains came into it, English influences and water. He might live near a waterfall, and other things that I only half heard because after a time, her voice turned inward and she spoke internally. I supposed it had to do with living alone.

I'd had difficulty entering L'Hostellerie. I'd fallen in love with the place and had spent weeks there, day and night, eating, drinking like a prince. And here I was now, too poor even to creep into the fixed-price brasserie. I didn't know what to tell them. If I said I couldn't afford it, they would perhaps feel embarrassed and there would be a certain humiliating stain on me. So I said the first thing that came into my head: 'I'm dieting.'

'It's not working,' said Marie Belle, the outspoken *sommelier*, looking not at my full plate but at my full body. 'You're fatter than ever.' She gave us a glass of strong dessert wine on the house. I might be fat but she might be lonely, I thought maliciously. In return for that cruel taunt, I'd let Fleur loose on her delightful husband, Francine's brother, the fish chef. I told Fleur he'd be worth a look. Or the Russian Sergei or the mountain guide. I asked what age Mr Right was supposed to be, but she thought I was making fun of her again, and said she'd drop the subject. I was relieved it wasn't Jay. For one mad moment I had thought it might be. Anyone would be better than that.

I was about to ask for the fish chef but both chefs came out of the kitchen to shake hands, pleased of the chance to talk about Paris. Fleur knew all the up-and-coming restaurants and some of the chefs personally. Francine gave us a delicious new addition, a dish of tiny coffee squares, dark coffee and milky coffee with the consistency of chocolate. These sweetmeats were served with the coffee as an alternative to the brittle burnt-sugar biscuit. But the *coup de grâce* had been the dessert, an iced celery mousse in a sea of cold frothy vegetable sauce.

They asked if I was buying the studio and I admitted I couldn't make up my mind.

'Well, if you've enough as it is . . .' The fish chef indicated I'd done the right thing. Fleur said she'd love to have a look so before the light faded we got a key from Juan Pamello.

'Oh, yes, definitely you should take it,' Fleur said. 'It's worth it at that price.' She had property all over the place and it gave her peaceful nights. She almost talked me into it. But then I'd be on an even more punitive budget. How many singing pupils could I get in the Pyrénées? If they were going to sing they sang anyway. And what would I do with the studio? Let it?

Colette's was full but not with Mr Rights. Officers from the army hospital joined the throng of curists and locals. The Colette lookalikes were primping and preening in the mirrors, their feet squashed into skimpy glamour shoes from the shop next door, shoes for dreams. In these, you skipped out like a fairy-tale figure and got your prince. Or you became like *her*, the mystery woman behind the bar. That, for most curists, was a better dream because it had some reality. Since Colette had moved in, the shoe sales in that shop had tripled and now they could afford a new lighting system, which turned on as you stepped near the window. The emphasis was on transparent styles, like glass, with gold-leaf pattern and very high gold heels. Prices had increased with the addition of the magic night-light. Not only that, if a customer, on impulse from dancing, romance or drink, desired a pair of shoes, Colette's staff had the key, could enter the shop at all hours and conduct a sale. Fleur loved the ones in the window: diamanté, long and slender. In these you'd never walk sensibly again. You'd be taken to wonderful places. She bought three pairs and the hunch-backed waiter handled the deal. I asked if Fleur thought he was especially sexy.

'Asexual,' she decided.

Colette had a new hairstyle, Grecian with a gath-ering of curls at the back and hanging down the sides. Her dress was the colour of deadly nightshade, and so tight – how could she breathe? She gave Fleur a second look, perhaps recognizing Paris, left the bar and shook hands with me. I was surprised. I'd only seen her do that with curists. I introduced Fleur and mentioned her rela-tionship with films, but Colette showed no interest. I asked if she missed Paris.

'Not at all. I can go any time. I just go to Perpignan and take a plane. You can go and come back in a day.' Then she went back behind the bar, her behaviour so matter-of-fact that she was like a proprietor anywhere in the world.

'The way she is doesn't match her appearance,' said Fleur.

I asked what she thought Colette was.

'It looks obvious, but it isn't. Maybe she's having a new start.'

One of the Pigalle men I'd seen weeks earlier, with the wig and bright beady blue eyes, winked at me. I nodded hello. I told Fleur he looked like a musician from one of the old clubs in Pigalle.

'Very old. They're not like that any more. It's all sex-machine *vérité*.'

Then the gloomy old man with the poodle joined the 'musician'.

'Is that her father?' I asked Fleur.

'Ninety-eight per cent impossible.'

It was a good, friendly crowd dancing, and as the night wore on, the crowd formed into a conga line, winding its way through the café and into the street, into the cool fresh mountain air and back again into the dark room, with the ball of light fluttering different colours on us, like confetti.

'It is rare,' said Fleur. 'A place like this. You don't find this in Paris any more.'

Before the night was quite over, the hump-backed waiter came to our table and said he understood I could sing. It was the owner's birthday. Would I mind singing 'Love Is the Sweetest Thing'? The accordionist would accompany me.

I felt quite nervous as the waiter introduced me. Naturally I looked at Colette as I started singing. The waiter indicated fiercely the old man with the poodle, so my eyes swung to him. He didn't look as though he was celebrating. Back I went to Colette but the Pigalle 'musician' rapped on the table and indicated Jean Gabin. I was now so confused that the singing wasn't up to much but Colette listened, smiling all the while. Whoever owned the café, she certainly had a lovely smile.

We went to Spain to the fabulous Motel Ampurdan and then over to the coast, to Cadaques, which Fleur had heard was chic. Then down to Gerona where I wished to linger but she did not. No waterfalls here. Then up to Olot, which was supposed to have that sort of glamorous water, a gorge, cascades, perhaps a waterfall, and I began to see the power clairvoyants and astrologers had – even over my life, because I was sitting in the car with her. Then we did an evening in the Hôtel Opéra, Toulouse. She chose the restaurant, which had two stars but which wasn't as good, I thought, as L'Hostellerie. Yet, for some reason the salad was unforgettable: very fresh lettuce leaves, with chopped green olives and chopped radish on a small flat white plate. Afterwards I always ate salad like that and not from a dish. The clients ate silently, reverently. It felt as though we were in church. The foyer of the hotel, full of Americans, gave Fleur a chance. There was even some kind of cascade. But she wasn't interested in a pick-up. Her eyes ranged every room, searching. My eyes were closing. We'd clocked up four hours' sleep in three days.

I noticed she changed her clothes and makeup two or even three times during the day, and pinned a large fresh flower in her hair. We filled the next day with cafés and bars, lunching in a Catalan restaurant in Perpignan that she'd read about and wanted to try. We drove towards Canigou, stopping at villages stacked against the mountain like playing cards. I said the wrong thing: 'Perhaps it's better to wait and let him find you.' She didn't like that: time was running out. The last night, and it started to rain and we were stuck in the apartment. Sunday night. What was open? We went to the old hotel in the main street and had an omelette and fresh vegetables. Pascale passed by and invited us for a drink at Le Zanzibar. On the way we stopped to say hello to Natalie and Robert. I wondered if the astrologer's selection could include Robert: a lot of women would think so.

Natalie was sad. Business was not good? Eric the chef? She wasn't saying. Then I saw Eliane come in and chuck a key on the desk and I saw how Robert brightened up. I didn't miss the wince of pain on Natalie's face. The way Eliane tossed the key. Contempt but something else. It had sexuality in it, that gesture.

Le Zanzibar was full of all those who couldn't sleep, who were lonely, who wanted more out of life. The cocktails tasted like most cocktails, harmless until we stood up to go. The rain fell, noisy and dismal, and we got back to the flat soaked and defeated. Even I felt cheated.

'You're trapped here,' said Fleur.

'That's not how I see it.'

'You must get a car and learn to drive.'

'I know I can't.'

She was irritated. 'But you haven't tried.'

Driving – it was just something I didn't waste time even thinking about. I could not drive.

'Then you'll have to sell this and move to Perpignan. You can't be stuck here.'

She was wildly claustrophobic, exhausted and strung out. It would all end in tears. I made some ginger tea, with plenty of honey and lemon, and encouraged her to get some rest. She assured me that she had had a good time. Then she realized she'd left her bag of magic shoes in either Le Zanzibar or the Hôtel Luna. I said we'd get them in the morning. She said this was the morning and she would have to leave at six to catch her plane. I did not relish going out into that storm again. I said I'd phone the hotel, the bar and ascertain exactly where they were.

'I'll go,' she said. 'I can't sleep anyway. And I love the rain. I love wildness.'

She went off down the stairs and I got ready for bed. I had discovered I didn't much like having guests and longed for the peace that would return to the apartment once Fleur had gone. I lit a candle, lay down on the sofa-bed to wait for her. I lay just looking at the candle flame, bending and twisting in the draught. When she didn't come back I supposed Pascale, still at Le Zanzibar, had offered more cocktails. I was thinking that I preferred wine to all other drinks and that I liked to drink slowly and not get drunk when suddenly Fleur was shaking me. 'Wake up. There's an Englishman who knows you. He's locked out of the Hôtel Luna and he can't get back into his house. Can he stay here?'

He was downstairs by the front door, soaked and standing in the rain. He was drunk. I explained that the hotel had a code system to get in. If he'd ever known it, he'd forgotten it.

'I'm Herbert Dunn.' He shook my hand.

I didn't know him, I thought.

He said he wanted to invite me to Le Zanzibar. I said he needed to go to the hotel and have a hot shower.

'I need a drink,' he said.

'Come on,' said Fleur, and I think she said, 'We only live once.' In this storm I thought the living bit wouldn't be long. I left them in the doorway while I got boring things like umbrellas, raincoats and boots, and we went to the bar, which at three a.m. was packed. They couldn't persuade me to drink anything other than sparkling mineral water, which took care of the first five minutes. Herbert said someone called Sean had his house key. Did I know him? I did not. I thought I knew most people. Sean was doing up his house and Jack was going to take over. I must know Jack. I didn't.

'But everyone knows Jack.'

The whisky seemed to sober him. He swept back his hair, straightened his wet jacket and I recognized the lawyer from Manchester, who'd fallen in love with Castel and bought a house near the pizzeria. And Marcel was building him a roof terrace.

Yes, I remembered him, his elegance, how he'd epitomized satisfaction, substance and success. He was someone who got what he wanted. I told him some of this, which made him laugh, a dry inward laugh. 'You're obviously no clairvoyant.' He ordered another round, and was at that stage in his drinking where he needed to persuade me to be sensible and have a proper drink. I thought, Are we looking at an alcoholic here? and stuck to water. Fleur made up for me.

I remembered he was professional and had a wife

who'd fallen in love with the house. 'Had,' he said. 'Had a wife.'

He told us he was a solicitor from Manchester and had bought the house in Castel for twenty-eight thousand francs. Before he'd left that first time, he'd run into Sean, a labourer, Irish, who said he'd get the house fixed up. It needed a few things doing. So he'd given Sean a down payment of two thousand pounds and left him his car to look after. Sean had said he'd take care of everything. Not to worry. Herbert had thought he'd be back within a few weeks but his business had collapsed due to some shaky investments, and he'd had to sell his country properties. His wife, meantime, had been looking for something cheaper for them to live in and had fallen in love with the estate agent. She'd gone off with him and Herbert had come back to the only thing he still owned. His house in Castel, however, was not easily available. He'd expected to find it finished. First, he couldn't get in. Second, when he did, it was full of Sean's tenants. Stuffed to the windows with the homeless. Third, Marcel's roof terrace had one flaw: instead of being flat, it dipped in the middle so the rain collected and was dripping into the house. The car had been crashed and Sean was nowhere to be found. Herbert had taken a room at the Luna and had done the only wise thing: got drunk. Meanwhile he'd re-met Jack – 'a good straight bright bloke' – also a labourer, and he'd had a look at the house and said Sean was a crooked shit and that he would take over. He'd move the squatters out, and to keep them out, he and his pregnant wife would move in. He'd get the house in order.

'So I gave him a couple of thousand to buy materials and to prop up the terrace.'

And that's when I knew I was listening to a complete loser. 'But what does Marcel say about all this?'

'He's useless. I've given him several hundred to draw up a plan for the terrace and to get the workmen to do it. He lets Sean do it. Then he says he didn't expect the rain.'

Herbert had to go back to Manchester immediately before the banks foreclosed on him. His wife had grabbed the remaining estate and he had nothing left.

'Your legal firm?'

'Bust.'

Not only a loser but unlucky. I thought he took it really well. He was quite cheerful and funny.

Pascale joined us, and along came another round. She didn't know much about Sean, except that he squatted in a large house with a palm tree and he called the whole area around it the Bronx. She'd seen Jack around and thought he was sensitive and, as far as she could tell, reliable. But how could she tell?

'So I'll leave him some money and put a phone in and then I can reach him and get progress reports.'

I thought that had about it the makings of more trouble.

'I paid twenty-eight but in the end it's going to have cost forty-eight.' He was drying out as far as the rain went and filling up as far as the liquor went and his eyes glowed, cheeks flamed, and he was good-looking.

Le Zanzibar had a policy inherited from Robert. As long as there was a customer, it stayed open. When we left it was coming up for daylight.

'We'll have a nice little breakfast,' Herbert said. 'But first, come and look at my house.' Which was fine, until we got there and he didn't have a key. Pascale knew where Jack lived and went to wake him up. Shivering, he joined us and opened the door.

The house was narrow and tall, and squinting with eyes from every crack and crevice. Mattresses on the floor, covered with rubbish and debris. Jack kept saying, 'Terrible. Terrible. I want to kill him.' Eventually, we arrived at the top, and the roof was dripping in several places.

'But what will happen to all the water that's collecting in that dip?' said Fleur. And at that moment she found out. The roof fell in and the water rushed down in a cascade. Here was her waterfall. And I had noticed that, as she stood beside Herbert Dunn, her eyes were no longer restless.

They stayed in the Hôtel Luna and I didn't see them for days. When they reappeared, Herbert said that out of bad some good did come, or something like that. Fleur was head over heels about him and he was heels over head about everything. In amongst all his adversity, he liked her. They decided to take the studio next to me, which wasn't such a bad idea: they'd rent it while his house was being finished. But Gato didn't want rent, he wanted a sale. And Herbert's wife didn't want half of the English leavings. She wanted half of the lot. So the Castel house was only half his.

'Look at it this way,' he said cheerfully. 'So are the problems.'

Chapter Twenty-eight

The *marginaux*, the homeless, the beggars, came to Castel. A charitable spinster gave them one of her houses just down from the Hôtel Luna where they could sleep, eat, cook, wash their clothes and receive vouchers for the supermarkets. They also put out the word, and professional beggars came from all over France, with their dogs and begging tins. Others, with tough punk hairstyles and attitudes, paraded between the Café de France and the town hall asking directly and sometimes aggressively for money. The mayor was left-wing and said that anyone could be anywhere as long as they didn't break the law. His opponent, a right-wing surgeon, called for an election. Castel was strongly divided on the beggar issue. Shop- and house-owners said that the charitable lodging should be shut and the beggars moved on. Pascale and Marcel said that unemployment was the problem and that we should all share it with these youths. Many of them were sick with a drug habit or Aids, they had no family, where could they go?

'To hell,' said Juan Pamello, who deeply disliked them. 'They've come here for the sun.'

He asked why the homeless, drugged, broke should

be on the streets. That was what the other side said too. Their view – kick their arses into work, the drugs should be a police matter. They should move on from Castel. It got so bad there were more beggars on the streets than other people, and the place was knee-deep with dog mess. I found two youths sleeping in the hallway and there was a constant smell of urine by the front door. I suggested to Madame Beaumarchais that we lock the door at night. She wouldn't hear of it. She said it had to be open so that her doctor could call if she needed him. Also, the postman in the morning. How could he get in? Was she a concierge suddenly? I reminded her that she got up at six, long before the postman did the round. Sophie, the hairdresser on the left of the front door, said, 'Don't bother arguing with her. The door will always be open.'

'Why?'

'For Eliane, of course. In case, after one of her long nights out, she has nowhere to sleep.'

'So where does she sleep?'

Sophie shrugged. 'Perhaps Madame Beaumarchais hopes it will be with her.'

I couldn't put that together, not remotely, but I did remember that when I was still in the apartment above L'Hostellerie, I had seen them across the road and how their shadows mixed together as they performed a secret act, one to the other, passing money? Drugs?

Another band of *marginaux* moved into a deserted country house or *mas*, and they, too, converged on the old part of Castel. They weren't begging, more taking the place over. They shouted and argued and drank a lot. The problem was that many of the local artists looked the same, acted the same. It was hard to tell who was who. Juan Pamello wanted them all run out of town. They were a health hazard. He found plenty of political resistance, and the intellectuals, too, were quiet and considerate to these homeless. The tradespeople wanted them burned.

Juan Pamello said, 'They get state money and then supplements from the mad spinster, who should be killed off, and then what they shake down from softies like Marcel and Pascale. One stopped me and asked for ten francs. Ten, mind you. Not just something. He was most specific. He was well-dressed and clean, and eating a very good baguette stuffed with salad, egg, ham, which must have cost him thirty francs. I said, "I have never yet seen a beggar as well dressed as you and eating better than I do. I'll tell you what. Come and work for me for a day and I'll pay you," and I thought he was going to faint. Even his tan went pale.'

I admitted that they made me nervous. I dealt with them as I did rough types in any city. No eye-contact. There was one, a young boy with a violin who stood in the hollow in the archway opposite. He played that violin divinely and people would stop and listen and leave him money and food. But there was a feeling of siege. The *marginaux* were active twenty-four hours a day. I couldn't see what was going to happen. Jack, who was now restoring Herbert's unfortunate house, said, 'It will never get out of hand. Don't worry.'

'But the police can't do anything . . .'

'They don't have to. The rugby club will sort it out. The *marginaux* are here, but they know if they go one inch over the line, that's it.'

He seemed to be right, because although more and even more appeared, nothing actually violent occurred. In the end, the shopkeepers won. They told the mayor they'd kick him out of office. They found the charitable spinster. I thought they would lynch her. She explained her intention had been to offer refuge for the poor of Castel, not for the whole of France. She agreed the refuge should be closed and after a period reopened for the poor of Castel, although nobody was actually sure who they were.

After the invasion the streets had to be cleaned and disinfected and most of the *marginaux* moved to the *mas* which in turn was closed after drug violence. A few lived in the car park in front of the Champion superstore on the edge of the town where they waited by the exit doors asking for money, and their dogs occasionally loped into the shop looking for food. But, on the whole, it was a friendly arrangement: the numbers were not frightening as before. But it left an unfriendly aftermath between Pascale and Juan Pamello. Marcel backed out. Pascale asked what I thought.

I didn't want to think. I didn't want it to be my problem.

'Then you're like everybody else. I'm disappointed in you.'

I said I didn't feel responsible for them and I didn't want them to screw up my life. If they were really poor I'd give them what I could. But I'd seen too much of it, the professional begging, and also the heartbreaking homeless in New York, with Jay. 'If you give to the first hard-luck story on East Fifty-second, you'll be broke and joining them by the time you reached Grand Central Station,' he'd said.

Pascale wouldn't let it go. 'So it's not your problem?'

I didn't answer directly. I was sick of trouble. Neither did I want anyone forcing me and bullying me again. I'd learned that. I said that as a property-owner I was glad I wasn't trying to sell my property when they were stuck in front of it. And that was all I had to say. But she wasn't finished. So I added that I thought they had banded together sufficiently to have their own survival system. That they didn't belong in Paradise.

'So you won't help them, even though many of them have Aids and are on junk. I know. I give them their methadone.'

And I thought of my son and how he could have been one of them.

'Of course I'd help them, Pascale.'

But with her, committed and absolute in her political views, there were no shadings of choice. Or discussion. I told her I couldn't even open my mouth with one point of criticism.

'Try it with the right,' she said. 'See how many shadings of attitude you're allowed there.'

Upset, I went to Madame Beaumarchais, whom I saw as only wise. She said, 'When has the world been fair? The charity house had a right to exist but some of the *marginaux* abused it. Never discuss politics. But if you really want to know what to feel, go and lie out there in the street and see who helps you.'

Later I even asked Marie. She said, 'People have to take care of themselves. We're all struggling.'

Fleur and Herbert stayed on in the Hôtel Luna where she did her agency business by phone to Paris. She was thrilled about Herbert. Some terrible caution in me, which I wished I didn't have, that I didn't approve of, refused to believe in this affair, stuffed with astrologer's predictions. It had fitted what Fleur had been told so she believed it. Herbert was in such a state that he couldn't fit into anything except the next bar. All I could say was, 'Fleur, he may not be the right Mr Right. He still has that wife.'

'She's run off with an estate agent.'

For some reason I didn't believe in an estate agent's love either, I suppose because I had only seen the shallow, semi-crooked selling side of one. Juan Pamello had done it for me: waxing lyrical over the cobbles and the stones, yet living in the acrylic Woolworth's house. I believed Herbert's wife would seek him out especially when she knew there was a Fleur around.

'But he says we'll live together and he'll give me a child.'

'Whose?'

She looked at me as though I was mad.

'He must be drunker than I thought. You're nearly fifty. He can't not know that. Can't you see he's not thinking straight?' I hated myself for being so petty and ordinary about her happiness. She had even considered selling her Paris business and starting something with him. She got happier and happier and then started thanking me for having allowed this even to happen. I kept saying, grimly, 'Fleur, please, don't thank me.'

Herbert Dunn had flair. He had some style and good bone structure, a deep throaty voice, beautiful almost long hair, hats that he could really wear and clothes that he enjoyed being in. He took to Castel, like a duck to water. He'd breakfast in the Grand Café in the sun and read the newspapers, then off to his roofless house to make phone calls and see what Jack was up to, then for a mid-morning drink in the Pablo. After lunch, mostly out of town and often out of France altogether, he'd take a walk, then a siesta, then a bath and the evening would start. Everyone knew his routine and he would have them share it at seven o'clock precisely in the Café de France. His first drink of the night was his favourite. He said he even tried to linger over that one. Then he'd move with his growing gang to the Pablo for the real drinking before dinner. The crowd could swell to at least twenty. Then life began. Clubs, dancing, bars, unconsciousness. He liked to meet as many people as possible and loved their lives, their stories, their looks, their dreams. He loved people. With one exception.

'I tried to get Marcel to refund my money. After all, it's hardly a roof terrace. It's at best a gap. He refused. He said it's Sean's fault. It had nothing to do with his plans. How I hate estate agents. Especially as my wife doesn't.'

He adored Madame Beaumarchais. It was she who'd first brought him to Paradise when he'd driven her from Toulouse. 'Of course, she knows what it's all about,' he said.

I asked what he meant.

'This place.' He couldn't be bothered to explain it. 'She's clever, really clever, not school bright, not social smart. She's truly really where it is.'

After all this I felt quite proud to be living above her.

The villagers were invited to his ritual drinking sessions and he listened to their problems as though he was still practising law. How he wanted to help Eliane, but she never asked him, and a little later Natalie.

Eric the chef was an ever-growing problem.

'Why don't they get rid of him?' I asked.

'They're frightened of him,' said Herbert. 'He's even making the pastries now. They can't even serve me a decent breakfast because he won't let them.'

'What about Robert?'

'He'd hardly serve anything. And he thinks all chefs are like Eric at heart.'

'But he's psychotic.'

Fleur thought I'd said psychic and looked intrigued.

'If you don't like his food he chokes you,' said Herbert. 'You can't send anything back. Now Natalie gives you a plastic bag with the menu just in case. Eric accosted the mayor the other day because he wouldn't eat the fish. He rushed out and shouted "What d'you mean you can't eat it? You asked for pork and you've got it!" And there's a new fashion started by the rugby club: Are you tough enough to eat at Eric's? Anyway, all chefs are touchy.'

But that wasn't Natalie's problem. In the marvellous courtyard, with little Canigou painted on the back wall and big Canigou in the sky, Robert had fallen in love with Eliane, one night when the candles were flickering and there was a full moon and flamenco music drifted over the wall from the café, and Eric was stomping to and fro discouraging customers and destroying business, and she'd sat alone with her moon face and rich glossy hair, piled up and falling down, and her breasts perfect through the silk of the new Dutch-lover-bought dress.

'He is mad for her,' said Madame Beaumarchais.

'There is no rhyme or reason to it,' said the village women. 'Natalie is a marvellous wife and Eliane a slut but there you are.' For some reason they blamed the mountain.

My phone stopped working and Madame Beaumarchais gave me one of hers. I asked how much.

'Just get me a bottle of Pernod when you next get taken to the border.'

I knew Dr Kat had forbidden her the strong stuff. Pascale had told me. 'Are you sure? What about wine?'

'Get Pernod. Eliane likes it.'

Then Garcia turned up, with a gang of Spanish taxi-drivers and their girlfriends, and we gathered around the piano and sang, as he put it, from the heart, until daylight.

Chapter Twenty-nine

Luis came to see me because Castel was halfway to Rennes-le-Château. Like a lot of people he had not got there. He sat at the kitchen table and I made him a tortilla. He took over, as he always did, because I could never ever get it right. And because he was there I didn't dare. He looked tired and had an Elastoplast over the corner of his eye and scratches on his face.

'But did you see Monsieur Privat? He owned the Tower Magdala and –'

'A sect or cult bought him out.'

'Where is he?'

He had no information.

'Did Raoul find anything in the presbytery? He was digging by the door.'

'I said I did not get there. But I am told they found nothing much, some Gallo-Roman vessels.'

'Did you see the tower at least?'

'I got as far as the village at the bottom of the hill and passed a small deserted chapel, and a cat sprang from its window tearing at my eyes. I only just fought it off. There was group of us but the animal chose me. I couldn't help but think of the Jewish centre which I had

been involved in starting. It was called Isaac the Blind —
in honour of the caballist in the Middle Ages. He had
been blinded by an animal. So I turned round without
ever seeing Rennes-le-Château.'

And during the evening he became irritated, which
was unusual. When I asked if he had found the dramatic
letters and documents in his family possession he said
simply, 'I want nothing more to do with this. Rennes-
le-Château belongs to the devil.'

I thought he was joking. He wasn't.

'And I went up there because of you,' he said. 'You
had stirred my interest again.'

It wasn't the first quarrel we had ever had.

I used to think sex was something he was just good
at but it had nothing to do with his heart. Age had
changed that. It was no longer so important but he
loved from his heart.

Monsieur Nadal saw him leave and, impressed, said,
'So you know him!'

'But you must know Can Mora?' said Herbert.

'Is that in Spain?'

'It's on the way to Amélie. Let's go,' and he paid for
the drinks. We were the last ones in the Castel street: it
was the absolute hour, the hour of lunch, which irritated Herbert more than anything. 'We can go eight
kilometres and we're in Spain and everything changes.
We can eat at three and stay all day. Here these people
are my best friends. They drink with me but they can't
serve me one French chip after two p.m.'

'So we go to Spain?' said Fleur.

'No, we go to Can Mora. They stay open until two fifteen.'

It was on the road to Amélie-les-Bains, an old building with a new terrace extension, full of little rooms where the tourists, the curists, the lorry drivers, the workmen, the criminals, the families, the politicians eat Chez Martine. This was the place.

Can Mora, on a bend on the narrow, treacherously busy road, had its parking place by the river, so you had to cross the road on arrival and on leaving, which was more of a feat. From time to time, customers who had either had a drop too much or hesitated too long had in fact just eaten their last meal ever. Even the owner's father-in-law had been squashed flat on a quiet Sunday night. The tavern was reached by a flight of worn steps and you entered through a squeaking wooden door with glass windows and old ads for drinks and soaps, into a dark room with long tables, covered in oilcloth, and men, lots of them, drinking litres of rosé and red and talking loudly from table to table. Nobody was ever excluded. This room was presided over by Martine, who if she didn't have the looks made up for it with money. She had a bulbous nose and didn't have time for prettying up. She worked from dawn to midnight. One afternoon a week she went joyously to the bank in Castel and unloaded the take, then had her hair done. It was said that her husband took both waitresses upstairs into one of the hotel rooms and had them together. As I got to know him, and then her, I hoped he did. Martine looked like a figure in a Brueghel painting. She loved men, mothered them, knew their secrets and weaknesses. She wasn't crazy about women. You could

do anything here: there was no sin except eating somewhere else. It was better to leave the country than to
be found folding a napkin at Le Pont in Amélie or
the pizzeria in Castel. She didn't mind L'Hostellerie
because that was crazy money. Even she'd been invited
there. I found her dangerous, especially when she was
pouring the Pernod. If the men wanted it she poured it.
Some of them would be legless and they left the tavern
that way, tried to cross the road and tried to drive their
car.

I did once say I thought she shouldn't serve it after
someone had reached a certain level of drunkenness.
'And why not, my darling? If I don't, they'll get it somewhere else.' Another time she said, 'Drink looks after its
own.'

Monsieur Nadal always took the car keys off his
drunken clients and told one of his waiters to drive
them home.

The food at Martine's was always marvellous; there
was never an off day. The dark cool room, the best
room, the inner chamber, the power base, was reserved
for the regulars. It had the bar and the till. The other
room was for the curists, the tourists, the middle class,
the lovers, the families. The terraced room was smart
with new furniture, a few plants and windows all
around. The other rooms were like private dining
rooms with tables close together, grandfather clocks, old
sideboards with vases of flowers, photographs in frames.
Can Mora was always full, every meal, every day of the
week. On Sunday there were two lunch sittings.

Martine's husband, a slim dark mysterious man who
looked like a young priest and as though he had

nothing in common with her, did the cooking, seemingly effortlessly. Two women helped Martine serve.
Rue was fat and Charmian was slight. The food was
fresh, copious and cheap. A three-course meal, with as
much wine as you could get down, cost fifty francs.
Rooms upstairs with breakfast were one hundred
francs.

Herbert was ushered through the dark room to the
terrace. Everyone stared at us, then nodded a greeting.
Herbert's hat sat back rakishly on his head and he wore
a well-cut midnight blue suit with a glamorous waistcoat. They already had a nickname for him: the gambler.
'They're not far wrong,' he said. 'It's better than the
loser. That comes next.'

Fleur didn't like that talk. She was ready to invest
some money and sell off a few bits of property but she
didn't want to save him. She wanted to save herself.
They could have what she needed: a home, a baby,
status. They could run a legal business for the foreigners,
buying in south-west France. Lawyers couldn't fail to
make money.

'Well, there's one sitting here who did,' laughed
Herbert. He was beginning to relax into this pause
between disaster and its consequences. This allowed him
to be the person he'd like to have been. In his midnight
blue suit with fabric so soft, luxurious as an angel's
wing, he did look like a gambler, on a Mississippi boat
a hundred years ago, with a marked deck of cards and
lots of enemies just one or two boats behind. Herbert
would never go into business and didn't know what to
do with Fleur. Or, come to that, with his wife and
family in England, the creditors, the press. So he did

what he was increasingly doing, ordered three Pernods, go easy on the water, while we looked at the menu. There was nothing much to look at, actually, because Charmian put down the fresh white paper on the table, the cutlery, water from the source and three plates of salad with cold meats and batter pudding. Very quickly she said, 'Chicken, veal, duck, green beans, potato purée or chips?'

I said, 'Fish.'

'Friday.'

We chose one of everything and a litre of the light rosé. The food was wonderfully cooked, and there was aioli sauce, tartare, and home-made pickle. Charmian sped from table to table as the rich, the poor, the bad and a few good ate hugger-mugger together. In the inner sanctum I could see the Pigalle musician from Colette's with the wig and beady eyes, sitting in a place of honour disputing politics and doling out scandal. He was funny enough. Martine muttered, 'Come on now, Monsieur Flavier. People will say you love the sound of your own voice.' The men laughed like children. Monsieur Flavier wisecracked back in slang and the chef came out to listen and join in the laughter. Monsieur Flavier's target was a Corsican I had danced with at Colette's. He sang beautifully. And he sang now. Then he said he had to hurry back to work. Monsieur Flavier didn't believe it. 'If you work and you say you are from Corsica then you are not a true Corsican. I've never seen a Corsican work. Your grandmother must have fucked a Japanese.'

'Is he from Paris?' I asked the waitress. 'Monsieur Flavier?'

'Castel. He lives in Castel,' and she flew by with arms full of pudding.

'Here, anything can happen,' said Herbert. And at that moment the door pushed open and in crowded a dozen firemen. 'Oh, my God,' said Herbert. 'If there's one catastrophe I can't bear it's fire.' And he looked quickly for the nearest exit. No one else took any notice. 'God they put their stomachs first,' Herbert said, angry in his panic. The firemen stood at the bar and the next thing their hands were full of glasses of aperitif wine. Martine speedily cleared a long table and laid it for twelve. They took off their helmets and undid their tunics and sat down to an extensive meal. The table was literally rocking with serving plates piled with food.

Herbert, annoyed at his early fear, said, 'Oh, she lets them in. It's after three. She turned me away the other day and it was only two thirty.'

Dessert was simple. Cheese, either Camembert or Emmenthal, ice cream, crème caramel, yoghurt or fruit. Once a week the cook made a dozen flans and on Sunday there was a delicious gateau and Rum Baba and slices of peppermint fudge.

Two timid curists pushed open the main door and looked around.

'Now we will see,' said Herbert, 'who she lets in and who she doesn't.'

It seemed they hadn't been before.

'They're French,' said Fleur, 'that helps.'

'She will let them in,' I said, 'they're the type.'

'No,' said Fleur. 'It will depend on the cook. She can't stretch him too far.'

I disagreed. This was where her power lay. It had nothing to do with that husband. Charmian, the waitress, greeted them, looked at the clock, said she would have to ask. The inner sanctum was staring at the couple. Was this their lucky day? Martine came out of the kitchen wiping her hands on a cloth.

'No,' said Fleur.

'Yes,' said Herbert. 'I bet a hundred on it.'

I joined him. Two hundred.

Jacqueline loved hesitation as long as she was doing it. Then she swung her huge body towards one of the smaller rooms. 'Come on follow me. But we do close at two fifteen.'

'I am going to remember that,' said Herbert, but it wouldn't do him any good. Martine let you in if you were somebody. Pascale, the pharmacist, always got in, even at midnight. So did Eliane because she brought distant grandeur and modern fuck-up and that entertained everybody. The police, the military and the paramedics always got in and so did drunks and curists. She refused all locals who knew she shut at two fifteen, all tourists passing through and those she found hard to place like Herbert, Garcia, Fleur and me.

Then some street types came in with harmonicas and bells on wood and sang mountain songs.

> 'Mount Canigou, you are fresh
> As the newly given present God sent.
> Especially in summer
> When your water is so needed,
> so icy.'

Jack came out of a side room and Herbert invited him for a drink. He was pale and lean with a very good body, highly strung and soulful dark eyes. His hair was cropped and he looked like trouble. I could see he could be moody and curt, quarrelsome and challenging. I'd be wise to avoid him. He had arrived in Castel seven years ago via Spain via Wales, and worked as he could, picking fruit, on the land, painting homes, rebuilding them, and now saving one. He played for the rugby third team and occasionally prepared the food for the first team. He had a French wife and daughter and an English girl-friend who was expecting their baby any day. He said Sean had really done the house in and when he found him he'd kill him. He discussed cheap ways of making one floor habitable. First he had to put a roof on and seal it. He was no fan of Marcel. 'Never let him say he will look after your place if you go away because he won't. And not only that, he'll let Sean in.'

I was surprised at how many English people there were.

'We meet every Saturday morning for a drink at the Pablo. Market day. Come along.'

I didn't think I would. Jack was tricky as hell, a disquieting acquaintance. He was powerful in his disap-proval. Put-down was his best weapon. I was sure Marie would know the reason for that. Mum and Dad hated him or each other. I felt intuitively that he behaved like his mother or, more, that his mother behaved through him. And later, when I saw her, I found out I was right.

He left us to get on with the roof in case anything else terrible happened, like more rain. 'If it gets into the electrics –' He made a *kaput* sign.

Fleur hadn't liked him either. 'I do not like thee, Dr Fell. Why is it, I cannot tell.'

'He's one of the best,' said Herbert, 'a real bloke.'

I wasn't at all sure about that either. Fleur said he looked stressed out.

'Of course he is,' said Herbert. 'He's stuck between those two women. Vampires. The English one will never let him go.'

I didn't believe it or agree with it. Nobody has to stay. They stayed.

'She's got her teeth in him, right to the bone. Poor old Jack. He can't even see his little girl.' Herbert was warming to his subject. 'What can I do to help him? I've said he can live in the house while he's doing it up.'

'Didn't Sean do that?' said Fleur acidly. 'Why don't you live in it?'

He said that, suddenly, he couldn't bear the responsibility. He just wanted a whole new start.

I knew how he felt. The women at the next table smiled and asked if I went to Colette's. One thought she had seen me there. And before long we were all talking about *la patronne*.

'She's amazing,' said one woman, 'and so strong. Up all night till five or six every morning. You and I couldn't do it. Not for three nights.'

'She *is* strong,' said her husband admiringly. 'Standing behind that bar on tiptoe literally.' And he imitated her. 'Looks like a –'

His wife nudged him – watch it.

'Like a goddess,' he continued. 'She does those curists more good than any cure.'

'Do you know her?' I asked.

'We certainly do. We stay there most weekends. We like to dance. We come from near Albi.'

I asked what the hotel was like, and they said good value for the price. About her private life they knew nothing. She was a good *patronne* and charged fair.

On the way out I stopped and said hello to the Pigalle musician, who was talking to Martine's two teenage sons, offering to take them fishing. I mentioned Colette's and he shook his head. 'They won't see me there again.' And I had the impression Martine signalled to him to be quiet because whatever else he was going to say remained unsaid.

Fleur and I took Herbert to the Café des Arcades, just in time for the first *thé-dansant* session. Colette was everything we'd said and Herbert was not disappointed. It was also clear that she liked him or, more, approved of him. He was what she was used to. She gave a wide smile and looked him steadily in the eye. She shook hands all round: she had a good, firm, strong hand. She was no fading lily, as Herbert put it. He was fascinated and would have asked her to dance but he caught sight of Jean Gabin. There was always a sense of protection around her. Today I decided I would speak to her, about Paris, the fifties, the clubs, her idols, but when I got up to the bar and in front of her, I couldn't think what to say. I had experienced that before when I had gone to see a guru. When I joined the queue I had twenty questions in my head, and forty by the time I got into the receiving room. Yet when I sat in front of him and he put his hands on my forehead I had none. And, in a way, questions ceased to exist the nearer Colette I got. Finally I said, 'Un crème, s'il vous plaît.' And Colette passed the request to the waiter, who brought the milky coffee to the table.

There was something classy about her, real inner classiness. She was born with it. Did she pretend to be a whore, a madam, as I pretended to be a singer?

The reaction to all this beneficent life, the hangover, came a few days later, and I thought if I saw one more wholesome thing, perfect blossom, snowy peak, I'd throw up. I needed greyness, cities, complicated people, bad deeds, the twilight life. Paradise had chucked me – Garcia describing his evening casserole, the daube sauce, all those gestures, just one too many. For a moment I'd have preferred a poisoner. And I ran down to Monsieur Nadal, but I had had it there too. I couldn't stay another moment. I couldn't bear the people, the claustrophobic dramas. I ran back to the apartment and packed to go. Then I realized that the day was beautiful. I'd stay another day.

Chapter Thirty

Lying ill in the bedroom, with the pleasing blue of the bed and white walls that soothed. Beyond the open window, a gentle young tree poking up like a friendly neighbour. Watching that tree I did not feel alone. It had something friendly about it. Even well I could see that. It seemed happiest in a light breeze and all its parts fanned out, swaying and dancing. That tree gave a sense of harmony, reminded me of harmony that I had long forgotten.

Beyond the tree, blue hills, one behind the other like a Chinese painting, and the shrine of St Ferréol clearly visible as though it was in the next street. The light and clear air seemed to pull things nearer. It was better lying here than in other places. Watching the sky, the weather changes, was as absorbing as any television programme. But I felt without energy, utterly exhausted, so low I became prey to depressive thoughts of the past, and how I regretted, mourned, lost chances.

Dr Kat was a problem from the start because he wanted to be a psychiatrist not a general doctor. He bustled in with the usual barking mad aggression I had encountered frequently in French doctors. 'And what's going on here?', suspicious, ready for attack. He put down his bag and looked around the room. Nothing to disapprove of there. The renovated floor pleased him and he smiled at the stones. 'Oh, so you have done up this old place. It's done very well.'

Then he turned to the less exciting, human part of the room and took my pulse, my blood pressure, and listened to my chest.

'It is very nice for Madame Beaumarchais having you living here. Someone on her level needs proper company.'

'Is she very ill?'

'She has had a very bad life at one time. But she knows that and knows she has to change.'

I longed to know what that was. He knocked my knees with a hammer. He gave me a ton of medicine and said I should stay in bed for three days, minimum. 'It's not serious,' he said. French doctors liked to give a *grand boeuf* cure because they thought that if they did not their patients would not be satisfied. Five of these, a spoon of that, an ampoule between, a suppository at night.

It had started as a virus. I had already seen that this part of the world produced some heavyweight viruses. Some real show-stoppers. If you had an immune system that could ward them off, you didn't have to know about them. If you didn't, you could be ill three weeks in four.

The fever went up but at least lying here I didn't have to do anything. Not like in London, where I had to get up and look after my husband, my son, and later go on and earn my living. The next day I was still too weak and I almost had to crawl to the lavatory. I was ill and the world became darker. It closed in, measuring me for a coffin. If only I could see Luis. Just hear his voice. He was so near, across the border, I could almost touch him. He was the most beautiful person I'd ever come across and, of course, someone like that would never settle for the isolation of one-to-one living, marriage, domesticity.

Madame Beaumarchais came in with a bottle of Crémant de Limoux. 'It's not really alcohol,' she assured me. 'People here drink it like medicine.' I warned her not to come near me. I was really ill and didn't want her to catch it. She scoffed, 'I'm too ill to catch anything else.' I didn't have the strength to open the bottle so she did it for me and had a generous glass herself. She talked about Dr Kat and how he treated her various ailments. Previously she had been operated on for cancer and would never go through that again. She thought Kat was all right otherwise she wouldn't see him.

It seemed to me that most of the inhabitants, if they became really ill, rushed to the acupuncturist Emile Loubet l'Hoste. He treated ten in a room, read your tongue, eyes, pulses. People came from all over the world to see him, and the hotels were full of his patients.

Madame Beaumarchais put a wet cloth on my head and said she'd prepare me some hot broth. She talked about her daughter, who had a good job in the government in Paris. Madame Beaumarchais had had two husbands, both wealthy: one owned a cinema chain, the other had been a minister during Giscard d'Estaing's presidency in the seventies. Madame Beaumarchais had known everyone worth knowing but enjoyed far more those who were not. She was sweet and attentive, and said she'd told Pascale to look in on me.

I stayed still like an animal in its lair, waiting for the illness to pass. Once up, I'd be energetic and hopeful again. I couldn't bear sickness and the self-absorption it produced. I acknowledged that everyone excepting perhaps saints and mystics, were self-absorbed but did their best to deal with it or hide it. Generosity, kindness, learning, it all helped, but the self-absorption was still there, part of survival. Perhaps it was the scaffolding that surrounds us. Maybe it could be dismantled. An act of faith would do it. But a sick person's self-absorption I disliked the most and was determined to resist it. In fact, I was ill so much I was almost ashamed and hid away. It wasn't something I talked about. I denied it as often as possible.

Lying there in the blue and white room with the blazing blue sky filling the window and the gentle tree, nature all generous and splendid, I was where I'd decided to be. This was it. Life's centre stage. No more hanging about in the wings. But I worried about Jay. It was a worry that never left me, however much I appreciated and loved the view, the atmosphere. I was afraid that he was suffering, but there was nothing I could do even if I was with him. I was, perhaps, the last person from whom he'd accept help. I waited until I felt strong enough, then got to the phone by the terrace and called Marie in London. She maintained that while he would not admit he was an addict there was nothing to be done. He was still insulated, cocooned, by drugs and had no ingoing lines. Nothing suggested was received.

'Shall I come back?'

'And do what?'

'Try to get him in to rehab.'

'He won't go.'

'He'll die.'

'The drugs stop him realizing that. You sound terrible. What is it?'

I got back to bed and my heart flapped around like a bird in a cage. I felt so bad I couldn't even cry. I'd be thinking about my son next.

Eliane came in with a tray of food from Madame Beaumarchais. I warned her not to stay. She, too, scoffed: 'I never get anything.'

The tray contained a medicinal herb soup, orange juice and toast. 'She'll cook you an egg. Do you want it boiled or poached?'

I said poached, but I couldn't eat anything and the food stayed on the tray.

'I'll go and tell her, but I'll have to wait a few minutes because she's got visitors.'

'Her daughter?'

Eliane shook her head. 'Men from Toulouse. Important.'

I could hear their voices, quite a few of them. I could smell the cigar smoke. 'Why are they there?'

'She's got a lot of business in that area.' She picked up the bowl of soup and fed me a few spoonfuls. 'This is what I do to my daughter. Have you got children?'

'No.'

'Never had?' She was surprised.

'Well, yes, I did. A son.'

'What happened?'

I shook my head. Some things I couldn't talk or think about.

Eliane was no stranger to the unendurable. 'You just

take what suits you best. What blots it out for while. And keep going.'

And she told me how she had been married at fourteen. It seemed everyone felt free to relive a bit of their past now that I was collapsed with fever. If I did hear, would I remember it? Or believe it?

'He wanted me to sleep with another girl and then join in. And then he got bored with that and wanted SM. He used to beat me until I passed out but no one believed it. He was so charming and he never left a mark. I tried to run away. He got me back. I wanted to kill him.'

'Did you?'

'No. Life beat me to it. He got stabbed in a fight in a casino. Out of gratitude I went with his killer. I had lots of men, believe me, but none as bad as that first one.'

'Couldn't you tell your father?'

'He killed himself when I was eleven. He was hanging in my bedroom when I came back from school. I found him. I cut him down but he was gone.' She couldn't talk any more about that. 'I married the second time to a South American millionaire. But I couldn't live over there. I feel the only place I can be myself even marginally is here. And he just fucked off in the end. My lawyer is trying to get me alimony.'

'How are you getting on with your apartment upstairs?'

'I'm not. I never finish anything. I did well at school and started my bacc. Did the first exams, couldn't finish the rest. I've never got over finding my father. Why my bedroom?'

'Why did he do it?'

'He hated my mother.'

'I bet you don't like people much. Men or women.'

'You've got it.' She smiled and took the tray out.

The men were still in Madame Beaumarchais's room when Pascale popped in. 'Everyone's got this virus. But not as bad as you. It takes a good three weeks. Really a month before the symptoms have gone.' She gave me two tubes of vitamin C. 'Take a gram every two hours.' She looked at the medicine Dr Kat had prescribed. 'Won't do you any good but it won't do any harm. I'll give you some stronger antibiotics. Anyway, I've got good news for you.'

'Good news?' By now I was delirious.

'They want you to organize the Christmas concert. The one who was doing it originally has got what you've got and he's really sick in hospital. Monsieur Nadal said you should do it and he'll pay you for your time. And he's given you these.'

She produced a bunch of roses. 'Your friend Fleur and Herbert have gone to Saint Cyprian Plage for dinner. When they come back I'll tell them to look in on you. I'm very happy. I'm in love.'

I said that was great. Was I going to get another confession because I was feverish? Definitely.

'I never thought I could be so happy.'

'Who is he?'

'Not he! She!'

'Are you –'

'Gay? Yes. Of course.'

'Who is it?'

She almost told me, then said, 'When you're better we'll go and celebrate.'

I couldn't get any peace. I tossed and turned on aching joints and painful bones. I wanted to be out of my body. Jay was in my mind, in the room, in the bed. I was delirious and he changed shape and became swollen and full of water. I dragged myself up and turned on the light, prayed, drank some water, took every kind of pill. And I deliberately resisted thinking about him. He came into my mind so I thought about Colette. This was my time. For the first time in my life. I had a chance to live for myself to do all the things I'd wanted and to be the person I wanted to be.

All night I heard the bird calling and by dawn I knew it among all the others. The bird called to me to leave, to depart from all this pain, exhaustion and distress, and go to new territories. After all, the bird made a long journey before winter and another in the spring.

I often heard that bird calling to me.

Chapter Thirty-one

Luis wasn't in Gerona. Without him it was the difference between the light and the dark. Even the glorious view of the river in the sunset and the houses at the water's edge couldn't change that. The last person I expected to see was Monsieur Nadal. There he was, crossing the canopied bridge. He was here visiting a cousin on business.

'We Catalans are all the same, one side of the border or the other.' He asked if I had been to Rennes-le-Château again and I realized it was strange that I hadn't.

'It's all a dead end, isn't it?' I said. 'No one really knows what happened.'

'Madame Matthieu knew.'

I was surprised he knew about her.

'That's not quite a dead end,' he said casually. 'You should go and talk to a butcher's wife, Pepita Carreras. She's not a dead end either.' He gave me her address. 'She was Madame Matthieu's friend.' We had a glass of ice cold greenish wine in the bar Boira and then another. 'I love this drink,' he said. 'To think I could ever give up.' He touched my hand, 'Good luck,' and was gone.

Señora Carreras was eighty-six and lived in the new

part of Gerona. She was bright, energetic and well above her marbles, as Jay would say, except that she was wearing a fur coat in this heat. She was the last link to the French woman and had been her friend since she was a young girl. 'I first saw her when I was ten. I was married at fourteen. My husband ran the butcher's near the town hall. She got her meat there. She was such a surprise, when you think of it. Living here all those years. She had a dry way of saying things. I looked after her practical errands. And I used to go to the house when she had an entertainment. A musical person from Paris sometimes. You would think she was well connected.'

'Where did she come from?'

'From the Aude district. Quite simple. She was a singer herself. Lots of admirers. But she never married.'

So I mentioned Luis and his uncle and she said she may have seen them. Her eyes were cautious now. I said Luis didn't want to talk about Rennes-le-Château any more although he had been so keen at the beginning.

'Nobody wants anything to do with it. It's as though a cover is being put over it, I imagine by order of the Church.'

'Did she know priests?'

'Well, she must have seeing the house was just behind the cathedral. As young Nadal says, it was convenient for priests, especially visiting ones.'

'I suppose we're talking about Saunier?'

'I didn't meet him. Not to be introduced. But I think the house was paid for by someone other than her. And especially bought. There was a reason for it.

Because a lot of money was put down. And the local people said there's treasure there.'

And then it was ended. She had nothing more to say. She even took off the fur coat, which relieved me a great deal. She'd open the window next. And I was sweating down to my shoes. I got up, soggily, to go. Then I remembered something. 'What connection does Luis' family have?'

'Oh, you'll never find out, not from him. Remember, he was a priest.'

'The Holy Grail?'

That made her laugh. 'More earthly.' And then I got it. 'Luis is her son?'

'Not unless he's had surgery. The last time I met him he was in his fifties or sixties.'

'But she had a child?'

'So they say.' Very dry now. 'A son. And he married and had a son himself. And they say that one had certain documents revealing man's purpose on earth and its end. But he never showed me. He has a charmed existence, that one.'

'Who is he?'

'Well, you wouldn't be here if you didn't know.'

'Does he know who he is?'

'I don't think he did.' They kept it from him. But now he does. He started digging into everything.

And although I asked her this way and that, Was Saunier Luis' grandfather?, she wouldn't say. In the end she said, 'If there were only answers there'd be no mystery. And life wouldn't be so interesting. Let's say they were both priests.'

Chapter Thirty-two

Going out in the morning could take a whole day. Go out of the front door at ten o'clock, turn left towards the Grand Café, beside which the main shopping street, the rue St Ferréol, ran down almost to the river, with a list of things to do and get, and the small singing lesson cheque, Francine always paid that way, to deposit in the Crédit Agricole, and after that the bus to Perpignan for the singing lesson and before even I had passed the *coiffeuse* Jacqui, there was Robert, had outstretched: 'It's a beautiful day. And how are your friends Fleur and Herbert?'

'But they stay in your hotel.'

'Our hours are very different, Madame.'

I moved on a few paces, right into Natalie's baskets and bags and plastic containers as she carried her shopping back from Casino. If Robert had been carrying anything it wasn't obvious. And she put it all down on the pavement because she wanted to know all the details of my illness and which doctor had been called, was he looking after me, and I shouldn't go to him at all but the one opposite her hotel, who was calm. I liked the sound of that. 'He listens to you. He gives you time. You should have called for me. I'm a nurse. Have you forgotten?' And she gave me a big kiss on the cheek with those huge carmine-painted lips, which left an imprint on my face, a sort of decoration. 'Come on Friday. It's Eric's night off. I'll make you a real consommé with egg and garlic. You need fattening up.' And she slapped my not insignificant buttock and laughed.

As I was passing the bookstore a mere ten paces on the owner ran out and asked if I'd come to the reading that night. Poems. That sounded short. I said I would. Pascale waved from the crowded chemist's. I was about to cross the street when Marcel stepped up beside me and said how was my friend Herbert and his house of ill-fortune. I wasn't getting into that, not those problems. I think he really wanted to know if I blamed him. He cracked a few hard jokes, like nuts, and was gone. Almost across the road, with the ownerless dogs running in a circle and Madame Marcel appeared from behind the flower stall and asked about my illness, my recovery, and then gave me a tiny kiss with her modest pink-painted ladylike lips, which left a second imprint, aslant near the first. Madame Beaumarchais left a third, a rich red juicy smudged pair of open lips below the other two.

When I had actually crossed the road and got to the Grand Café I sank into a chair and had to have a Coca-Cola for energy. 'Put some rum in it,' said an English voice, and there was Herbert having a substantial breakfast. 'Of course I want to live here, for the rest of my life,' he said. 'Can I do it?'

Then off towards the post, and I met the arrogant French painter who looked like a *marginaux*, then Jack, then Sergei, then a *marginaux*, then Fleur, and finally I got into the bank and the manager wanted to see me and shut me in his airless office. There was no air, not a molecule. He told me how privileged he was to have me as a customer. Then he told me the rules of French banking. The one I caught on to – no overdraft.

At last I turned into the Pablo and Monsieur Nadal said, 'All those lips have kissed you. So you're well loved.' And we discussed the rehearsals for the Christmas concert, which would be given on 18 and 19 December and then in Spain for Epiphany on 6 January. Most of the singers were local, including two of his waiters, various clerks from the banks, Maître Aznar, and Pascale. The songs were Catalan, with a sprinkling of French. Other singers, thirty in all, from all over Castel, were forming a chorus. 'And I thought you could teach them in English a carol or two. And also, perhaps, one of your own songs. That you've written yourself. We have guest soloists to be announced.'

Of all the problems the worst was that I couldn't understand Catalan. He said that didn't matter as long as the pitch was right. He offered me a *verre* and said the mountain wind, the *tra montana*, was coming. It could sing in his bones. 'Shut your windows and the shutters and keep all doors closed, and if you're outside cover your face.'

I believed he liked my voice but his reasons for giving me the job were not musical. He suspected that I was short of money and wanted to help. 'It'll be fun, you see,' he said. 'And it will establish you here.'

I was very pleased to accept and we had a bottle of champagne.

On my way back I met Juan Pamello and then Sophie, the hairdresser, then Jacqui the hairdresser, the waiter from L'Hostellerie and Jack. He stopped me and his smile was nice enough. 'Johnny Halliday's coming here to sing.'

I looked pleased? Grateful? Blank? He waited apparently for a better reaction.

'Johnny Halliday?' He looked teasingly at me.

'Yes, I've heard of him.'

'Oh, I thought it was more than that. Don't you know him?'

I had actually met him with Jay but I wasn't going to tell a non-friend this. 'Why do you ask, Jack?'

'People say you were married to him.'

'Which people?'

'How can I remember? You are a dark horse.'

And he walked on. I thought, be careful. There is always a worm in Paradise. Jack wasn't big enough for a snake.

By the time I got back to the doorway I'd had quite a few drinks and could feel the effect as far away as my toes. I could see the day fast coming when that would have to stop. It was a habit. I felt it could become trouble.

Garcia got out of a car and rushed towards me waving his arms like windmills. We embraced, very pleased to see each other. He was on his way from Spain to his boat in Toulouse.

'Let's at least have lunch,' I said. 'I've found a really good place.' And I told him about Can Mora.

'Oh, definitely. I love it there. I'll just go and clean myself up. And we must shut all the windows, dear

Madame, because the *tra montana* is coming and it's a bad one.'

I remembered suddenly that I had no winter clothes. 'How cold does it get here?'

'Never cold. It's sunny every day. You can eat outside, have your lunch in the sun, throughout the winter. The evenings, you need a fire.'

I'd lingered too long in the doorway. It was time for Herbert's pre-lunch drink so we crossed to the Café de France and joined his gang of ex-pat English. Jack and Sergei were having a discussion, which became animated. Jack turned to Herbert, whom he knew would give his support. 'He says I've cut him up. I haven't shared the job on your house with him. I can't hold his hand all the time.'

Sergei, in voluble French, explained they always cut each other in. It was their law.

'But I'm not just working for you,' Jack told Herbert. 'I'm living there and so protecting your property.'

'You saved me,' said Herbert. Then he turned to Sergei and offered him a drink. It was the first time the Russian had been known to refuse. He was too angry.

'Every time I get work on the grapes I cut Jack in. I got him the job cooking for the rugby club. He can't cook but I'm worse and they don't know what they're eating after the tenth drink.'

'Sit down, sit down.' Herbert got up and put his arm around him and coaxed him into a chair. 'You're funny and I love funny people. So why don't you work at the Hôtel Luna? I'll get you a job.'

'Doing what?' said Jack, alert. Was Sergei becoming a rival?

'He'll take over from Eric.'

'But he can't cook,' laughed Jack.

'Since when did that matter?'

I thought Herbert had found a place in which to play God. I thought he was chucking around a little too much power, lord-of-the-manor stuff. Pride before a fall. I was tight enough to say it aloud. And I think Herbert, although busy with the boys, heard the remark and understood it was meant for him, because after that he was cooler to me. Garcia joined us, and in spite of being in Castel for a quarter of every year he didn't know Herbert, Jack or any of the English.

The side room at Can Mora was filled with curists. It was comfortable and safe and warming, and felt like being in a womb with Mummy providing the food and Daddy doing the cooking. Everything was all right and always would be. And today it was mixed fish – *parillada*, grilled peppers, meatballs. And Monsieur Flavier, the Pigalle singer, came and shook my hand.

'I hear you're doing the Christmas concerts.' He gestured, not bad. His gestures were deft and elegant. And then I realized he had only one arm.

'Why don't you come along and sing?' I said.

'I don't sing,' he said.

'But you are –' I nearly said – a musician. 'From Paris.'

'No. I'm from the north. Lille.'

I felt disappointed. 'But I thought you came with the couple at the Café des Arcades.'

'I lodged there and I had all my meals there on arrangement. But now I'm here.' And he shook hands all round and left.

'He's one of the toughest guys in the whole area,' said Jack. 'He's only got one arm, a tin plate in his head, half of the rest of him is synthetic – but, my God, he's strong.'

'He probably has to be,' said Herbert.

'I saw him get hold of a pig of a man twice his size and weight, half his age, and with that one arm chuck him out of the Grand Café. After that, no one messes with "Bon Bon" Flavier.' Then Jack turned to me. 'Since when are you doing the Christmas concerts?'

I chickened out and said I hadn't decided if I'd do them.

'You must have some power behind you and not far behind.'

I disliked him so much I could have choked him. But Jack was one of those slippery types who come on aggressively and slide away before you can respond. He punched, you punched back, but he wasn't there. Now he was smiling. Offering me his pudding.

I noticed that Fleur didn't say much any more. She looked tired, and her face had coarsened slightly from late nights and all the drinking. Her yellow and gold clothes now included white and it all went together beautifully.

'How did "Bon Bon" Flavier get injured?' I asked Jack.

'Car crash. Years ago. He worked as a steeplejack. Did all the high building work and always thought he'd fall. It's the most dangerous work in the world. And he earned a fortune. He did the stuff the others wouldn't touch and he didn't fall so someone has to crash into him at a hundred miles an hour on the ground.'

'It's an incredible thing, destiny,' said Herbert. And we all felt a little quiet around that subject.

'Well, it certainly isn't destiny that got her the Christmas concerts,' said Jack, and laughed so that we all saw how good-humoured he was. Just as I was about to confront him or snub him or squash him, he became very nice. He said something sincere, friendly, and he was all right after all. And I decided he was just moody and left it at that. He talked enthusiastically about his plan to buy a large house and turn it into cheap flats for the casual-labour guys like himself. 'We have to stick together to survive.'

'That's not what you were saying earlier to Sergei,' said Fleur.

He ignored her. 'Sergei reckons I can get council support.'

'I doubt it,' said Herbert. 'Why should they help the English?'

'It's a free market, Herbert.'

'Only when it suits them.'

'What do you think?' Jack asked Garcia.

Garcia did an enormous shrug and didn't answer. He, too, hadn't said anything. With these people he was not out of his depth: he wasn't even in the water.

'What next?' said Herbert. 'A drink, a dance? The Café des Arcades and Amélie? There's another *thé dansant* at the Castle. Let's go there.'

A group of young French at the next table overheard us. 'We're going somewhere special. It's just opened. Just over in Spain. Come with us.'

'Dancing?' said Herbert.

'Everything.'

'Then let's go.' As usual, Herbert paid and would not accept even a contribution from Garcia.

Somehow everyone got into three cars and sped along the motorway, turning off at the first exit after the border. I was sure we were going to end up in the brothel, which had afternoon tango dancing, but the French carried on kilometre after kilometre into the wilds of the country. Then we arrived at electrically controlled gates, a private drive to a minor palace at the edge of a lake, and jazz, the old style, drifted up from open windows.

The interior was white, plush, sophisticated thirties, and air-conditioned, with lots of ferns in tubs, and engraved mirrors. Although it was five in the afternoon glamorous couples danced on the circular floor lit from beneath. Everyone was beautifully dressed except us.

'Are we in heaven?' said Herbert.

'We can play that too,' said the Maître'd. He led us to an even darker part of the dark room where we would feel less uncomfortable.

'It's very expensive,' said Garcia to me privately.

'It's for Americans,' said Herbert. 'It's *The Great Gatsby* — Scott Fitzgerald — somebody's dream. Who owns it?' he asked the French. They didn't know.

The jazz band was good. Everyone agreed on that. 'Someone To Watch Over Me', 'Dinah', 'Smoke Gets In Your Eyes'.

Herbert danced with Fleur. He bought a second round of cocktails, which he thought would lift our strange but rather broken mood, something lovely that was captive. Fleur felt it and started crying.

'It's the *tra montana*,' said Garcia. 'It's going to do us

all in.' Then to me he said, 'Let's get back out in the sunshine. This isn't our sort of thing.'

Herbert insisted on knowing whether the owner was influenced by Scott Fitzgerald. The maître d' said the club was run by an American, who didn't enjoy what was on offer in the area so he had made his own enjoyment. Meet Mr Shine.

'Where is he?'

'He lives in Castel.'

'Shine?' No one had ever heard of him.

Jack saw Garcia get up and sensed I was about to leave with him. 'But wait a minute. We've got a real singer with us.' And he approached the band. 'Any Broken Hearts To Mend' came to an end and Jack grabbed the microphone. 'She's supposed to be good. From London. Miss Jane but not plain Jane. Let's hear her.'

And he clapped and so did the elegant crowd. So I got up and I had to be good. And all the time I was singing I heard that bird calling, the special one, 'Fly away before it's too late.'

The applause was everything I'd wanted and the maître d' escorted me over to a side door where a large mournful-looking man waited. 'Monsieur Shine,' whispered the maître d' reverently.

'So you're a torcher. What luck. You're going to work for me.'

Chapter Thirty-three

We stood, an ill-assorted group, outside the Crédit Agricole as Herbert went to the slit in the wall. He slid in his card and punched numbers. We were on our way to the sea for dinner, then a party on Monsieur Shine's boat. For some reason I was holding Fleur's arm and I wanted to say, Let's stop all this. Garcia nudged me gently. 'Excuse me, dear Madame, but I'm going home now.' He winked, indicating, don't tell the others, and he edged off into the pale evening light, down towards Maître Aznar's office and left up the one ugly street in Castel, with its ordinary buildings and nothing atmosphere. Herbert's card came back but that was all. He turned to us, arms raised in surrender.

'Trouble?' said Jack, his eyes very bright.

'Well, you know women – just as I'm beginning to. She's obviously blocked my credit line.' He turned to me. 'My wife.'

We all stood quiet, each trying to come up with some solution.

'I'll have to go back to Manchester. I'll get the next plane,' said Herbert.

Fleur said immediately. 'I'll lend you some.'

He wasn't having that. 'What does that make me?'

I didn't believe it, the shut slit. I'd seen Jack's eyes. I knew he was behind in it, his idea. Dump Fleur. He was Shakespeare's Iago right here in the Pyrénées. I thought, Stay away from him.

'Well, let's go into Spain,' said Herbert, 'and we can do the fat lottery.'

'Get real,' said Jack. 'I'll drive you to the airport.'

I still had hold of Fleur's arm and walked her away in the direction of my apartment. Herbert shouted something about having a drink. We didn't turn round.

'Let's go and pack your stuff,' I said, 'while he says goodbye to all the bars.'

'We owe quite a bit at the hotel.'

'Let Jack pay it,' I said angrily.

Jack was all the things I had escaped from. The rivalry, jealousy, power games, insincerity, ruthlessness that I'd suffered in Jay's world. And here it was, in this small place, literally shoved in my face. I hadn't dealt very well with it around Jay. Maybe I had to do better this time. But I thought it was strange that this modest little haphazard group could present the same troubles and challenges, although on a smaller scale. And because I could even think that way I'd always be in trouble.

Fleur had her bags packed and a flight booked before I'd even got up the stairs to my apartment. I said I'd go with her to Perpignan airport. The last plane for Paris left in ninety minutes.

'And how will you get back? You don't drive?' She gave me a note for Herbert and I knew she'd paid the hotel bill. She kissed me and ran down to her rented car.

'He was Mr Right, you know. Who said Mr Right was for ever?'

Next day she rang from Paris and said she was glad to get back to meditation, yoga, the spiritual path. How she'd missed it. I thought that perhaps we should have done some of that in Castel and let Mr Right and his followers do the drinking.

Herbert didn't leave. There he was, having a substantial breakfast in the Grand Café and a mid-morning drink at the Pablo. I no longer joined him and stayed away from that group, using my singing lessons as an excuse. Eric was removed as chef in the Hôtel Luna and Sergei took his place. A board outside the hotel announced, 'kitchen under entirely new management'. According to Natalie, Jack had got the rugby club behind the move. Then Eric couldn't argue with them. And Herbert behind Jack, had paid for a new billiard table in the rugby clubhouse. Eric had gone away. She pointed at Canigou. 'Into the mountains.'

'What do you think of Jack?' I asked. My first mistake. This was the beginning of involvement.

'He's been around for years. I see him in the streets.' Then she looked at me and laughed. 'He's not for you.'

'He's not for anyone,' I answered roughly. Second mistake. Who said she kept her mouth shut?

I could see that Herbert was delighted by Jack. There were blokes and there were girls. The blokes were good and sometimes bad but they were still blokes. The girls were the enemy. Herbert disappeared into Jack's drama, wallowed in it. It made him forget his own.

As I got off the bus from Perpignan Jack approached me, all smiles as though he was my best friend. He was carrying a huge wooden engraving, which he'd found in an abandoned house. 'I'm going to make a sitting room for Herbert, for the winter. This will go over the fireplace. And I'm doing the roof. Come and have a look.'

I said I was in a hurry but I'd come round another time.

He walked along beside me. 'Come and have a drink.'

I realized all this nice attention was for an un-nice reason. I might as well get it over with. We chose the Pablo and sat inside. I ordered sparkling water. He had a beer. The wind was getting up.

'Has Shine been in touch?' he asked.

I said he hadn't.

'Apparently he lives in Castel but I've never seen him. He's loaded.'

I said I hadn't seen him either.

'You should work for him. You'll be set up then. Why bother with the small stuff?'

'Do you want to organize the Christmas concert, Jack?' I said directly.

'Of course not. But you shouldn't.'

'Why not?'

'You're not a local woman. You've got nothing to do with their music. You're not one of them.'

'Music's universal.' I was so angry that I was foolish.

He closed his eyes in contempt. My better self said, Avoid him, walk away. So I stayed and said, 'Yes, you'd like to do it. You'd like to be a lot of things you're not.'

He said, 'Are you trying to say I want to be you? I'll tell you this. I'd be a better woman than you any day.'

I got up and put fifty francs on the table. 'I'm doing the concert, Jack. So what are you going to do about it? Send round the rugby club?'

His eyes looked bad and too black in the pale face. And then an elegant hand flapped on to my shoulder. 'My two best friends in the world, drinking without me.' And Herbert sat down in a chair.

'I'm not drinking,' I said.

'Don't be so damned silly. Of course you are. Waiter. A bottle of your best white.'

The wind raged, howled and sped down to the sea, taking with it roofs and trees and lamp-posts. I stayed in – as did everyone else – amazed the house could withstand the violence. I prayed for the gentle tree and wished I could reach out and hold on to it. It swung as far as the ground on one side, to the wall on the other, a pendulum about to break. Then the electricity went. The phone lines were down. The water stopped. Madame Beaumarchais, Garcia and I sat by her kerosene stove drinking hot tea with ginger and honey and she told us about her youth in Toulouse, taught by nuns, father owned horses. It seemed a short youth. Then Garcia had his turn and talked about his cab-driving in Paris.

'You must have driven her – Colette at Amélie?' said Madame Beaumarchais.

'I wouldn't be surprised,' said Garcia. 'I thought I knew her.'

'She ran a club in Pigalle.'

'How do you know?' I asked.

'Eliane told me. La Culotte.'

'My my!' Garcia shook his hand for 'hot'. 'I know that place. That *is* a club! In the rue Droui.'

'She got busted for serving champagne without a licence. Eliane said the club was behind a lingerie shop.'

'That's right,' said Garcia. 'Underwear in the window, provocative, expensive, and the private club behind. One of the hottest places in the area. But I'd be surprised if she didn't pay a drinks licence. She'd be paying everything else. The police, the peddlers, the *mec*, the politicians. No, I don't think champagne is the reason she left.'

'So why did she go?' I asked.

'Who knows?' said Garcia. 'She keeps herself to herself.'

'And that's what you should do,' said Madame Beaumarchais looking at me. 'You can't do that concert. Marcel's wife wants to do it, so does Maître Aznar, and a young Catalan coming over from Spain has got far more knowledge of the music, and they'd want her to do it rather than you. Monsieur Nadal should never have asked you. He doesn't usually make mistakes.'

Garcia said all that was a little hard. After all, he'd heard me sing at Shine's place.

'Singing is one thing. Being here is another. And she wants to be here.'

And I thought how right she was.

The wind roared so much we bent over involuntarily. It was like being in a war zone.

'It'll last for three days,' said Madame Beaumarchais.

'Six,' said Garcia.

Suddenly Madame Beaumarchais got up. 'You

haven't got anything to wear. For the cold,' she said to me. 'Come in here.' And she led me into her vast bedroom. In the middle, rails of clothes. Clothes to dream in. Silks, furs, wool, linen. She pulled out a black cashmere jacket with a little sequin decoration on the front. And then a calf-length light brown skirt with a tight waist that swung freely, reminding me of the young tree at my window. She dug out a box of lace-up boots and selected black suede. She told me to try them on. Everything fitted almost perfectly. I was quite surprised, since I was much bigger than her. 'They're not yours?'

'My daughter's.' And she added a brown cashmere shawl. 'And now just be here. Take my advice.'

I didn't sleep that night. Painful thoughts churning over. It was like London again. Who said a small town was good news, however beautiful? Eventually you got down to its elements and they were no different, but less diffused. I hadn't played it cleverly. I had to have far more inside me for this kind of existence. I decided I'd go away and live *en pension* by the sea on a different coast and try again to get my life together. I heard Madame Beaumarchais's phone ring, as it always did, at seven o'clock and I realized the wind had stopped. Suddenly there was peace. I opened the shutters immediately and the tree was still there, so loving and faithful like a good friend. I was so grateful I almost cried.

Then I made breakfast and, as usual, looked out at Mount Canigou. The sky looked mean, full of clouds and eminences I'd never seen before. I wrapped the cashmere shawl around me and started down the stairs for the newspapers and the post. Then I stopped, and just stood on those ageless stairs, enjoying the feel of the wooden rail, cool and thick, and the light in shafts from the skylight.

Chapter Thirty-four

People came from England in ones and twos, and their visits thankfully, were short. I'd changed, didn't belong to that world any more and preferred the people in Castel. Now that I'd given up all idea of the Christmas concert I'd started writing songs again, collecting songs from the mountains, and I sent some to Jay. I didn't want a royalty just a straight pay-off, if he was interested, but I didn't get a reply. Then another visitor who I didn't expect knocked on the door. My ex-husband. He was thinner and more serious. He looked as though he'd shed more than flesh. Ideas, hopes, concepts, memories. He'd spent over two years in Ireland, teaching. As always he did not sit on anything but crouched on his heels. He had enviably long tendons. After a few polite pleasantries, he said. 'It all went wrong for me after –'

I knew what had come after. 'Don't talk about it!'

Then he said, 'Marriages do break up after the loss of a child. The statistics are high on that.'

He waited for me to disagree. I waited for the reason he'd come. It wasn't to join my new life. He wanted to stay in Ireland.

'Who is she?' I had to ask but wished I hadn't.

'One of my students. Young, bright. It doesn't matter. I want a divorce.'

I said yes. And he left.

I sat on the new Provençal-patterned sofa and after a while it gave me such pleasure, this bright, white-walled sanctuary with the lights just right, the mountain flowers on the fridge and the space. I never thought I'd get pleasure from a room. I was so pleased I didn't know what to do so I got some paper and started sketching a net curtain, the shutters half open against the night sky, the throbbing squat fridge with the dark printing on the door, which made it look as if it had a friendly face. The fridge might belong to Eric and he did not have a friendly face.

So the past, that past, was quite done and over. And I went on sitting in the room and, after a time, a sense of peace came from the lights, the shutters, even the noisy fridge. It was a sweet peace that was present in this room and more comforting than any person, as real as perfume. But further back than the divorced, the dead past, were the Bohemian years and Luis, and not even Luis himself could take that away. And the feeling of peace was a solid thing that I could find at any time. All I had to do was let go and just be.

They were still clearing up the debris from the *tra montana*. I saw Herbert having his breakfast, not on the terrace any more, but inside the Grand Café. The portion looked rather less than usual. 'My wife's got very nasty so I've got to go back and face the music. Liquidation, et cetera. But she doesn't know about the flight fund. I've kept that a secret for years and I'll come back and live off that.'

'In your house?'

'Hopefully.' He lingered over the syllables.

'Not ready?'

'Not exactly. The wind blew the roof away – the one Jack put on. It's not his fault. Who thought we'd have a wind like that? Now all we need is rain to come again and that'll be it. I've given him some emergency money to fix up the bathroom and just one room and to put a tarpaulin over the whole house if necessary. It's cost me nearly sixty thousand so far.' He sounded quite cheerful about it. 'But now Sean's shown up and he's put out that Jack has taken over his – well, territory, I suppose. There's so little work around I quite understand.'

'Perhaps Sean could replace Sergei in the hotel kitchen? I understand it's not all it should be round there.'

'Sean owes me for the car and the phone and the roof terrace and other little matters. But I feel sure we can sort it out between us. I have to think that.' He paid his tab – a month's breakfasts, two thousand francs. 'I'm paying Jack up-front. The baby's due any day and he has to get a few things. If it's a boy he'll call it after me. And probably Monsieur Shine as well, if he gives him work.' He laughed. 'You mustn't mind Jack. The mountain wind did his nerves in. There are people like that. They go completely mad. He wasn't right for days.'

I said I had nothing against Jack. He just brought me too near to what I'd left.

'You don't want to go back into the old battles?'

'I have to avoid them.' And I realized I did. We shook hands and he said he'd be back in a couple of weeks and we'd get on with the real business of living.

Monsieur Nadal brought me a beautiful lamp for the narrow bit of passage as you came in through the front door. A lantern of different-coloured glass, it transformed this area, which Luis had wanted sealed off. It had been the one dull patch in the apartment.

'Johnny Halliday's coming to give a concert. Here in Castel.'

I told him about Jack's rumours. 'They say I was married to him.'

He laughed. 'Perhaps they hoped you were.'

And I told him I'd known Jay. Had they got it muddled up? And how did they know one way or the other?

He pointed to the phone. 'Someone listens to you speaking when the back door is open. Sound carries. They heard you talking about Jay and concerts and maybe you mentioned Johnny Halliday. Of course they are curious about you.'

'So who is it? Madame Beaumarchais, Garcia, Eliane, the hairdresser, the bookshop?'

He didn't have a clue. 'At least it's a nice rumour. Think what they could say.'

He said Maître Aznar was now doing the Christmas concerts. Did I want to sing in them?

I declined.

'But you'll come on Christmas Day and sing for me. That's a promise.'

*

The middle-aged couple got up from the pavement table at the Café de France as I came out of the front door. They waved to me as though they knew me.

'Do you live in this beautiful house?' the woman asked.

I agreed that I did.

She introduced herself as Helen and her husband Don. They had a house in one of the new villa communities on the other side of the river. They said it was wonderful and they'd never live anywhere else. They'd retired two years before. But every time Helen visited the centre of Castel she always looked at my front door. 'I love the door-knobs, old-fashioned, substantial. I used to sit over in the café and stare at them and long to touch them.'

So I invited them to see the apartment, and she fell as in love with it as I had, eight months before. 'You're so lucky. This old house, really old. All this atmosphere. Things you can touch.'

And again she walked along the oval from the front door to the kitchen, amazed by all the views. 'I'd give anything to live here,' she said.

And Don, who would give her anything, offered me thirty thousand francs there and then.

Chapter Thirty-five

Pascale drove me to Can Mora for lunch. As soon as Martine saw her, customers were swept aside and Pascale was led to the best table in the middle of the terrace room. How I longed to eat in the dark inner chamber with 'Bon Bon' Flavier and the regulars and Pascale had the power to arrange it. She was respected above everyone else because she wasn't a doctor. She was neutral and saved lives. She told the truth about the medicines prescribed. And she was the one who handed out these medicines and had to get them right. But she preferred the terrace. Before we'd even got a glass of wine to our lips, customers flung themselves upon her with questions and tales of horror and she handled each one and managed to order lunch. Then Martine asked her about an old man living on the outskirts of Castel.

'Is he dying?'

'From the medicine prescribed I would say so.' Martine crossed herself. Pascale said lightly, 'But we're all dying. He got there first.'

Martine went away mopping her eyes.

'She must be fond of him,' I said.

'Fonder of him dead. He's left her his entire estate.

Do you want mashed or chips?' She knew them, how she did.

'I worked in Paris but then I was offered the head job here. And I'm back with my family. My mother's got –' There was such a noise I couldn't hear what it was, but said I was sorry. The rugby team had arrived at the same time as five policemen.

Pascale came from an established Catalan family. She'd known she was gay since she was twelve.

'Do they know here?' I asked discreetly.

'I hope so.'

Then 'Bon Bon' Flavier came across, shook hands and said his new medicine was no good. When it was going to rain he could feel it in every part of him, the parts he had left. Pascale told him to drop by that afternoon and she'd look out something more effective.

Quickly I mentioned Amélie-les-Bains. His eyes were frosty. 'I gave them my friendship. I was with them every day, every meal, and then one day, out.' He accompanied that with a gesture.

'Why?'

And Martine chose to pass by and said, 'Because you talk too much.'

He turned to the whole room and said, 'I talk as I want. I've looked death in the eye too often for anything else. She is worse than him. She's had a terrible life. Drugs, the bottle, the street.' He couldn't think of anything worse to say so he added, 'And without makeup. My God! She looked seventy.'

'How old is she?' asked a curist.

'Sixty at least,' said 'Bon Bon'. 'She's had this operated and that padded and that taken away.' His hand ran over his body like a spider. 'She's had more operations than me. And she's not married to that brute. She's married to the old guy with the dog.'

I asked if he was sure. He didn't listen and carried on with his testament. 'He put up the money for the place. They all live together opposite in two apartments but she spends her nights with the old one. They've got a daughter and pretend it's the bouncer's. It's the old man's I can tell. By the eyes. She's gone to the bad as well.'

'What's she doing here?' asked a rugby player.

'Running. But they'll get her. You can't run from Pigalle.'

'She's a showgirl,' said one of the policemen, 'in the Lido club.'

'Never,' said 'Bon Bon' Flavier. 'The nearest she's been to that stage is in the alley round the back. She's terrible. I know. I know her mother. She came to visit. A very classy woman. Real class. And money. Jewels. Wow.'

Martine grabbed his arm and began to lead him back to the inner room to safety. He said, 'It's going to rain. I can feel it in my bones.'

I could see what Monsieur Nadal meant about rumours and how the ones about me were not that bad.

A male curist said, 'The woman, whatever she is, she's amazing.' With his hands he described a woman's curvaceous body. 'How does she do it at her age? And up all night. Three or four in the morning. And she's still there at ten sharp doing the books.' They always mentioned her age, the men. She looked as though she should have been thirty. That's what her face suggested. There were no lines or wrinkles.

I turned to Pascale. 'Do you know her?'

Pascale paused and laughed. 'How can I know her? I'm in love with her.'

Marie phoned and said Jay was all swollen up. Perhaps I should see him. I couldn't keep running away. She was like the older dictatorial sister I'd never had. Well, I had her now.

'You're the one who says I should stay away. Remember?'

Her memory was personal and suited her argument. 'Let's all get together for Christmas, all right?' and she sounded more friendly.

Then Jay called. He said it was nothing; it was something swelling in his veins.

'Marie said she'd put me in the car and drive me to your mountain and that would do me good. She said that was the best.'

I dared to ask if he had considered rehab. I got no thanks for that. 'I like the song you sent about the mountain. How it brings people to it, the ones it wants, and they act out its drama. Is that true?' He said he'd send a cheque. I said, Have it as a Christmas present.

The wind had damaged the gutters and the terrace I shared with Garcia, and stones were missing. There was a leak from the roof because slates had been dislodged and water dripped into Madame Beaumarchais's bedroom. She said we'd have to send for the mason to fix it all up and gave me an estimate of the cost.

'But what about the insurance?'

'They won't pay for this.'

Then I noticed Eliane's name wasn't on the list. Madame Beaumarchais was quick with an answer. 'She can't pay. You let her down. And you have to pay now. The water's dripping into my bedroom. Come and look.'

I refused. 'But the water's coming from the roof. That's because she's got no windows or doors. It's got in, the rain. It's her problem.'

Madame Beaumarchais started to shout and rage and got very over-excited. The basic thing was that I, or rather Marie, had taken away Eliane's choice of alternative finance.

'What about the Dutchman?'

'Why should he pay when it's your fault?'

I made a deft exit, still holding the estimate for the work, and went straight up to Garcia. He read it and turned pale. 'I can't pay all this.'

Madame Beaumarchais had worked it out according to the size of each property. His was double mine so double the price. Gato would pay half of what I did but, as it was, we all paid too much because we paid for Eliane, who owned the same percentage as Madame Beaumarchais.

'She thinks she owns the house,' he said quickly.

'Eliane?'

'Both of them. Madame Beaumarchais thinks we're some kind of inferior lodgers lucky to be here. That garden out there and the courtyard — we're also supposed to use that. Eliane queens it over us because it was her grandmother's house when they were wealthy. But times change. And Madame Beaumarchais is in awe of Eliane because she has the one thing she hasn't – class.'

Remembering the mother, I thought it must all have come from the father's side.

He invited me to sit at the kitchen table and got out a large pair of spectacles. He reread the estimate. 'We'll have to go to a lawyer.'

'Can't we just get together and –'

'No. They'll win. Between them they own the greater percentage of the house so have the majority vote. And Eliane believes she'll get this house back as hers. She will never let it go. And who has to pay for it? That's what Madame Beaumarchais is making us do. She's got us cornered.'

He was very upset and I said I was sorry to worry him. I asked if Madame Beaumarchais had money.

His face creased with the ludicrousness of the question. 'Every month,' he whispered, 'men come from Toulouse. They give her the profit of her various establishments.'

'Which are?'

'Gambling, I hope, my dear Madame. But it might be the oldest profession. That's what I twigged when I saw the rail of clothes. I hadn't realized they weren't hers. Perhaps they're what she dresses the girls in, the working girls.' He looked at me. 'Belong to her daughter? How could she have a daughter as big as you? The men phone every morning with the night's takings.'

'What shall we do?' I was whispering too.

'We should have a *syndic*.'

'What's that?'

'A tenants' and owners' association so we vote on every issue. But she won't allow it because she'll always protect Eliane.'

Was it Marie who'd said – neighbours! Rent the

L'Hostellerie apartment. Could she have been right, after all?

'You see, Eliane thrills her.' His face was pale and his hands were trembling. His share, what with the new roof, would make anyone tremble. 'It's nothing like you might think. It's on a much higher level. Madame Beaumarchais admires her, would like to be her, so it ends up we have to pay for someone else's obsession. Juan Pamello should have let you in on this when he sold it to you. He knew what he was doing.' He went out on to the terrace and kicked around at the stones.

'No one pays for my problems.' He pointed up at the dark stain on the ceiling, which had puzzled me on my first visit. 'Eliane's washing-machine overflowed.' Then he pointed to a crooked beam. 'Eliane's croupier boyfriend threw the fridge across the room. Then he threw it out of the window. Then he threw the mother's boyfriend through the window. I can't tell you what I've suffered.'

'What does your wife say?'

'Oh, she hates it here.'

'You were discreet about that.' I was quite angry with him.

'Why should I spoil your view with my experiences?' He stopped suddenly and gasped. 'But she's a poor young girl with a child to bring up. So,' he lifted his arms, 'I put up with it.'

'But we're going to be poor *old* people if we don't watch it,' I said.

'We'll go to Maître Aznar,' he whispered. 'Walls have ears'.

And I thought about the *pension* idea up in the

north of France, away from all the mystery and seduc-
tiveness. A bracing reality with no shadows.

And the thirty thousand was suddenly very attractive.

'Bon Bon' Flavier went into the Grand Café at noon
every day to lay bets on races. He was lucky. Even with
the lottery. Especially with fruit machines. He'd said it
was because of all the metal inside him.

I sat opposite him without being invited, and he
wasn't exactly easy about it. Walls have ears and cafés
had eyes and this village thrived on gossip. Ignoring his
unease I asked, 'What about the Café des Arcades in
Amélie?'

'They're on the run definitely. I did everything for
her. She threw me out. No one gets near them.'

'Was she a prostitute?'

'Everything. But very high up finally. And that club.
Everyone went there. Including Saleras. But she's very
sad. She loved Saleras, was crazy about him – you know,
the flamenco star. She thinks one day he'll come here
and get her. I said, If the others can't find you how can
he? She's been through everything. Illness, abuse, addiction. She's been in a hospital, in the other hospital.' He
touched his head. 'Depression. I've seen her cry. I've
held her like this.' He showed me how he'd held her.
'But I'll never go back. It's funny because, and I don't
mean any offence, she reminds me a bit of you.' He
shivered. 'Rain's coming. It's already in my bones.' He
saw Eliane crossing over from the Casino. 'She always
wears the same clothes,' he said contemptuously. He
turned away. He didn't like her.

I got up to go. He said, 'They always stick together. You'll never win.' He turned towards the house. 'Wolves never eat each other.'

I caught up with Eliane on the stairs and said Madame Beaumarchais wanted money from everyone, which was impossible. And couldn't Eliane at least close the door to the attic so that the rain didn't get in? And put in some windows. Even wooden ones.

She said she would. She was sweet-voiced and gentle. She said again how she was having the house accepted as a listed building so as to be allowed a grant to do the whole thing up. 'It's valuable property. They all stayed here. Picasso, Braque, Krémagne, Soutine . . .'

For once, I was more concerned with the present day. 'But who will pay your share of Madame Beaumarchais's estimate?'

'I will!' She rose up, eyes fiery. 'I pay my way. I do, after all, own the façades.'

Pascale heard some of it. 'She's in the shit. Her mother won't pay. The croupier won't. The Dutchman can't. Madame Beaumarchais will.'

Pascale said everything 'Bon Bon' Flavier had recounted was untrue. She laughed. 'They threw him out for gossiping and he's hurt. She worked in the cinema. French films. Then she got ill and they came here for the climate. I know because I prepare her medicine.'

'How's it going? I mean the love affair not the medicine.'

'One-sided. But I know men are not her fix. She just plays with them. But if she was a working girl, a prostitute, it would bring the number in this area up to . . .' She counted thirteen. 'And they say that has something to do with Canigou. That's what they say.'

At first I thought it was television, a dramatic episode in an afternoon soap. Madame Beaumarchais had it on unusually loud. But the players were right there in the house and the show was too live. Eliane was shouting and raging at Madame Beaumarchais. 'How dare she order me to do things in my own house? I told you at the beginning, don't let her in!'

Madame Beaumarchais shouted back, 'She bought from the postman. It's legal.'

'You could have got it stopped. You know you could. Shut her up or get her out.'

It wasn't the nicest conversation I'd overheard.

Later Madame Beaumarchais said that I mustn't mind Eliane, that she had a terrible temper, and that the mountain wind burned her skin up. I wondered if Helen and Don, the English couple, were going to do any better.

Garcia was going to Bagur, and he didn't mind going further into Gerona and making a detour. He said he'd wait for me if I wanted, but I was sure I would see Luis. Garcia gave me a detailed plan to get to his house if I wanted to spend a few days at the coast. I didn't see Luis. His friend in the second-hand bookshop said he was out of town, government business.

I needed to ask Luis' advice. Not only about selling the apartment but about my whole life. In that moment I needed confession. He was, after all, a priest.

By chance as I turned into the old hotel where I'd

decided to wait for him, the receptionist with the cinder black hair was coming out. 'Oh, so you're back.' She chose to remember me this time. Looking too deeply for comfort into my eyes she said, 'He gave up being a priest because of you.'

I was beyond surprise. More than amazed. I waited for her to continue. There was no doubt that she would.

'You kept coming back. He fell for you and decided he wasn't strong enough for the priesthood and his vows.'

'Oh, no, Madame.' I had never felt so full of dignity and strength. 'You've got it wrong.'

'I doubt it!' she said.

'He fell from grace long before I started coming back. The moment we met. That's when it was consummated.'

And I decided not to wait in the old hotel. I felt that her bitterness came from a more personal place than even religious belief.

Chapter Thirty-six

The rain fell straight from the sky, relentless, on and on, hour after hour, day after day. It fell, not from clouds which, after all, emptied eventually, but from some higher vengeful altitude. Limitless, was how it manifested itself on earth. The atmosphere in the apartment in turn became damp and invasive, the colours looked muted. It set up a feeling of alarm. Could the house sustain all this water? Could the town? Just crossing from the front door to the Grand Café soaked you through so thoroughly that you might as well go on to L'Hostellerie for a meal or down to the old hotel in the rue St Ferréol. The house smelt of damp. The hallway gleamed with a greenish light and looked like the inside of a cave, dank and dripping. All kinds of things had washed up in there and were spawning and growing in this extraordinary time. For the first time I felt uneasy because I was trapped. Of course I couldn't drive – of course there was no railway, just the shell of what had been a lovely station. Who did I really know here? The weather kept everyone in, snug with their families or just in. I considered calling the local taxi and going down to Spain. I thought of the Motel Ampurdan in Figueras. That famous restaurant that Dali and the Catalan writer Joseph Pla had loved, full all the year round, crammed with atmosphere, elegant yet discreetly formal and the owner Señor B with his scathing, endless Catalan wit. I felt safer there. But the roads were hellish. And, in fact, I'd heard from Eliane that the taxi was doubling as a funeral car in the cortège for Monsieur Maurice's wife. She'd been driving back from Lourdes and was drowned when a quite minor river burst its banks. Monsieur Maurice owned a restaurant called La Goutte d'Eau – a drop of water. People tried not to think of the irony but it made them quite hysterical, this flagrantly ironic tragedy, and the ceaseless rain. It did in their nerves, so that laughter, normally rigidly suppressed, bubbled up like air in water. The manager of the Crédit Agricole bank, one of Monsieur Maurice's regular clients, shook with unseemly mirth. Wiping his eyes, his dripping face, he said, 'The poor man runs a business called a drop of water and his wife is washed away in a flood. What does that mean?' and again he was overcome with inexcusable, inappropriate laughter, storms of laughter. What did it mean? This irony that grief turned hilarious? I wondered if we'd laugh as much if he, the manager of the farmer's bank, met his end under a ton of horse shit.

I sat on the brightly patterned sofa and the white walls started to close in. I moved to the spindly café chair in the kitchen, then to the clothes chest in the bedroom. To calm myself I looked towards Mount Canigou but it wasn't to be seen. Cloud, the whole sky, hung down over the streets. When I'd sat on everything and found no respite I tugged open the back door and stood on the terrace. I tried not to think of Marie's final threat, which had seemed laughable at the time. Just wait till it rains. I thought about phoning her, resisted the weakness. She'd known and, of course, I hadn't, how pushed into isolation you can be when inclement weather and a foreign village conspire together. I loved the place but love wasn't enough. I didn't belong among them. I was rootless, except at the bank. A sudden wind sent rain stampeding down the street. The street-lamp lit up the diagonal lines streaking endlessly from the sky. The wind stopped and the rain swung back like a curtain. It fell on and on, heavy, impenetrable, unceasing, just like curtains, muffling sound, subduing light.

I could see Madame Beaumarchais sitting in her usual place at the kitchen table eating a chicken and vegetable casserole and watching television. The rain had got on her nerves drastically. She shouted at Eliane. She yelled at me to shut the street door when I went out. How could I? The wood had swollen.

'Speak to me in English!' She insisted.

'But you don't understand it.'

'No. But I can't bear your French.'

She sent Eliane sloshing through the village for newspapers, spicy sausage from her favourite butcher, new medicine, apparently homoeopathic: it didn't interfere with her pleasures. Eliane brought back a variety of wines and a strong, medicinal-smelling liqueur. Their longed-for weekly car trip to the duty-free shops at the frontier for bottles of Pernod, had had to be cancelled. That didn't help Madame Beaumarchais's mood. Eliane said the flat land towards the coast was under water and streets in Perpignan cut off.

There was no sign of the rain stopping. I had put a red mullet in the oven and boiled some rice. Then the lights went out, so did the stove. I went downstairs and fixed the fuse in the hallway box. I couldn't, it seemed, have the lights on and the radiators on and the oven. I turned off the radiators and some lights. The oven did not come back on. It was definitely off. The fish would be next. I threw it in the lavatory.

Now it was dark and I put on all my sweaters and sat in the kitchen trying to write the new songs. I couldn't write a thing but I pretended everything was all right and the original joy and gaiety were still present. But I was becoming unnerved and lonely, and next I'd start thinking about the past and then I'd be really done for.

Finally I went splashing down to the old hotel for dinner. I was the only customer and the food was lousy. Yes, you had to have a strong sense of self-reliance on nights like this.

The owner, Pepe, rubbed his legs with liniment in front of the wood stove. He was a hero to the Catalans because of his Spanish civil war activities, but he was no cook. Usually his daughters handled kitchen matters while he, always wearing the black beret, sat remembering the old Spanish days with his cronies. He remembered in the secret muttered talk that they'd all had to get used to during Franco's regime. I asked where the daughters were.

'In bed. Where else?' he gestured at the rain and spat. 'It makes me think of the plague. It's like the locusts. It's biblical.' He said that during the civil war he'd walked from Spain through the Pyrénées into France, always at night bringing the fugitives into Castel giving them safe houses. He'd been rained on by bullets, by hailstones, ice. Never anything like this. He was horrified by Monsieur Maurice's loss. Yes, he'd been to the funeral and soon there'd be another one. The wet had done in his blood-flow. He mentioned some medical names and threw in a couple of hospital horror stories. 'I always carry in my pocket the names of the doctors I don't want to touch me. There is one hospital I will not be dead in. I'd sooner die on the roadside. Or with Pascale in the pharmacy.' He felt that was inappropriate and crossed himself and muttered Monsieur Maurice's name. 'I told him to call the restaurant something else. Water. A drop. You can say that again. It didn't even let up for the funeral. Has he offended God or Neptune? Poor man.' He remembered my dessert and stuck a dish of crème Catalan on the table. It shivered and shook. There was something indecent about it. Then I tasted it. I preferred to go straight on to the coffee.

Every night since the tragedy he'd seen Monsieur Maurice sitting in his restaurant alone and gloomy. 'Last night I couldn't bear it so out of respect I went in for a meal. There was just me and someone passing through from the coast. Monsieur Maurice served a perfectly good *coq au vin* in excellent sauce but before I'd even tasted it he started telling me again about the floods and his poor wife and then he was crying and it felt all wrong to go on eating. So I settled for a quick coffee and a brandy. Now it's impossible for any of us to go in there because all he does is cry. Yet it's impossible not to go in because he looks so pitiful. He'll feel abandoned and cry more.'

'Couldn't you just have an hors d'oeuvre?'

'Why should I do that when I'm in the business myself? It makes sense to go for his specialities because he's French. We Catalans cook food differently.'

I thought tonight's meal would be hard to place geographically.

He gave me a Spanish liqueur containing forty-two herbs. It sat on the dinner and kept it down. I paid him the equivalent of three English pounds and he opened the door to the street. I stepped out into the night and gasped. It was as though someone had thrown a bucket of water over me. The old man cursed. 'It's a catastrophe.'

There wasn't a cat or even a rat on the street. Bits of branches from the plane trees rushed down the gutters. The old man pointed at a cloudy object like a broken plate. 'Ice from the mountain.' My shoes filled with water and sank down to the street, invisible below, pulling me with them. At this rate I'd be walking out of Castel on webbed feet. Suddenly I stopped pushing through the gale. It was all right. Being here. Yes, better than that. I felt jubilant. I wanted to dance along the street singing the Gene Kelly song. I wanted to jump and spin and laugh and celebrate life. I believed I'd passed some test or other. The mountain was pleased? I waded carefully back towards the house. And there under the street-lamp, across the flooded roadway, was the only other person out on such a night.

Luis the Spaniard stepped forward, said my name. Yes, the mountain was pleased.

Chapter Thirty-seven

We huddled together laughing, on the narrow bed. The rain drummed against the shutters. It had stopped being like an endless curtain, and was now attacking everything.

'My God!' he said. 'This could only happen when I finally get here to see you. You are like some comet trailing a strange – change.'

I didn't like the sound of that.

'But an enigmatic, mysterious comet. Good? Bad? Who knows?'

'I could say the same about you.'

'No.' He'd stopped laughing. 'You know, I'd have made you happy if I could.'

The next morning the rain stopped briefly and we waded across to the Catalan food shop. As we bought ham, salad and wine a sad procession passed the window: Jack, Sergei and members of the rugby team carrying chairs, sofas and a soaked mattress.

'Whose are those?' I asked.

'Herbert's,' said Jack. 'The rain has gone through floor after floor. It's got into the electrics. And by mistake Sean ran his bulldozer into one wall. The place is a write-off. How are we going to tell him?

We'll put his stuff in the Hôtel Luna to dry out.'

Luis and I went to look at the forlorn house, which was open to the sky. Sean's tenants had now moved in on the lower ground floor. They said, to bail out the water.

'He's been taken. Right from the start,' I said.

'Of course,' said Luis. 'You can't walk in and buy a place and leave it to strangers to look after.'

I could see the sight of that house depressed him.

As he didn't drive either, we took a taxi to Colette's. The rain had started, but fine, penetrating, like a mist. As usual Colette was behind the bar but so different. She'd cut her hair. The shock made me say, 'You've changed.' I felt offended. She looked like anyone else now, except she was beautiful. Perhaps perfection had got too much for her. Then she came around the bar to shake hands with some drenched regulars and she was wearing tight cowboy jeans, a shirt, a denim waistcoat. The boots were high-heeled. She was one of the only people I'd ever seen who could wear jeans at that age. They suited her, fitted as immaculately as her skirts and dresses. The hair was designed to flow backwards, meeting at the nape of her neck like a 1950s Tony Curtis DA. She looked got up as one of the boys and I wondered if Pascale had been lucky in love after all.

Luis saw Colette. He saw much more than that. 'She's come here to breathe and look at the mountains and feel the sun. She's been in too many airless dark rooms in hot hotels with too many strangers and she's longed for purity. The dream of it. That's how she got through those years.'

As always, she stood to advantage in front of her shelves of coloured bottles. But now I saw her as someone sealed against rumours.

Luis was amazed I'd given up so easily on the Christmas concert. 'Why didn't you fight?'

'With what?'

'You wouldn't have said that at sixteen in Pigalle.'

'I've changed.' I tried to laugh.

'You're bigger, that's all.'

And he said he'd teach me some precious Catalan songs passed down from his grandmother. They couldn't but see the value of those. And I was to go straight back to Monsieur Nadal and reclaim my rights.

And he decided suddenly we should go up into the mountains and he'd sing them into a tape and teach me the rhythms. And we went up to the top of Canigou and stayed in a monastery and I felt he'd taken me higher than I'd ever been.

> Mountains of Canigou, fresh you are
> And God-sent as a present.
> Especially now in summer
> When the waters are icy.
> I've spent six months here
> Without seeing a born person
> Except for a nightingale
> Which out of its nest was singing.

The second was about a bird as well. Coincidence? A message from the mountain?

> Nightingale, you who are on your way to France,
> Put me under the protection of your mother.
> Ask her blessings for me.

The night I'd got back from the mountains I was woken by a sound. It was not one I'd heard before. It sounded like a machine. Fully awake, I sat up. Everything quiet. The church bell chimed four. I supposed it was the bakery starting up and I lay down. Then it was there again. A loud, snoring noise. Madame Beaumarchais? I went to the window. It did not seem to come from below. More from the passageway and cupboard in my flat. Was it a trapped animal? The cupboard revealed nothing. Was it something on the stairs? I opened the door. The sound had stopped.

The next morning as I climbed the stairs I thought the two front doors, mine and Gato's were too close together. I had never thought that before. That afternoon I heard the snores again. They were coming indisputably from beyond the bedroom wall. Gato had let the studio.

Madame Beaumarchais said she knew nothing about it. Gato owned the property, always paid his share of the house expenses. He could let it to whom he wanted. And when was I going to pay mine? The roof had to be fixed. By law I had to pay my share.

Garcia had seen the lodger. He described him as fearsome and rough-looking. And, as he spoke, suitable noises came from the other side of the wall. A hacking cough, spitting and some oaths. His unlocking and relocking his door was like the soundtrack from a fifties prison, death-row movie. We waited till the heavy footsteps scuffed their way down the stairs. It wasn't the most optimistic sound.

'He never had good lodgers but who would stay in there? Usually they're drug addicts. Two to the room with Alsatian dogs.'

I thought he was joking. I hoped he was joking.

'They pee all over the stairs.'

'Why don't they take them out?'

'Not the dogs, Madame, and they turn night into day. The fights, the music!'

'What did the postman do?'

'He used to go mad. He'd go and kick that door and tell them to shut up. He threw one of them into the street. There was a huge row. They were drugged up, dogs whining. Augustin's children woke up screaming. And then Eliane's household upstairs started fighting.'

'Monsieur Augustin was lucky to sell the apartment,' I said.

'Blessed, Madame. He said it was his luckiest day ever. Do you think I don't want to sell mine?'

Madame Beaumarchais said that the lodger didn't worry her. I should have made up my mind and bought the studio like she'd advised.

'Why didn't you buy it?'

'I have no money. Only my pension.' She didn't look as though she was lying. 'And I have to help Eliane.'

Monsieur Nadal said Gato had waited a reasonable while before renting out the studio, because he didn't want to be seen to be doing it out of revenge.

That night I sat on the edge of the bed while the lodger moved about between his bathroom and his bed. He didn't do anything extraordinary. It just sounded too loud. And then the springs of the sofa bed screeched as he lay back and cursed.

And suddenly I thought, It's Eric the chef. It has to be.

And the bird, its voice I knew among all the others, called to me to leave, to depart.

Luis came back quite unexpectedly and asked if I'd presented the songs. I said I could not.

'Then you should leave here. Get out.'

Of course Marie had been right. I was in the same predicament as Herbert. You moved into a place you didn't know and you asked for all you got. You either took it or you didn't. I'd decided to take it and make it work. But Paradise had its rules. You stayed in your bit and you didn't take the bits that weren't yours.

Luis had brought me another song. I hoped it was about a bird again.

> When I was five my father
> Took me to the boat and told me,
> When you grow older
> Beware calm times.

I told Luis that if it was right for me to sing I would. I told him how I'd started my career in New York, in the Village. I'd been there a few successful weeks. And that was when my son had the first drug problem. I'd had to rush back for him. I always felt guilty. My success at the expense of my son. And then, later, I had to keep thinking, Don't feel guilty about being happy.

'This isn't the right place for that attitude. Not at the foot of Canigou. The mountain questions you, challenges you. You have to come up with the answers.'

I didn't believe that. In the past I had believed anything he said.

'In the end the mountain moulds you. When I was a child I thought it was the nearest thing to God that I knew. Perhaps there's another way of being happy?' And he took my hand.

I thought at this stage of things I'd have to kiss a lot of frogs before I found the prince.

The bird was singing and it seemed to be perched on a branch of the young tree. I told Luis to listen to that bird. What was its message?

He laughed. 'Get out before it's too late. The saddest thing to hear – the bird has flown.'